Advance Praise for *Backyard Bounty*

As usual, Linda Gilkeson is spot on with her trademark down-to-earth advice to Pacific Northwest Gardeners. If, like me, you sometimes find your vegetables bolting before their time and falling short of your expectations, if you're wondering how climate change is affecting what you should plant and when, if you're perplexed about pollination and the impact it is having on your garden's productivity, struggling with organic pest management, or wondering how to achieve year-round bounty in your outdoor space, you'll find these pages brimming with seasoned wisdom and practical common sense.

—CAROL POPE,
Editor, *GardenWise*

Once again, Linda Gilkeson has enriched the gardening literature of British Columbia with a book that is generously thorough and thoughtfully written. *Backyard Bounty* is ideal for beginner gardeners, and essential reading for serious enthusiasts!

—MARK MACDONALD,
West Coast Seeds

Backyard Bounty delivers a straighforward, practical guide to growing an organic food garden in greenhouses and containers as well as in the open garden. In detailed directories to individual vegetables and fruit Linda covers all essential information from choosing varieties to harvest and storage as she anticipates common problems and equips the reader to prevent and deal with them. No guesswork here.

—HELEN CHESTNUT,
garden columnist, *Times Colonist*

Linda Gilkeson has paid some tuition in the garden. *Backyard Bounty* is remarkably thorough, from roots to pests to pruning to crowns, and it inspires even the experienced grower. Just like homemade soil for a bedding plant, this book is loaded with the richness we need in order to feed ourselves.

—LYLE ESTILL, author of
Small is Possible: Life in a Local Economy and
Industrial Evolution: Tales from a Low Carbon Future

Whether you have a small or large lot, little or plenty of time, this book shows you how to grow your own toxic-free fruit and vegetables the whole year round. From preparing the ground to harvesting and storing the ripened produce, all is clearly explained. An invaluable book for novices and experienced gardeners.

—BARRY ROBERTS, Past-President,
Master Gardeners Association of BC.

With *Backyard Bounty*, Linda Gilkeson has written the ultimate book filled with practical, interesting and sound advice. She takes the reader from the soil to harvest and everything along the way — growing your own bounty has never been easier.

—JEFF DE JONG, C-FAX 1070 Host
'Gardening 101'

BACKYARD BOUNTY

The Complete Guide to Year-Round
Organic Gardening in the Pacific Northwest

Linda A. Gilkeson, Ph.D.

NEW SOCIETY PUBLISHERS

Printed in Canada. Second printing April 2011.
New Society Publishers acknowledges the support of the Government of Canada through
the Book Publishing Industry Development Program (BPIDP) for our publishing activities.

Inquiries regarding requests to reprint all or part of *Backyard Bounty*
should be addressed to New Society Publishers at the address below.

To order directly from the publishers, please call toll-free (North America)
1-800-567-6772, or order online at www.newsociety.com

Any other inquiries can be directed by mail to:
New Society Publishers
P.O. Box 189, Gabriola Island, BC V0R 1X0, Canada
(250) 247-9737

New Society Publishers' mission is to publish books that contribute in fundamental ways
to building an ecologically sustainable and just society, and to do so with the least possible
impact on the environment, in a manner that models this vision. We are committed to doing
this not just through education, but through action. Our printed, bound books are printed on
Forest Stewardship Council-certified acid-free paper that is **100% post-consumer recycled**
(100% old growth forest-free), processed chlorine free, and printed with vegetable-based,
low-VOC inks, with covers produced using FSC-certified stock. New Society also works to
reduce its carbon footprint, and purchases carbon offsets based on an annual audit to ensure
a carbon neutral footprint. For further information, or to browse our full list of books and
purchase securely, visit our website at: www.newsociety.com

Library and Archives Canada Cataloguing in Publication

Gilkeson, Linda A.
Backyard bounty: the complete guide to year-round organic gardening
in the Pacific northwest / Linda Gilkeson.
Includes index.
ISBN 978-0-86571-684-1   eISBN: 978-1-55092-474-9
1. Organic gardening — Northwest Coast of North America.   2. Backyard
gardens — Northwest Coast of North America.
SB453.5.G538 2011   635'.048409795   C2011-900049-0

NEW SOCIETY PUBLISHERS
www.newsociety.com

MIX
Paper from
responsible sources
FSC™ C016245

Contents

Acknowledgments

The information in this book is the sum of far more than just my own experience. It is thanks to many people over the years that have shared their gardening enthusiasm, knowledge and most importantly, their questions, that I have learned so much about growing food in this climate.

I am grateful to Elizabeth Cronin who took many of the photographs in Chapter 9 and has always been generous with permission to use her images.

Further thanks are due my gardening companions: Charlotte (a fairly good guard dog), Quirk and Quark (the two recycling hens), and a multitude of (nameless) beneficial insects.

Introduction

With so many gardening books published every year, why write another one?

One reason is to provide a guide to organic gardening in our coastal Pacific Northwest climate, which is like no other on the continent. For tomatoes we are limited to about the same growing schedule as other northerly regions, but go out to my garden in January and you will find it full of carrots, beets, leeks, celeriac, lettuce, spinach and other leafy greens, cabbage, Brussels sprouts, kale and much else besides. With a planting season that lasts for six months and a harvest season all year round, our plants and planting schedules (and even our pest problems) are unique.

Gardening the easy way leaves me time to sit in my favorite lawn chair and enjoy the view.

Another reason is the popularity of my talks and classes on the theme "Grow the most food in the smallest space (with the least work)." This book expands the topic into a detailed guide to high-yield, low-maintenance food gardening. I wrote this for busy people with little time to garden and for anyone who wants to learn how to grow a lot more food in whatever space they have.

When I was a child, vegetable gardens and a fruit tree or two were common features in yards, and how to garden was common knowledge. That's not true today. So another aim in writing this book was to provide basic information that would help new gardeners successfully transform their collection of seed packages into a delicious harvest. Growing an organic food garden is a practical skill anyone can learn: it doesn't have to involve a lot of work and certainly doesn't require a big investment in special products or equipment.

I have to confess that, for me, food gardening is really about pleasure. I want everyone to enjoy the delights of fresh food harvested straight from the garden and to reap the health benefits of a bountiful supply of organically grown fresh vegetables and fruit. That's the biggest reason why I wrote this book!

CHAPTER 1

OUR GARDENING CLIMATE AND HOW PLANTS GROW

This chapter covers basic information to help take the guesswork out of growing vegetables and fruit in the Pacific Northwest coastal climate. It starts with an overview of the climate and weather along the coast, followed by a review of how plants grow, flower and fruit.

Gardening in the Coastal Climate

What's different about gardening on the Pacific Northwest coast? The climate here is characterized by mild winters and warm summers. Only rarely is it too hot in the summer to grow the vegetables that do well in cool conditions (such as broccoli, lettuce and peas), yet it is almost always warm enough to allow warm-season crops to be grown reasonably well in most gardens. This is actually a wonderful place to garden because so many

FIGURE 1.1. What's for dinner in January? Carrots, kale, Komatsuna, Brussels sprouts, parsley and radicchio.

1

vegetables can be harvested fresh out of the garden *all winter*. Because garden beds can produce food all year, you can grow a surprising amount in a small area—and you don't have to spend the time that gardeners from less "fortunate" climates do preserving food for the winter. (When those gardeners move to the Pacific Northwest, it can take them a while to adjust to the idea that our planting season lasts for six months and our harvesting season lasts all year.)

Microclimates on the Coast

Within this generally mild climate, the varied geography of the region—from mountains to seashore—holds many local microclimates. The complexities of West Coast geography mean that the USDA climate zone maps are not much use here. While roughly USDA Zone 8 for much of the lower elevation coast, there are large differences in local microclimates.

These microclimates differ in:

- total rainfall and the timing of rainfall;
- amount of local fog, marine clouds, and direct sunshine each year;
- average low winter temperatures, frequency of frosts and snowfall;
- the average warm temperatures in the summer.

The effect of all this is that two gardens only a short distance apart may have the same average annual temperature, but quite different gardening climates. A garden close to the ocean or the Strait of Juan de Fuca will have cool summers with more fog than a garden a short distance inland, but the winters won't be as cold. Gardeners may need a greenhouse to ripen tomatoes in an oceanside garden, but winter crops such as broccoli and salad greens will grow beautifully without one.

Rainfall patterns also vary widely around the region. Gardens in the rainforest microclimates will receive far more rain than gardens in the rain shadow of the Olympics or other coastal mountains only a few miles away. (A rain shadow is the dry zone on the opposite side of a mountain range from the prevailing direction of wind and rain; as storms pass, they dump rain on one side of the mountain, leaving little to fall on the other side.)

And then there are the variations in weather. Influenced as the coast is by the El Niño/La Niña weather patterns of the Pacific Ocean, some winters are much colder or wetter than others. A feature of winters in the south coast of British Columbia and north coastal Washington State is the occasional Arctic outbreak. These blasts of frigid air break out of higher latitudes and roar down the coast, bringing brief periods of much colder-than-average temperatures. There may only be one or two such outbreaks in a winter, and they usually only last for a few days at a time, but this weather pattern can be very damaging to unprotected vegetables in the garden.

Effects of Elevation

Elevation affects microclimates, but not always in obvious ways. The higher the elevation, the lower the minimum temperatures are in the winter. But higher elevations also get more snow. With an insulating blanket of snow providing cold protection, overwintering plants often have a *better* chance of surviving an Arctic outbreak at *higher* elevations than at sea level. With precipitation falling mostly as rain at lower elevations, the ground is often bare during cold snaps, so plants are less protected.

Higher elevation gardens (up to 1,000 feet), if they are on open slopes, can sometimes have a longer frost-free growing season than valley gardens

Know Your Garden

For a small investment in a minimum-maximum thermometer and a simple rain gauge (or a straight-sided tin can), you can keep weather records for your own garden. The records will become more and more useful as the years go by because they will show you the *range* of temperatures and rainfall in your own garden. Adding notes on sowing and harvest dates and other gardening observations will make the records even more valuable. Lee Valley Tools sells a large hardbound 10-year garden journal with spaces for 10 years of notes for each date. Now that I am used to putting all my garden notes in one place, I couldn't do without my journal.

because cold air flows down the hillsides and pools in the valleys. On very still nights, the air may be even be a few degrees warmer at higher elevations than down in the valley due to temperature inversions. This can be an advantage for higher elevation tree fruit production because there is less chance that a late frost will kill the blossoms of peaches and other early flowering fruit.

Gardening in the Future

My parents always had a backyard garden when I was a child. Back then, we turned on the overhead sprinklers to irrigate whenever the garden looked dry, we never worried about whether or not bees would pollinate flowers and, of course, we didn't worry about global climate change because is was unknown. But the world has changed and this affects how we garden:

Climate change: By now, most people are aware of the increasingly unpredictable weather that is the result of changing global climate. As the global atmosphere warms, it holds more energy and more water vapor, which means an increased potential for stronger windstorms and heavier rainfall. Extremes of heat and drought are also more likely (most of the warmest years on record have occurred in the last decade). To adapt, gardeners must be prepared to moderate the impact of unusually wet/dry/cold/hot weather by screening plants in a heat wave, throwing plastic over winter crops in unusual cold snaps, staking plants for high winds, and mulching to insulate the soil. None of these methods are difficult or expensive, but they require a gardener to pay more attention to the weather and how plants respond to it.

Water conservation: Where once water was simply applied as needed to keep gardens producing in the summer, in many regions conserving water is now an important — and sometimes critical — issue. Gardeners must learn how to use irrigation water most effectively and without waste, which includes collecting rainwater and recycling gray water.

Loss of pollinators: When I was a child, no one hand pollinated squash, fruit trees or other crops. The many species of native bees and other pollinators were "out there," so we didn't even think about it. Since then, the loss of native pollinating insects and domestic honeybees has meant that pollination is no longer guaranteed.

The Basics of Plant Growth

You might be tempted to skip this bit, but I urge you to read on because so many crop problems that perplex gardeners have to do with growing conditions (weather, nutrients, irrigation) that affect plant growth, flowering and fruiting. When plants do weird things — such as bursting into flower when they shouldn't — we need to understand why, so we can avoid it in future.

Requirements for Growth

Photosynthesis in plants is a truly amazing process. It allows plants to take energy from sunshine, carbon dioxide from the atmosphere, and water from the soil and turn it all into sugars. Inside the plant, another process, called "respiration," uses those sugars to make the building blocks of plant cells: fats, carbohydrates and proteins. Some necessary elements such as nitrogen and sulfur come from the soil through the roots and move up through the plant in water. Surprisingly, most of the weight of the solid material that makes up a plant actually comes from carbon in the atmosphere rather than from nutrients in the soil.

Sunlight Is Essential

To make a very complicated story simple: exposure to sunlight is vital. Vegetables and fruit need bright sunlight for as long as possible to produce the building blocks that make leaves, seeds, roots and fruit. Leafy greens can grow adequately — though slowly — with half a day of direct sun each day, but most food plants do much better with eight hours of direct sun in the summer.

The efficiency of photosynthesis depends mostly on light level, but it also depends on temperature;

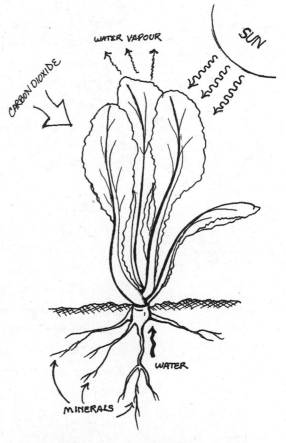

FIGURE 1.2. How plants grow: With energy from the sun, carbon dioxide from the atmosphere, and water and minerals flowing upward from the roots, plant cells produce the building blocks that become leaves, flowers and seeds.

the process goes faster in warmer conditions. When it is really hot, the balance between photosynthesis (making sugars) and respiration (using sugars to make other components) gets out of whack—and plants are stressed as their stores of sugars are used up.

Plants Are Mostly Water

Water is an essential ingredient in photosynthesis. The movement of water from the roots to the leaves (called "transpiration") carries nutrients from the soil up through the stem and out to the photosynthesis "factories" on the leaves. When the water reaches the leaves, it evaporates into the air and cools the plant.

Plants must have a film of water around their roots so nutrients from the soil can pass into the cells of the roots. If this film dries out, even temporarily, fine root hairs die back, and growth stops. Plants may be so severely stressed by a brief check in growth that even if they survive, they may never be as productive as they would have been.

Soil Has a Supporting Role

The soil physically holds up plants and anchors them. It is the source of water and many of the essential major and minor elements needed for photosynthesis and respiration.

Soil also contains a complex community of organisms that range in size from microscopic bacteria to (relatively) huge earthworms. This vitally important community includes the decomposers that digest organic matter and release nutrients in forms that plants can use. Other soil microorganisms actively protect the health of plants by colonizing roots and protecting them from attack by microorganisms that cause disease.

The larger soil inhabitants include insects, mites, nematodes, earthworms, slugs and snails, crustaceans (e.g., pillbugs), millipedes and centipedes. While a few of these characters attack plants, our gardens couldn't do without most of the others. For example, bacteria have more nitrogen in them than other living things, so when larger organisms eat soil bacteria, their poop is rich in surplus nitrogen, which becomes available to plants.

And, as earthworms and other creatures move through the soil, they aerate and enrich it with their excrement. The soil *surface* is also the hunting ground for predators, such as large, purplish-black ground beetles, centipedes and many kinds of spiders.

Plants Need Nutrients

Plants need three elements in large quantities for growth. These primary nutrients are: nitrogen (N); phosphorus (P); and potassium (K). There are also secondary nutrients: calcium, magnesium and sulfur. While plants take up smaller amounts of these, they are no less important for growth.

A third group of nutrients is essential too, but in extremely small amounts. These "micronutrients" or "trace elements," include iron, manganese, chlorine, zinc, boron, molybdenum and copper. The tricky thing about this group is that most are toxic to plants in large amounts or if soil conditions (such as acidic soil) make them too easily available to plants.

Chapter 3 covers nutrients from the soil in greater detail and describes how you can make them available to the roots of plants.

How Plants Grow

Plant growth depends on external factors such as weather, sunlight and nutrients as well as on the internal workings of the plants.

Annuals, Biennials, Perennials

Vegetables are mostly either annual (go to seed in the first year of growth) or biennial (go to seed the second year). Many crops (lettuce, radishes, mustard greens, beans and squash) are annuals wherever they are grown, which means they will flower and produce seeds in the same summer if left in the garden long enough. Practically speaking, however, in the Pacific Northwest all garden vegetables can be treated as annuals, which means we can harvest crops the same year we sow the seeds.

Crops such as carrots, cabbage, kale, leeks, beets, Swiss chard and parsley are technically biennials. Left to their own devices in the garden, they would have a two-year life cycle. From a spring planting they continue to grow all season without going to seed. After spending the winter in the garden, they send up a flower stalk the following spring. The seeds ripen in the summer and then the plant dies.

Some plants that we treat as annuals, such as tomatoes and peppers, are actually *perennials*; in a subtropical climate or heated greenhouse they could continue to produce flowers and fruit year after year. Tender herbs, such as sweet basil and sweet marjoram, are also perennials, but they are often grown as annuals because they are not hardy enough to survive outdoors over the winter.

There are a few hardy perennial vegetables, such as artichokes, French sorrel and asparagus. And of course, all fruit trees, grapes, berries and rhubarb are hardy perennials in the garden.

Effects of Temperature

Plants grow best when it is warm; when it turns colder, growth slows, then stops altogether. The cut-off point at which growth stops differs among plants. Frost-hardy vegetables continue to grow (very slowly) even in the winter, whereas heat lovers, such as corn or melons, pack it in and die. Eventually, when the days are shortest and temperatures are cold enough, all plants stop growing.

Perennials, such as fruit trees, have a natural dormancy in winter. They drop their old leaves in the fall and withdraw the sap from their stems so they can survive very cold weather without damage. They won't suddenly start to grow if there is a brief period of warm weather in mid-winter because they also need the lengthening days of spring to break the dormant state and stimulate growth. Leafy vegetables, on the other hand, are just resting in the cold; they can take advantage of warm spells in a mild winter to resume growing a bit.

How well plants withstand winter temperatures depends on when — and how quickly — it turns cold. As days get shorter and temperatures gradually drop, plants "harden off," becoming used to the cold. If there is unusually cold weather in late November, before plants have hardened off completely, they can be injured by temperatures that wouldn't hurt them in mid-winter.

In spring, if there has been mild weather for a month and plants start to grow again, a late cold snap can cause far more injury than the same temperatures would have done earlier.

At the other end of the thermometer, as temperatures rise, plants grow faster—but only to a point. When it is too warm (above 82–95°F/28–35°C, depending on the crop) plant growth slows or may even stop temporarily. To avoid a disastrous loss of water, plants have to close the pores (called "stomata") on their leaves during the hottest part of the day. This also shuts down photosynthesis; plants cannot start making food again until it is cool enough for the pores to open. So a prolonged hot spell means a prolonged inability to make food.

Growth and Flowering

While they are young, vegetable plants should be growing quickly. This period of vegetative growth gives the plants more leaf area (more capacity to photosynthesize) and bigger roots (more access to water and nutrients from the soil). If all goes according to plan, by the time conditions are right for them to produce flowers and fruit, plants will have accumulated enough food reserves to support a good crop.

For vegetables such as lettuce, leafy greens or root crops, the vegetative growth period should be as long as possible because we harvest the leaves or roots, not the flowers and fruit. For these plants, fertile soil, high levels of nitrogen and regular watering helps prolong their vegetative growth period. For fruiting plants, however, such as squash or tomatoes, a long period of leafy growth isn't desirable, because it delays flowers and fruit.

Once a plant switches over to flowering mode, its vegetative growth slows, at least until

FIGURE 1.3. A tale of two squash: The plant on the left was sown April 6th; the plant on the right May 6th. Vegetative growth of the older plant was stunted by being held too long in a pot. Now it is flowering, but it is too small to carry a crop.

the fruit is picked. If a squash plant or a very young fruit tree, for example, is allowed to carry fruit while the plant is too small, the plant has to stop growing leaves to put energy into the fruit. To avoid this, simply pick off early flowers that form when plants are too small.

Several things can cause plants to flower:

- Day length is a signal to some. At these northern latitudes, spinach, for example, resolutely flowers in response to the long days of June no matter how early or late it is sown in the spring.
- Temperature is a signal for others. Biennials flower only after experiencing the cold of winter; other plants flower in response to the heat of summer.
- Stress from a poor nutrient or water supply, from being root-bound in a small container, or from unseasonably cool weather can cause plants to flower prematurely (see "Vernalization," below). This is why it is so important to grow seedlings under good conditions, and to do what you can to avoid stressing them.

Vernalization (or Why Vegetables Unexpectedly Go to Seed)

Vernalization is a plant's response to low temperatures that results in flowering. After the cold of winter, biennials normally send up their flowers. But if a seedling is big enough, a spring cold spell can fool it into behaving as if winter has passed, so it sends up a flower stalk instead of waiting (as it normally would) until the following spring. Crops readily vernalized by cool temperatures in the spring include beets, Swiss chard, cauliflower, cabbage, onions, leeks, celery and celeriac. Temperatures of 5–10°C (40–50°F) for one to two weeks, for example, are enough to cause onions to flower.

Plants can only be induced to flower if they have grown large enough to have some food reserves to devote to flowering. If the cold period happens while seedlings are still tiny, they won't flower because they are too small. Plants don't have to be very large, however, to respond to cool temperatures. Onion sets larger than a nickel and cabbage or leek transplants with stems the thickness of a pencil are big enough to be induced to flower by a cool spell. The larger the seedlings are when the cool weather occurs, the less time it takes to cause them to switch to flowering mode.

Vernalization is a particular problem for coastal gardeners eager to get a jump on the season. In our mild climate, it is often possible to sow seeds of hardy vegetables as early as February. If there is a nice long period of mild weather, these early seedlings grow big enough that a late cold spell (and we always seem to get a late cold spell!) can cause them to flower. You don't see the flower stalks immediately, but the plants get set on a growth path that will result in too-early flowers later on.

Vernalization is also a problem if you try to get a head start by starting seeds indoors too early. If you a do a good job of growing large, healthy transplants and set them out early, it can take as little as a week of cool weather to induce them to flower. Our spring weather is so variable that it is more reliable to start seedlings later and plant out small plants that can tolerate a late cold spell.

FIGURE 1.4. A Leek flowering in response to a cool spell that happened shortly after transplanting. Only the largest one has gone to flower, but if they had all been larger, they might all have flowered this summer.

Pollination and Fruit Set

For many vegetables, flowers are only important if you want to save seeds. For fruiting plants, however, such as tomatoes, squash, apples or blueberries, there can only be a crop if the plants flower and the flowers are fertilized.

Pollination occurs when the dust-like pollen from the male parts (stamens) of the flower reaches the female parts (pistils) of the flower. The flower is successfully fertilized when the pollen grain sends a pollen tube into the egg cells in the ovary of the female flower. Most vegetables and fruit have flowers with both male and female parts in the same flower. Most are also self-fertile, meaning that pollen from the same flower only has to drop onto the pistil within the flower for fertilization to proceed. Bean and pea flowers, for example, are already pollinated by the time the flowers open.

Many species of bees as well as other insects have a vital role in pollinating flowers. As they collect nectar and pollen, they move the pollen from one blossom to another. Bumblebees, because of their large size, also vibrate flowers as they work, which causes the pollen to fall onto the pistil inside the flower. People can be another pollinating agent: gardeners can hand pollinate flowers to improve fruit set or to make sure seeds they save are true to the variety.

Some crops, such as squash, cucumbers and melons, have separate male and female flowers on the same plant. They depend on bees (or people) to carry the pollen from male to female flowers. This is also the case for kiwi fruit, which has male flowers on one plant and female flowers on a separate plant. Corn has separate male and female flowers on the same plant, but it depends on wind to shake the pollen from the male flowers at the top of the plant onto the silks of the ears (female part) lower on the stalks. Other plants

FIGURE 1.5. No pollen equals no squash. The shriveling small zucchinis at the bottom of the picture were not fertilized.

Were Your Squash Flowers Pollinated?

Many disappointed gardeners want to know why their squash plants produce flowers but no fruit. It happens because the flowers were not pollinated. The flowers need bees to pollinate them, but wild bees are scarcer now and few people keep domestic honeybees in populated areas anymore. Bees are also less active in cool weather, so flowers go unpollinated when it is cool and rainy. The bottom line is that nowadays gardeners need to know how to hand pollinate flowers (for instructions, see the entry for squash in Chapter 10, A to Z Vegetables).

pollinated by wind include tomatoes and grapes. The flowers are self-fertile, but they need the wind to shake the pollen onto the pistils within the flowers.

Despite having flowers with both male and female parts, many varieties of fruit can only be successfully fertilized if the pollen comes from flowers of a different variety. This is called "cross-pollination," and it complicates your choice of what to grow in a small garden. Without a suitable variety for cross-pollination, flowers of apples, pears and many other fruit can't be successfully fertilized. Some crops, such as blueberries, do have self-fertile flowers, but cross-pollination by other varieties helps to increase the amount of fruit set.

FIGURE 1.6. A honeybee working a flower. Bees are called "nature's sparkplugs" because without them, many plants can't start to produce a crop.

Fruit without Fertilization

Parthenocarpic varieties of plants set fruit whether or not the flowers were successfully fertilized. For example, the early tomato varieties, Oregon Spring and Siletz, can set fruit when it is too cold for tomato pollen to successfully fertilize the flowers. The unfertilized flowers develop seedless fruit; later, in warm weather, they produce normal fruit.

Long English cucumbers also set fruit without pollination. In fact, greenhouse growers take care to avoid letting the flowers be fertilized. They remove all male flowers and screen bees out of greenhouses because fertilized cucumbers have a bulbous end instead of the long slender shape desired.

What's Next?

I imagine you are wondering whether you really need to know all this and when we are going to get to the hands-on gardening information. I have spent so much time on vernalization and pollination biology because in my experience those are the two biggest sources of grief for gardeners in this climate. When plants bolt prematurely or flowers go unfertilized, it results in a partial or even complete crop failure — and there is nothing more discouraging after all the work you put into to the garden.

Now, on to planning that garden!

CHAPTER 2

PLANNING A PRODUCTIVE GARDEN

Vegetables and fruit are all sun lovers: the less direct sunlight there is, the slower they grow. Sadly, the amount of sunshine is the factor that you may have the least power to change (especially if it is your neighbor's house that is blocking the sun!). Happily, you can improve many other things—soil

FIGURE 2.1. Vegetables and fruit need as much sun as they can get during the growing season.

FIGURE 2.2. Late August peas happily growing at the shadier end of the garden in the summer.

depth and quality, drainage, and irrigation—so before you pick your site, start with finding out where the sun shines the longest in your yard.

The ideal site for a garden is where it will receive full sun for 6–8 hours of the day from March through September, when plants are most actively growing. But also keep in mind that for plants harvested from November to February, the best location is where they also have the most protection from cold and wind.

Lettuce and salad greens can grow fairly well in gardens that offer about half a day (4 hours) of good sunshine during the summer, but tomatoes and other heat-loving crops must have more than that. The midday sun is the most important. Most gardens get direct sun in the middle of the day from May through July because the sun is so high in the sky at midday. Some fortunate people have gardens in open sites that receive sun all day, but most of us have to work around obstacles that block the light.

As the angle of the sun and the length of day changes over the year, the amount of sun reaching a garden depends on neighboring buildings, trees and other objects. With the sun low in the sky in December, even a low fence casts a long shadow (if the sun ever comes out, of course). It is too cold for plant growth anyway, so exposure to direct sun isn't that

Will Anything Grow in a Shady Yard?

If you have a spot that gets half a day of direct sun over the summer months, by all means experiment with growing some vegetables. Start with lettuce, spinach, arugula or Chinese cabbage and other leafy greens—and be patient: the less sunlight the plants receive, the slower they grow.

important in mid-winter. For example, my garden receives only about 1½ hours of direct sun in December due to a neighboring mountaintop, but my winter crops do fine.

Get to Know Your Garden

Even in a small yard, there are microclimates that can make a difference in which crops will grow best there.

Light and shade: Some parts of the garden are more shaded than others, and this changes over the season as the angle of the sun changes. Tall crops eventually shade other plants once they reach their full height, so there may only be certain places where they can be grown (usually along the north side of a garden). The places that receive the most sun should be reserved for heat-loving crops.

Useful places might exist that you haven't thought of as garden space. When the sun is low in the fall, it can reach under decks, porches and building overhangs that may have been shady in mid-summer. Such protected spots can make good places for hardy greens to spend the winter. (You can transplant them from the main garden in late summer.) And don't overlook the possibilities in your flower beds: many vegetables are beautiful and look lovely mixed with flowers or even by themselves in ornamental beds.

Soil drainage: While you can grow summer vegetables on low-lying, wet ground by planting late, after the soil has dried out, such sites are not good for growing winter vegetables. For these crops, either choose a site that is already well-drained or improve a poorly drained site — by installing a raised bed, for instance.

Air circulation: The flow of cool air depends on the terrain. You may find "frost-pockets" in slightly lower spots where cold air settles on clear, cold nights in spring or fall. When there has been a light frost overnight, note where the frosty patches are in your garden. These won't be good spots for the most frost-sensitive crops (such as cucumbers or squash). These are also likely to be the coldest areas of the garden in the winter, so avoid planting overwintering crops in these areas, or reserve these places for the hardiest plants (such as kale, corn salad or parsley).

Garden Bed Design

Gardens are as personal and varied as the people who make them. Authors of garden books are an opinionated bunch, and we all swear by our own ways of designing gardens. But, really, plants don't give a hoot about that; they seem to grow fine regardless of human opinion. Personally, I'm glad I didn't read a lot of gardening books when I started gardening because the amount of work some people go to would have stopped me in my tracks. Since this book is about my own intensively planted, organic, low-maintenance, year-round coastal garden, that's what I am going to describe. But ultimately, the best design for your garden is the one that works for you.

Permanent Beds

Growing crops in permanent beds is popular in this region for good reason. Compared to a garden plot that is tilled from edge to edge every year, there are several advantages to permanent beds:

- Once beds are laid out, pathways and growing areas don't change over the years.
- Only planted areas need be fertilized, watered and weeded, which saves work and resources.
- Soil in beds doesn't become compacted, because you don't have to walk on it.
- It can be easier to control weeds between beds when the pathways are permanent.
- Permanent pathways provide a refuge for beneficial insects that eat plant pests.

FIGURE 2.3. Permanent beds are very productive and save a lot of work.

A Stable Home for a Gardener's BFF

Ground beetles eat slug eggs, root maggots and other garden pests. Because they are territorial and long-lived (for an insect) they appear earlier in the season and in higher numbers in gardens with undisturbed areas. They use these areas as refuges while garden beds are being dug and planted.

Beds can be any length or shape, but should be narrow enough that you can reach the center easily without stepping off the pathway. Four feet is a width most people find workable. If the beds are too wide, you will end up walking on them, which defeats the purpose.

Beds should also be designed with the irrigation method you plan to use in mind (see Chapter 4). Despite our long, wet winters on the coast, there is a dry period in the summer when plants will need some irrigation. The drier the summer climate is where you are, the more important this consideration will be.

FIGURE 2.4. A common ground beetle—one of the good guys you want to encourage to live in your garden.

Do you need raised beds? Permanent beds do not have to be raised beds. Whether you decide to build up the height of the soil in raised beds depends on your site and on personal preference. Garden beds must have soil at least 12 in (30 cm) deep. A depth of 18 in (45 cm) is better — and deeper than that is better yet. If the soil in your garden is very shallow, you can increase the soil depth and also improve drainage by building raised beds.

Raised beds usually have sides to hold the soil in place. The sides can be made of any material, including untreated wood (scrap lumber, utility-grade cedar boards), recycled plastic landscape timbers, or stone, brick or concrete blocks. Treated wood is not acceptable for certified organic growers, and no one should use wood treated with creosote, pentachorophenol or chromated copper arsenate (CCA). These are toxic chemicals that can leach into the soil and should never be used around food crop. Some people now use borate

FIGURE 2.5. Well-built stone raised beds give excellent results.

pressure-treated wood, which is a considerably more benign wood treatment. I would still advise lining borate-treated wood with heavy plastic before filling in the soil to make a barrier to prevent leaching into the soil. Where pillbugs (see Chapter 9) are damaging, you might not want to use wood anyway because rotting wood attracts them.

Raised beds have several advantages:

- They provide improved drainage for the root zone in low-lying, wet soils.
- They can be used to terrace steep slopes so the soil is held level in a bed.
- Soil warms more quickly in the spring, which is particularly desirable in cool, foggy regions and for gardens with heavy clay soils.
- Beds several feet high can make gardening more comfortable for people who have trouble bending down to ground level.
- Gardens can be built on rocky surfaces (or concrete or asphalt).

Raised beds also have disadvantages:

- Plants generally need more irrigation in the summer dry season.
- Soils may be too warm and too dry in mid-summer, especially sandy soils that are already well-drained.
- They take work to build and maintain, and they require some investment in materials.

For many gardeners, the choice comes down to personal preference. You may find that raised beds suit some parts of your garden, but not necessarily the whole garden.

Pathways

Paths can become weedy messes if not maintained. As you might expect, I try to keep maintenance to a minimum. Here are a couple of ways to handle the pathways between garden beds:

Permanent sod: You can sow the pathways with lawn grass or white clover to make a permanent sod. If you make the pathways wide enough to accommodate a lawn mower, you can maintain them by mowing. This works better for permanent beds without solid sides because the mower wheel can ride along the soil edge of the bed, giving a clean cut. Once a year, you'll need to re-cut the edge along the sod with a spade or edging tool to prevent the sod from taking over the bed. This method isn't quite as low maintenance for raised beds with sides because the mower leaves an untrimmed strip along the sides where the wheels travel.

Mulches: Another option is to use a thick, more or less permanent mulch on pathways to control weeds. You can use wood chips, shredded bark, leaves, straw, newspapers, landscape fabric, or any combination of these. Laying a solid mat of newspapers along the path and covering it with a layer of wood chips gives a neat appearance and lasts for the whole season. For the small, intensively planted space I have now, narrow, well-mulched paths have been easy to maintain; they look good and don't require periodic mowing or clipping.

Pathways are much easier to manage when you use a drip or seep irrigation system as opposed to sprinklers. Without overhead watering, there is considerably less weed growth in pathways.

Breaking New Ground

In the first year or two of a new garden it usually takes extra work to establish the beds. You might have to put up a fence, build beds, or bring in more soil. There's no way around it: this takes work. But, the long planting season on the coast means that not all of your beds have to be done at once. Get one done and plant it before building another. If you plan on building five beds, you can make one every month from March through July and plant as you go.

To make the job of converting lawn or weedy sod into a new garden easier, cover the area with a thick mat of newspaper or sheets of cardboard, old tarps or other light-excluding materials to smother the sod. Ideally, you should do this in the fall, but three months ahead of time works too. A huge, thick pile of leaves left on the spot over the winter will have the same effect. When you smother the sod in place, it won't have to be removed and the dying roots benefit the soil by adding organic matter. You won't believe how much easier this method is than digging up sod!

If you *do* have to remove sod, shake as much soil from the roots as you can, then compost the rest. That layer of soil still clinging to the roots is the best topsoil you have, so you will want to return it to the garden eventually.

Choosing What to Grow

Now that you know *where* to garden, it is time to figure out what to grow. If you have limited space, you might want to concentrate on a few favorite vegetables or special crops that are expensive or hard to find in the market. Some gardeners, for example, don't bother with potatoes or carrots because they are relatively cheap and always available. I do grow them, however, because the flavor of a carrot right out of the ground is irresistible, and tiny new potatoes are a gourmet treat.

Start with the Easiest Plants

Some vegetables are easier to grow than others in the coastal climate. If you are a beginning gardener, the vegetables on this list are usually good ones to start with:

- lettuce and other salad greens
- onions from sets
- garlic
- plants in the cabbage family (broccoli, cabbage, kale)
- summer squash (zucchini, crooknecks, patty pan)
- beans
- peas
- beets, radishes, turnips, rutabaga
- potatoes
- spinach (sown as a fall crop)
- Swiss chard
- parsley
- annual herbs: cilantro, dill

In addition, perennial herbs such as chives, thyme, sage and mint are easy to grow, as are hardy perennials like French sorrel and rhubarb.

Some vegetables grow well in the coastal climate, but are a bit more of a challenge:

- carrots germinate slowly, so it is difficult to get a good stand of seedlings.
- cauliflower is very sensitive to cold, heat, lack of nutrients and irregular watering.
- leeks, onions from seed, celery and celeriac have to be started indoors very early (it is easier to buy transplants if you can find them).
- globe artichokes need special care to survive the wet winters (see entry for artichokes in Chapter 10).
- asparagus takes up a lot of space and needs high fertility.

Vegetables that need a long warm season are usually the most difficult for coastal growers to manage, especially along the ocean and straits where it is much cooler than in inland areas. The following can be particularly challenging to grow on the coast:

- tomatoes
- sweet and hot peppers
- winter squash
- cucumbers
- melons
- eggplant
- sweet corn

All but sweet corn either have to be started early indoors so they have time to mature, or you must buy transplants in the spring. Also, some of these — winter squash and sweet corn, in particular — can take up a lot of space.

Among the fruit, strawberries are the easiest and most reliable to grow. If you have the space, blueberries, currants and gooseberries are not difficult either. Raspberries and other bramble fruit thrive in this climate, but they do require pruning and training to keep the canes within bounds.

Among the tree fruit, apples are probably the most reliable, but all tree fruit (and vine fruit, like grapes and kiwi) are more challenging than other crops: varieties must suit this climate; some have cross-pollination requirements; they all take up more space than vegetables; and they require at least some pruning (or a lot of pruning) every year.

Choosing Varieties

Within each of the many kinds of vegetables and fruit, there are hundreds to thousands of varieties on the market, each with different characteristics. (Strictly speaking, to a botanist, a variety is a naturally occurring plant type, while a cultivar is a specially selected or hybrid form of the plant. I will stick to the term "variety" to cover both for the purposes of this book.) By some counts, there are over 7,500 tomato varieties worldwide, ranging from pea-sized yellow ones to gigantic green-and-red-striped fruit. Among lettuce varieties, there are leaf lettuces, buttercrunch, Romaine and iceberg types — and all come in a variety of leaf shapes, textures and colors. Some are adapted to spring planting, some tolerate summer heat, and others are frost-hardy.

So, how to choose? Read the seed descriptions in catalogs, particularly those from local and regional seed suppliers; they will have pre-screened many varieties to find the best ones for the region. Ask local gardeners (join a

A Cautionary Note

If you are tempted to grow interesting varieties from international seed houses or heirloom seed banks, do some research first on what they require. Some vegetables are sensitive to day length, such as onions, spinach and Chinese greens; varieties adapted to the southern United Stages (e.g., southern California or Texas) might not behave as desired at our latitude, which has much longer days in June. Short-day onions, for example, may only form small bulbs in a region with long days. Many heritage varieties of tomatoes, sweet corn and winter squash need the long, hot summer of the midwestern and southern United States to mature. Varieties from British and Dutch seed suppliers, however, usually do well in the Pacific Northwest because of the similar climate and latitude.

local garden club or veggie group). Some of my favorite varieties are the ones I've grown from seed given to me by neighbors.

Keep trying different varieties. After a while, you will discover which ones you like the most for taste, how well they grow in your garden, and other characteristics.

When you are perusing the descriptions in seed catalogs, here are some things to look for:

Climate and season adaptation: The coastal zone is relatively cool in the summer, with few really warm days. Therefore, look for "short season" or "early" varieties of tomatoes, corn, peppers, cucumbers and melons. In the cooler, foggier parts of the outer coast, even the earliest varieties may not ripen unless they are grown in a plastic tunnel or under row covers to trap heat. If your garden is in a warm, protected location on the inner coast, though, you might find you can grow some of the warm-season varieties that take longer to mature.

For winter vegetables, look for descriptions of cold hardiness and suitability for winter conditions, such as "frost hardy" or "stands all winter." There are large differences in cold hardiness among varieties of leeks, lettuce and other leafy greens, endive, broccoli, cauliflower and other crops. Choosing the right varieties can make all the difference in the success of your winter harvest.

Days to harvest/Days to maturity: Where seed catalogs give a number after the variety name, it refers to the number of days from planting to harvest. For example, "Redwing F1,

FIGURE 2.6. For hardy varieties of leeks and leafy greens, winter temperatures are no problem.

110 days," means that this hybrid onion would take 110 days to mature under ideal conditions. For most crops, the days are counted from the time the crop is seeded. For commonly transplanted crops, however, such as cabbage or to-matoes, the days are usually counted from the date of transplanting.

Since growth rate depends on temperature, soil fertility and water supply, how long it will take a particular variety to mature in your garden can vary from the number given — often by quite a bit. The "days to harvest" figure is most useful as a guide for comparing varieties: a 110-day variety will obvi-ously take longer to mature than a 90-day variety.

Open pollinated vs. hybrid plants: Open pollinated, or OP, varieties are like purebred animals, which have both parents of the same "breed." Seeds of each successive generation should produce plants that look and taste just like the parents. A great advantage of growing OP varieties is that you can save their seeds.

There are many excellent OP varieties, well adapted to the coastal climate. Some of these, the "heritage" or heirloom varieties, are tried and true ones that have been grown for many years. Opinions differ on how old a variety has to be to be called a heritage variety. I was recently surprised to see Sugar Snap peas billed as a heritage variety because I remember when they came out as a new thing in the 1970s. That certainly made me feel old!

Many vegetables and some fruit varieties are hybrids. Hybrids should show the term "F1" as part of their name (sometimes seed suppliers omit this). It means that the parent plants come from two different "lines" of that crop. When the male from one line is used to pollinate the female from a different line, the next generation of plants (the F1 generation) has a unique blend of characteristics from the parents.

There are many excellent hybrids that give good results in home gardens under a variety of weather conditions. Hybrids, like cross-bred animals, tend to be more robust due to the phenomenon known as "hybrid vigor." The main problem with hybrids is that you can't save seeds, because the next gen-eration won't necessarily have the same characteristics as the parents.

I grow a few hybrids because they have characteristics I haven't found in OP plants. For example, the hybrid zucchini Radiant F1 is resistant to powdery mildew. In my garden, it continues to produce a crop for 4–6 weeks longer in the fall than OP varieties, which are susceptible to mildew. It is difficult to save squash seed, and I only use a few seeds each year anyway, so I don't mind buying a package of hybrid zucchini seeds every 5 or 6 years.

Disease resistance: The moist, cool climate of the coastal region favors many plant diseases. Fortunately, among the many varieties of fruit and vegetables are some notable for their disease resistance. Growing disease-resistant varieties is the easiest and most effective way to avoid many plant diseases (see Table 2.1 for examples).

FIGURE 2.7. Leaves of powdery mildew-resistant zucchini (center) are undamaged even though they are surrounded by infected crookneck squash leaves.

Table 2.1. Varieties of fruit and vegetables resistant to plant diseases of concern on the West Coast.

Crop	Disease	Examples of resistant or tolerant varieties
Apples	Apple scab	Akane, Bramley's Seedling, Elstar, Enterprise, Fiesta, Jonafree, Liberty, Macoun, Mutsu, Prima, Priscilla, Red Free, Sunrise, Wagener, Wolf River, Yellow Transparent
Beets	Cercospora leaf spot	Kestrel F1
Cucumbers	Powdery mildew	Sweet Slice F1
Grapes (table)	Powdery mildew	American hybrids: Himrod, Golden Muscat, Interlaken, Reliance, Sovereign Coronation
Peach	Peach leaf curl	Frost, Pacific Gold, Renton
Peas	Powdery mildew	Cascadia, Sugar Lace II, Green Arrow, Oregon Giant, Snow Green
Peas	Pea enation virus	Cascadia, Sugar Lace II, Sugar Ann, Oregon Giant
Potatoes	Late blight	Fundy, Kennebec, Sebago and others
Potatoes	Potato scab	Sieglinde
Spinach	Downy mildew	Space F1, Samish F1, Olympia F1, Tyee F1,
Zucchini	Powdery mildew	Radiant F1, Paycheck F1; Soleil F1 (yellow)

Careful reading of variety descriptions will turn up information on disease-resistance characteristics. It is a good idea to cross-check with various seed suppliers (online catalogs are great for this), as some don't list disease resistance. For example, Sweet Slice F1 cucumber is widely available, but the fact that it is powdery mildew-resistant is not always listed.

Disease Resistance Terminology

Some varieties are listed as "immune" to a particular disease, meaning they won't be infected even if conditions favor the disease. Others are described as "resistant," meaning they are less likely to be infected; if they are, infections will likely be minor. Varieties listed as "tolerant" can be infected, but should continue to produce reasonably well unless conditions are highly favorable for the disease.

How Much to Plant

Quantity is something that is very hard to judge when you are new to gardening. Over time, of course, you will learn how much your household generally uses of each crop.

There is a big difference in space requirements between a summer crop and the winter version of the same vegetable. For example, 2–3 square feet of lettuce and salad greens for a small family is plenty for each successive planting in April, May and June. For winter salads, however, one big planting in early August has to last all winter, so you might need an area about five times larger (i.e., 10–15 square feet). The same for carrots: 4–5 square feet of May-sown carrots might be plenty for summer eating, but if you want fresh carrots all winter, in early July you would need to sow a larger bed to last you for 6–8 months of eating.

If you aren't sure how much to plant, for summer crops I suggest you start with the following space allotments:

- One square foot for each tomato, pepper and cucumber plant; three to six plants of each usually provide enough for a small family's fresh eating. Grow more plants if you plan to make tomato sauce, pickles, etc., to store.

- 2–4 square feet each for these fast-growing vegetables: lettuce, other salad greens, scallions, spinach, Chinese cabbage.
- 8–12 square feet for vegetables that occupy the beds all season: beans (one pole bean tepee takes about 8–10 square feet of soil area), leeks, broccoli, kale, cabbage, Swiss chard.
- 20–40 square feet for each of the "big" vegetables: that's a patch of 20–40 sweet corn plants, three summer squash, or three winter squash.

Crop Rotation

Rotating crops means that you don't follow one crop with another crop from the same plant family (see Table 2.2). Where you grew potatoes last summer, you wouldn't plant tomatoes this year, because they are both in the nightshade family (Solanaceae). This complicates garden planning, but not too much. Some sources recommend leaving 3–4 years between plantings of the same family. For a home garden, not only is this unrealistic, but for a lot of vegetables I think it is also unnecessary. You might only have certain places that suit tall crops or heat-loving crops, leaving little ability to rotate these to other beds.

That said, the most important plant families to rotate are the carrot, cabbage, nightshade and onion families because they are most at risk from insect pests or disease (see Table 2.2). To simplify crop rotation, try to grow plants from these families together in blocks (e.g., all cabbage family members together). Luckily, some important families for winter crops (goosefoot, sunflower and valerian families) are low risk, so you can plant or interplant them anywhere, anytime.

When crop rotation is important (and when it isn't):

For pest insects: Crop rotation helps to avoid damage from the few insect species that attack the roots of the crops in this region. Because the larvae (immature stages) attack the roots, you only have to avoid planting another susceptible crop for as long as it takes those larvae to become adults that will fly away to other parts of the garden. So don't follow a carrot crop immediately with more carrots, because you might encourage a carrot rust fly attack. After a couple of summer months, though, the adults will have flown away, and you can plant carrots in that bed again if necessary. Other pests in the soil, such as wireworms, pillbugs and climbing cutworms, attack a wide range of plants, so crop rotation doesn't help control them (for more on pests and diseases, see Chapter 9).

For diseases: Some serious plant diseases are caused by organisms that can stay dormant in the soil for several years (17 years, for clubroot!). If you have had plants infected by a soil-borne disease, you should avoid planting related plants in the same place — for as many years as possible. Get help in identifying the disease problem, however, because some (rusts, for example) are spread by the wind, not in the soil, so crop rotation is irrelevant.

For fertility: Growing the same crop year after year depletes the soil of the nutrients used by that crop, which is why you see recommendations to alternate "heavy feeders," such as potatoes or corn, with vegetables that enrich the soil with nitrogen, such as beans. While this is important in agriculture, I don't think it really matters for a garden, because you can easily dig in enough soil amendments to compensate for nutrients used by a previous crop.

Making the Most of the Space You Have

Land is expensive, and few people can afford the large lots or rural properties that make it possible to have a large garden. However, the point of this book is that you don't have to have much space to grow a surprising amount of food, especially if you adopt some of the intensive methods described below.

There are several ways to increase productivity so that your garden is full of food most months of the year:

Grow more plants in the same space:

- In fertile soil you can grow vegetables closer than the spacing recommended on the seed package — sometimes much closer. A bonus is that densely planted crops help control weeds by shading them out.
- Grow vegetables in beds, rather than spaced out in rows: you waste much less space on unproductive rows and have a smaller area to weed.
- Within a bed, set individual plants in a staggered pattern, which allows closer spacing while giving each plant room for its roots.

Table 2.2. Vegetable families for planning crop rotation.

Plant families [older names appear in brackets]	Family member plants	Relative nutrient demands	Root pests and soil-borne diseases in the coastal region*
Carrot family Apiaceae [Umbelliferae]	Carrots, celery, celeriac, parsnips, parsley, cilantro	Light	Carrot rust fly
Cabbage (Mustard) family Brassicaceae [Cruciferae]	Broccoli, cabbages, Brussels sprouts, kales, cauliflower, Chinese cabbage, mustards, arugula, kohlrabi, radishes, rutabagas, turnips	Heavy (leaf crops moderate)	Cabbage root maggot; clubroot disease
Nightshade family Solanaceae	Tomatoes, peppers, eggplant, potatoes, ground cherries, tomatillo	Heavy	Soil-borne wilt viruses; nematodes
Onion family Alliaceae	Onions, leeks, garlic, shallots	Moderate	Onion maggot; several root diseases
Goosefoot family Chenopodiaceae	Beets, spinach, Swiss chard	Light	Leafminers
Grass family Poaceae [Graminae]	Corn	Heavy	
Gourd family Cucurbitaceae	Cucumbers, squashes, melons, gourds, pumpkins	Heavy	
Pea family Fabaceae [Leguminosae]	Beans, peas, lentils, chickpeas, clover	Light (soil builders)	Pea leaf weevil
Sunflower family Asteraceae [Compositae]	Artichoke, lettuce, endive, Jerusalem artichoke, salsify	Light-moderate	
Valerian family Caryophylleae	Corn salad	Light	

*Note: This column only shows diseases and pests unique to each plant family.

Table 2.3. Examples of close spacing.		
Crop	**Inches/feet**	**Centimeters/meters**
Onions, garlic	3–4 inches apart	8–10 cm apart
Celery, celeriac, leeks	6–8 inches apart	15–20 cm apart
Squash—3 plants per hill	3 feet between hills	1 m between hills
Broccoli, cabbage	12–16 inches apart	30–40 cm apart
Peas, beans	1.5–3 inches apart	4–8 cm apart in rows

In the first years of a new garden, the soil might not be fertile enough to plant too densely, so keep an eye on how your plants look. You might need to give them a dose of liquid fertilizer a few times over a summer to keep them growing well. Thin the plants if it looks like they are struggling. Over time, as you continue to add compost and other amendments, your soil will improve and you can grow plants closer together.

FIGURE 2.8. Weeds don't have a chance in densely planted beds. I was too busy to weed this bed all summer (the few weeds trying to hang on are along the edge).

Take advantage of vertical space. Crops with sprawling vines take up more space on the ground than their roots do in the soil below. Trellising them off the ground opens up more space for planting:

- Stake up tomatoes, cucumbers and melons or train the vines on a trellis. (You can make slings of cloth to support melons so they don't pull the vines off the trellis.)
- Grow pole beans instead of bush beans; they produce more over a longer season in the same amount of space.

- Use the space along fences and walls to grow plants you can train vertically, such as beans, grapes and kiwi vines.

As well as using vertical space, sometimes you can use non-garden space to accommodate plants temporarily. For example, you can plant winter squash (most are notorious ramblers) where you can direct the vines between corn plants, under fruit trees, over a patio or other non-garden space.

Avoid wasting space on unproductive plants: Gardeners soon learn that a small patch of lettuce can provide a lot of salad, and that radishes shoot past their prime in days. To avoid wasting space on crops you won't use, sow smaller amounts of the quick-maturing vegetables at 2–4 week intervals. That way you don't have too much of any one vegetable to deal with at one time, and you can enjoy a longer harvest of vegetables in prime condition. The coastal growing season is quite long for crops that thrive in cool conditions, making second, third, or even fourth plantings of peas, lettuce and cauliflower possible (see Table 2.4 for other examples).

FIGURE 2.9. An astonishing quantity of pole beans grows in a few square feet of space.

Table 2.4. Examples of succession planting.	
Crops	**Schedules**
Radishes, lettuce, mixed salad greens	Every 2–3 weeks until mid-August
Peas	Monthly, late March to end of June
Sweet corn, early variety (65–70 days)	Two-week intervals, early May (started indoors) to mid/late June
Bush beans	Three weeks apart, mid-May to late June
Cauliflower, spring/summer varieties	Monthly, March (started indoors) to late July
Potatoes, for harvest as new potatoes	Two or three plantings between March and June

Get Rid of Surplus Plants!

It seems like a waste to discard unused plants—but it isn't nearly as much of a waste as an unproductive garden bed. Give the vegetables away or pull them out (and make a note not to plant so many next time). But if you do overplant, you can console yourself knowing they will make great compost or mulch.

Keep trying out different planting dates for your favorite vegetables: you might discover how to enjoy them longer. It was only after years of sowing peas in early spring (having given up on them as a fall crop), that I discovered how well they do when sown in mid-June in the shady end of my garden. I now enjoy peas through October!

Minimize the time garden space stands empty: A Dutch grower once told me "never leave a space empty more than a day." In our climate, this is quite possible. Many vegetables for winter harvests can be sown immediately after spring crops are finished. For example, the earliest sowings of peas, radishes, lettuce and other salad greens are usually exhausted by July. Garlic (planted the fall before) and onions (from onion sets) are also harvested by mid-July. So July is a perfect time to sow hardy greens, such as

Table 2.5. Approximate dates when early crops are finished.

Planting date and crops	Harvest usually completed
March–April-sown peas, lettuce, mixed salad greens, radishes Early garlic (planted the previous fall)	1st week of July
March–April planted onions (from sets), Chinese cabbage, cauliflower, carrots May–June sown lettuce and greens, radishes Main crop of garlic (planted the previous fall)	3rd week of July
May-sown bush beans, cauliflower, carrots Sweet onions (from March seedlings) Early potatoes	Late August

kales, Komatsuna and leaf beet, which will occupy the garden bed until the end of May the following year.

Be ready to fill gaps as they arise by keeping a small area in one of your beds as a seedling nursery. Crops such as cauliflower or corn, for example, leave empty spaces in the bed as they are harvested one by one. You can fill these spaces immediately with seedlings of lettuce, kale, Chinese cabbage, leaf beet and other plants if you already have them started in a nursery bed.

You can also use the seedling nursery to make a winter crop planting schedule work when crops that should be finished are lingering later than expected. A cool summer can jam up the schedule for hardy vegetables that should be sown in July. But you can start your winter crops in a seedling bed (or in flats) and move them to growing beds when space opens up. It depends on the crop, but most transplants can be set out 3–4 weeks later than they

FIGURE 2.10. A small seedling bed provides transplants to fill gaps or get winter crops started while you are waiting for their space to open up.

would be seeded directly. This buys you an extra month to allow a crop still occupying a bed to mature. Or, because local nurseries are beginning to carry winter crop seedlings in the summer, you can skip sowing seeds altogether and just buy transplants to fill gaps as needed.

Interplanting: Some combinations of vegetables can share the same garden space. Plants that occupy different root zones or mature at different times make good partners. For example, lettuce, which has short roots and grows quickly, can be tucked in around a variety of larger, deep-rooted vegetables. The lettuce is harvested and gone by the time the other crop needs the space. I never plant lettuce separately anymore because there are so many places to fit it in among other crops.

One of my favorite combinations is planting lettuce between Brussels sprouts, which, because they grow quite large, need to be widely spaced. The same goes for winter cauliflower and winter broccoli, which occupy garden space in beds from mid-June to the following spring. When they are still small, interplant them with lettuce (or other salad greens). Or, plant cauliflower and broccoli between cucumbers or melons. The low vines shade the soil, which is good for the cauliflower and broccoli roots in the summer.

Some of my other favorite combinations:

- Leafy greens (Swiss chard, Chinese cabbage) can be planted in alternating rows between root crops (carrots, beets).
- Green sprouting broccoli (a very large, productive summer broccoli) can be interplanted with early cauliflowers, which are harvested by the time the broccoli expands to fill the space.
- Radishes sown sparsely in carrot beds break the soil for the carrots and are half grown by the time the carrots germinate.
- Lettuce grows well between newly planted strawberries or asparagus.
- Onion sets planted along the edges of garden beds mature in mid- to late July and leave the space to the other crop.

Whatever the combinations you try, be alert to how the plants are growing. Thin or remove the interplanted crop if the main crop is struggling or supplement with a feeding of liquid fertilizer as needed.

Underplanting: Also called "relay cropping," underplanting is starting the next crop in a bed before the previous crop is finished. It works particularly well for fast-growing greens (corn salad, lettuce, spinach, leaf mustard), which can be sown underneath warm-season plants that will be finished in the fall.

FIGURE 2.11. Interplanting Brussels sprouts with lettuce for two crops in one space.

For example, in late August, I lift up winter squash vines and broadcast corn salad and lettuce seeds over the soil. The seedlings grow well in the shade of the vines and are a good size by the time cold weather puts an end to the squash.

You can underplant squash, cucumbers, melons, tomatoes and peppers. To avoid disturbing the new crop, cut the spent plants at the soil line rather than pulling them out.

FIGURE 2.12. Squash vines underplanted with corn salad broadcast over the soil in late August.

Developing a Planting Plan

I hope your head isn't spinning with how complicated this all sounds. Garden plans can be as simple or as complex as you want, but the more planning you do, the better use you will make of your garden space. I find a plan really helps me be sure I save enough space for winter crops that won't be sown until mid-summer.

Here are my suggested steps in developing a garden plan:

1. Make a list of what you want to grow. Check your seed collection to make sure you have enough of each variety for the year's plantings.

2. Sketch a plan of the garden beds, marking areas that might be limited to certain crops. For example, I look for:

FIGURE 2.13. The same bed after the squash were removed, ready to produce salad greens all winter.

An Example of Intensive Planting

Here is an example of how interplanting and underplanting worked over the course of a year in one of my garden beds:

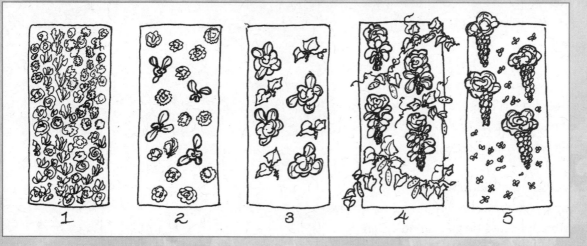

1. April: Set out mixed lettuce seedlings.
2. Early June: Set out Brussels sprouts plants between the remaining lettuce. About half of the lettuce has been harvested by this time.
3. Late June: The lettuce is all done. Set out cucumbers plants between the Brussels sprouts.
4. August: Gently lift the cucumber vines and broadcast corn salad seed under the living vines.
5. October: Cucumbers are all done and vines removed. For the rest of the winter, the bed is occupied by the mature Brussels sprouts plants with corn salad covering the soil between them.

For the purpose of figuring out the crop rotation for this bed, the only plant family of concern is the cabbage family, which at various times occupied most or all of the bed. Because of the risk of overwintering root maggots in the soil, I didn't plant any cabbage family vegetables in the bed until late summer of the following year.

- sunny, warm spots: best for tomatoes, squash, cucumbers, corn;
- areas with less sun: could grow lettuce, peas, Chinese cabbage;
- places for tall crops: on the north side of the garden for corn or pole beans;
- areas with well-drained soil: good for overwintering crops;
- areas under roof overhangs or decks: suitable for winter crops sown in August, such as spinach and winter lettuce.

3. Next, identify the space needed for winter vegetables because planting these at the right time is critical. That means beds have to be empty and available when it is time to plant. Decide where the big blocks of winter crops are going to go, and note when they should be planted (for a suggested planting schedule, see Table 8.1). For example:

- Carrots, beets and other root vegetables for an 8-month supply (seed July 1).
- Cabbage family: winter broccoli and cauliflower, cabbages (transplant to growing beds in July).
- Hardy lettuce and other leafy greens (winter lettuce, kales, leafy mustard, Swiss chard and leaf beet, arugula, radicchio, Chinese cabbage, Komatsuna, etc.) (seed late July to early August).

4. With the winter crop beds reserved, decide which early and short-season crops (e.g., onion sets, early lettuce, radishes, peas) you can fit into those spaces before you need the beds for winter crops. You don't have to plant these beds, of course, but it makes the most use of garden space if you do.

5. Now go ahead and assign the rest of the crops to the remaining garden space. Try to keep together plants in the four most critical plant families (carrot, cabbage, nightshade and onion) to make it easier to rotate crops (see Table 2.2). Pencil in where each crop or family of crops could go on your plan.

6. When you are happy with the plan, you might want to make a chronological list of what you will plant. See Chapter 8 for a step-by-step year-round planting schedule.

FIGURE 2.14. Plan to have space open for sowing winter crops. These beets (background) were sown July 1st; the lettuce and endive (foreground), August 8th.

7. Keep records so you can perfect your planting plan next year. I know we all think we will remember what was planted and how it went — but next season rolls around and we are left scratching our heads. So, really, write it down! When I finally indulged in buying a 10-year garden journal (from Lee Valley Tools), I found it so much easier to keep good records of planting dates, garden plans, harvest dates, pest problems and favorite varieties (and failures).

The Simplest Plan of All

If you have a level, sunny area for your garden large enough to lay out five or six parallel beds of equal size and sun exposure, you can develop a plan that you can use year after year. Essentially, you develop a plan for each bed that you can shift over by one bed each year. For example:

- You might have one bed for nightshade family crops that has vine tomatoes staked up at the north end, bush tomatoes and peppers in the middle, and potatoes at the south end (because they are low growing and won't shade the other crops).
- The next bed over might have pole beans and peas at the north end, bush beans at the south end, with the peas followed by winter greens.
- The next bed could have sweet corn at the north end and squash and cucumbers on the south end.
- One bed could have all kinds of cabbage family crops and blocks of Swiss chard and other greens, and,
- The last bed could be devoted to leeks, garlic, onions and other roots.

Next year, you could use the same plan, but shift it over by one bed. In this example, the beans and peas would move to the bed where the nightshade crops were growing, the corn and squash would go to where the beans and peas were, and so on. This would give you a crop rotation cycle of 5 or 6 years.

Once you figure out how much of each crop you need and the succession plantings to make the most of the space, you will have a perennial garden plan.

CHAPTER 3

PREPARING THE SOIL

The Ideal Garden Soil

The best soil for a vegetable and fruit garden is deep, fertile and well drained. Prime agricultural land has these characteristics, but the soil in your garden plot might start out far from this ideal. Not to worry — even the worst soils can be amended to grow a garden. The better your soil conditions are to start with, however, the less work it will take to make it into a productive garden.

Soil chemistry is a complex subject. Fortunately, if you follow a few basic rules for managing soil, you can grow a perfectly good organic garden without getting too technical. Think of the soil as a living, breathing, densely populated community of organisms (roots, fungi, bacteria, insects, mites, worms, and a lot else besides) living in a moist, dark world. Keeping this community happy, rich and busy is the essence of organic gardening. If you can do that, you will reap the rewards of a thriving garden.

Deep soil: A garden should have soil deep enough to provide a root zone that anchors plants and allows roots to reach sufficient nutrients. A small annual plant like lettuce can grow in a foot of soil, if necessary, but obviously a fruit tree has much a larger root zone.

On natural, undisturbed land, there is a top layer of soil (the topsoil) that is several inches to over a foot deep. This is usually darker than the layers of soil below (the subsoil) because it has more organic matter in it. Ideally, there is a thick layer of topsoil sitting on subsoil that is several feet to several yards deep. If your soil profile is like this, you are fortunate indeed!

It is more likely that when you start digging up the yard for a garden you will discover there isn't an obvious topsoil layer — or there is, but it is only an inch or two deep. Unless care was taken to preserve topsoil when the building was originally built, the topsoil was probably mixed up with excavated subsoil (or even stripped off and sold). The builder may have then trucked in a soil-like substance to spread on the yard areas after construction. It could be a thin layer, barely enough to grow grass (which can grow in practically anything). This situation is all too common, but it can be remedied: If there is hardly any soil before you hit gravel, rock or very stony subsoil, you could build raised beds and bring in good soil to fill the boxes. If there seems to be a foot or two of workable soil, but it is of poor quality (it is light-colored, for example), use the soil you have and enrich it with fertilizers and other amendments.

Fertile soil: Good garden soil has an adequate supply of the major and minor nutrients as well a good supply of organic matter. It also has a healthy community of soil organisms. You won't be able to see the smallest microbes, but they will be there and thriving if conditions are right.

Plants use three elements in large quantities for photosynthesis and growth processes. These are called "primary nutrients":

- **Nitrogen:** This is the main element for plant growth, and plants use it in greater amounts than any other. Nitrogen promotes rapid leafy growth and is a key building block of protein in plants. Microorganisms breaking down organic matter in the soil release nitrogen in a form usable by plants. Until there are good levels of organic matter in the soil, nitrogen is most likely to be in short supply. So, in the first few years of an organic garden, you usually need to provide some extra nitrogen during the growing season

- **Phosphorus:** This promotes flowering, fruiting and strong stems and roots. Phosphorus doesn't move around much in the soil and isn't leached out by rain. Soils often have sufficient phosphorus, but it isn't necessarily available to plants, especially in acid soils (see *Our Soils Need Lime*, page 61). We usually need to dig in additional phosphorus to make sure there is enough in the root zone. Even so, availability depends on a good supply of organic matter in the soil and a healthy community of fungi and other microorganisms.

- **Potassium (potash):** This element regulates the production of proteins and starches and makes for sturdy plants. It plays an important role in plant disease resistance and heat and cold tolerance. Potassium can leach out of the soil with heavy rain, but the more organic matter there is in the soil, the less likely this is to happen. Root crops need more potassium than other vegetables.

Plants also need "secondary nutrients": calcium, magnesium and sulfur — in smaller amounts, but they are no less essential. A third group of nutrients are essential too, but in very small quantities. These "micronutrients" or "trace elements" are iron, manganese, chlorine, zinc, boron, molybdenum and copper.

Well-drained soil: Soil organisms and plant roots suffocate in waterlogged soil. Poorly drained soils can grow good summer crops that are sown after the soil has dried out, but such soils won't be good for winter or early spring crops. Plants suffer if they are planted where water stands for more than 24 hours. When it rains day after day in mid-winter, however, water may pool anywhere temporarily. As long as the water drains within a day after the rain stops, plants should be fine.

Poorly drained soils can be remedied by installing subsurface drainage. This is costly and may not be possible on small properties because there is nowhere to direct the water. The most practical solution often is to build raised beds tall enough to elevate the main root zone above the water line.

Soil Texture

The ideal soil has balanced proportions of clay particles (the finest), silt particles (medium-sized) and sand (largest particles). These balanced soils are called "loam" soils; they are the gold standard for horticulture. I don't know why I bother bringing this up, though, because so few gardeners are lucky

Special Case: No Soil?

If you don't have a patch of soil to cultivate, try for a plot in a community garden. Or, if you have a sunny deck or balcony, many vegetables can be grown in containers (see Chapter 7). If you have a large sunny area, but it is paved or covered with gravel or rock, you could still have a productive garden if you invest in building large planters. Planters should be at least 2 feet deep; they can be any length and any width as long as you can easily reach to the middle. Put a 6-inch layer of gravel in the bottom to ensure drainage before shoveling in the soil. Buy the best soil available, and mix in a generous amount of compost, leaf mold (well-rotted leaves) and other organic matter as you fill (1 or 2 parts compost to 9 parts soil).

FIGURE 3.1. In the absence of good garden soil (or for convenience), building raised beds with deep soil works very well.

enough to start with loamy soil. It is good idea, however, to have some idea of the texture of your soil so that you know how to improve it and the best way to irrigate it.

Sandy soil: Sandy soil feels gritty when rubbed between your fingers and may have small stones mixed in. Such soils are strong (don't compact easily), well aerated, and usually well-drained. In the spring, they warm up quicker and can often be worked earlier than loam or clay soils. The downside is that they don't hold water and nutrients as well as loam. This can be greatly improved by adding organic matter and fertilizers.

Clay soil: Soil with a high proportion of clay feels slippery and leaves a sticky coating when you rub the wet soil between your fingers. Clay soils are "heavy," meaning dense and easily compacted. They are sticky when wet and make hard clods if they are cultivated when wet. The upside is that clay particles hold water and nutrients well and make them available to plants. They are excellent garden soils once amended with coarse organic matter and, if necessary, coarse sand, to improve aeration and make the soil easier to handle. Before investing in sand, though, get to know the soil and see how things go with compost and other fertilizers. If you do decide to bring in sand, it should be coarse, sharp builder's sand (the kind used for making concrete), not river sand, which is smooth and packs down when wet. Put on a 1 inch (1–2 cm) layer and dig it in.

Soil Structure

In an ideal soil, the tiny particles are clumped together in larger crumbs with stable air spaces between them. This structure dictates how quickly water drains through the soil and how well oxygen gets to roots and soil organisms. Humus, which is the dark brownish residue of decomposed organic matter, coats soil particles and sticks them together (as well as releasing nutrients). Soil particles are also clumped together by the activity of earthworms, microorganisms and roots, especially the roots of grasses.

The point of this information is that you can destroy soil structure by careless cultivation. Excessive rototilling, for example, dashes apart the crumb structure. As the structure collapses, the soil becomes compacted, which slows drainage and the movement of air. Cultivating while soil is too wet also destroys structure, particularly in soils with a high proportion of clay. When such soils dry out, there are often rock-hard clods to contend with, or you are left with a hard crust on the soil surface.

Organic Matter

Organic matter provides slow-release nutrients as it is broken down by earthworms and microorganisms in the soil. And slow release does mean *slow*: studies show that the rate of nitrogen released from mature compost can keep increasing for at least 8 months after it is dug in. It continues to release small amounts for much longer, which is why gardens fed with compost every year become more fertile over time.

No matter what type of soil you have, the one thing that improves every soil is organic matter: coarse organic material improves aeration in clay soils; fine, well-digested organic matter (humus) improves the moisture and nutrient-holding capacity of sandy soils. The humus in the organic matter improves soil structure and makes nutrients available to roots.

Sources of organic matter for urban gardeners:

Homemade compost: Use it when it has become dark, crumbly and well digested. Apply a layer of 1–2 inches (2–4 cm) annually (more on this, below).

Commercial compost: Several brands of composted fish and wood waste are made on Vancouver Island and in Washington state (see Resources). Some are certified for organic growers by the OMRI (Organic Materials Review Institute). They are available bagged or in bulk quantities. There are also bagged mushroom, steer and poultry manure composts (these are cheaper, but quite inferior to the fish composts).

Municipal compost: Some municipalities collect yard waste, compost it, and sell the finished product back to residents by the bucket or bag or in larger quantities. Because the sources of material are unknown, this compost is not allowed for certified organic growers. There have been problems in the past with herbicide residues in such compost in the United States; however, this is much less of a concern in municipalities that restrict pesticide use by residents.

Leaf mold: Pile any kind of leaves in a bin for the winter, and you will have leaf mold by spring. A deep mulch of leaves applied to garden beds in the fall decomposes on the spot. All kinds of leaves are fine, including oak and bigleaf maple. Black walnut leaves should be composted first to break down the juglone in the leaves, which inhibits the growth of some kinds of plants.

Two other sources of organic matter are animal manure and green manure (discussed below), but for most gardens, I recommend sticking with the above sources.

The Manure Problem

Older garden books always talk about digging in "aged manure." These days, it is pretty rare for an urban or suburban dweller to get ahold of livestock manure. If you *can* get cow, chicken or pig manure from a commercial farm, you must compost it carefully in a well-turned, hot compost pile before using it. Disease organisms that cause serious illnesses in people, such as *E. coli, Salmonella* and *Campylobacter,* are now common in the livestock industry. It is no longer enough to pile manure and wait for it to "age."

If you can get rabbit, goat, sheep or llama manure, you can dig it in without composting it first. These manures are lower in nitrogen, so they don't burn plant roots, and they do not carry the risk of human disease that other manures do. They should be composted before use, however, if there is a lot of straw, sawdust or shavings mixed in with the manure (more than 10% of the volume). Many gardeners find it makes the most sense to buy bags of composted and pasteurized manures at garden centers. These don't carry the disease risk that raw manure does.

Horse manure: For many people in suburban areas, the most readily available manure is horse manure. Even though it isn't a disease risk, there are reasons to compost horse manure before using it:

- Many seeds pass right through a horse's digestive system, so the manure is a source of agricultural weeds you may not have had in your garden. It usually has bedding mixed in with it. How much and what kind will dictate how long it should be composted. Straw bedding composts quickly, but if there is a lot of sawdust or wood shavings, the manure should be composted for about a year.

- Most horses are given de-worming medication regularly. Although much of it stays in the horse, there may be some in the manure right after worming. These products are usually avermectin-based products, which are extracted from cultures of a soil microorganism. The compounds break down quickly, but composting for 3 months ensures the worming products have entirely disappeared.

Green manure: These are living crops, such as fall rye or clover, grown for a short time and then dug into the soil. While this is a practical way for growers to boost organic matter in a field, I do not recommend green manures for backyard gardeners for several reasons:

- Most people with small, intensively planted gardens don't have the space. If you are growing food year-round, the garden is filled with crops much of the year, so it is difficult to include green manures in the sequence — and why waste the production time? You can add all the organic matter the garden needs in the form of leaves, compost and mulch materials.

- A cover crop is tricky to manage because it must be dug in when it is a few inches to a foot high, while it is still lush, green and easy to dig. A delay of a week or two results in a crop that is too tall and woody to be a "green manure," because it is nearly impossible to turn under. What could be more discouraging?

- Where wireworms are a problem (and they are widespread in this region), green manures can make the problem worse because the adults like to lay their eggs on grasses (see entry for wireworms in Chapter 9).

Compost

One of my goals in writing this book is to banish "composter's guilt." I believe this widespread (in gardeners) anxiety comes from comparing those ideal instructions found in garden books with how it really happens in a home garden. When I ask people in my gardening classes, "Who turns their compost regularly?" it is rare to see even one hand go up — and that one usually belongs to an energetic new gardener going by a book (written by someone who works too hard!).

After years of making "proper" compost when I had a market garden, followed by decades of *intending* to make good compost, but not quite getting around to it for my home garden, I finally realized my gardens were not suffering. In fact, yields appeared to be increasing, not decreasing.

I often just leave crop waste on the ground where it grew. Up until this year, I piled the rest into a bin to decompose at a leisurely rate. Now that I have a couple of chickens, I heave everything in their run first and let them go over it. Every month or two, I fork the well-shredded material mixed with manure into a bin beside the run to finish composting. Easy as pie!

Following are some notes on the various methods of making compost, starting with the simplest. Although it has been many years since I bothered with hot composting, I have included a procedure to follow in case you have farm manure to compost.

Sheet composting: This is how nutrients are recycled in nature: organic material lying on the surface of the soil decomposes in place. The material disappears as it is consumed by worms and other organisms. Green, soft materials disappear quickly, while drier, woodier material is broken down more slowly. When leaves and other materials are used as mulch, they continuously break down and feed the soil.

I routinely leave green crop waste, such as pea vines or bean plants, on the ground and transplant seedlings for the next crop through the mulch. In fact, you can leave any material on the soil under the plants to decompose, including pulled weeds, lower leaves of cabbage or squash, leaves from harvested corn or cauliflower plants, etc.

An extreme variation on this is "lasagna" gardening, which involves spreading layers of crop waste, peat moss, leaves, manure, spoiled hay or other organic matter on the soil surface until it is a foot thick. The layer takes the place of soil; you plant directly into the mix. This method works, but you

FIGURE 3.2. The wire compost bin holds layers of crop waste, horse manure and leaves. Kitchen scraps are composting in the closed composter.

have to be able to get ahold of *a lot* of organic material—and have a means of hauling it to the garden. While this is a "no till" method, it is not a "no work" method.

Cold composting: Most home compost is made using this method: simply pile materials in the compost bin as they become available and leave them there. After about a year, pull apart the pile and use the well digested, crumbly brown material in the center and bottom of the pile. Undigested stalks and other coarse material that hasn't decomposed goes into another bin to become the bottom layer of the next pile.

You can build a more organized cold compost pile if you can stockpile enough materials to build a pile all at once (see below).

Cold composting won't kill weed seeds. It also won't kill all plant disease organisms, although it does kill those that can't survive on decomposing plant material.

Hot composting: This labor-intensive way to make compost results in a pile that heats up and is ready in months. If piles are carefully made, turned and managed (see below), the temperatures reached during the heating phase of the decomposing may be high enough—and last long enough—to kill plant pathogens and weed seeds. This is the only way that cow, poultry or pig manure from commercial farms should be composted.

The Well-Organized Compost Pile

A good time to make any compost pile is in the fall, when there is usually lots of garden waste, leaves and other material available at the same time. Whether you are going to leave the pile to compost slowly (cold composting) or keep turning it to make hot compost, the decomposer organisms need:

- **Good ventilation:** The organisms that digest organic material take in oxygen and get rid of carbon dioxide, so build piles with good ventilation. An easy way to ventilate the center of a pile is to build the pile with a length of wide plastic pipe (a 4-inch drain pipe works well) standing in the center. Pull the pipe out when the pile is built, leaving a donut hole in the center. Some people make a cylinder of wire mesh and leave it as the core of the pile.
- **Moisture, but not too much:** In the summer, make sure the pile doesn't dry out. Over the winter, cover the top of piles with a plastic tarp, a sheet of plywood or other material so that it sheds rain.
- **Balanced ingredients:** Use whatever materials you can get most easily. Ideally, materials used to build the pile should roughly balance nitrogen content with carbon content: "Brown" dry materials tend to be higher in carbon and include bulky materials such as straw, mature crop residues, corn stalks and shredded paper. "Green" materials are higher in nitrogen and include fresh garden trimmings, most fresh manures, leafy weeds and kitchen waste. Try to layer twice as much brown material as green material in the pile. Some materials already have a good nitrogen-to-carbon ratio: leaves, ground-up tree trimmings, and horse manure (as long as there is a minimum of sawdust or shavings mixed in) can be used in any quantity.

Bins or Piles?

Either works fine. Bins, however, usually look better in a landscape setting than an open pile. A good size for a pile or a bin is about 4 × 4 × 4 feet (a meter square by a meter high). Bins can be as simple as cylinders of fence wire or more sturdily built of wood, plastic "wood" or other material. Beloved of composting enthusiasts, a system of three side-by-side bins allows you to turn compost from one bin to the next and have an extra bin to accumulate material until there is enough to make a pile. Sides of bins should be slatted to allow air circulation.

Composting don'ts: Things *not* to put in a compost pile include pet poop, dairy products, meat, bones, fat and oil. Starchy or sweet kitchen scraps attract rats to open bins, but can be composted in rat-proof composters. Don't put wood ashes or lime into the compost pile either. It makes the compost more alkaline, which depletes the nitrogen content (in the form of ammonia lost to the atmosphere).

Note: The "green cone" type of composter is meant for disposal of pet waste, meat and other materials. The contents should never go into a compost pile or be used on a food garden.

Seedy weeds in the compost? Even the hottest compost piles are rarely hot enough to kill weed seeds. Here are two ways to approach this:

- Just go ahead and throw the weeds on the compost pile, anyway. In the future, try to pull weeds before they flower. Better yet, keep your soil mulched to smother weeds and inhibit germination of seeds so there won't be weeds to worry about.
- Keep a "seedy weed" compost separate from the main garden compost. Use this compost where the seeds won't get a chance to germinate, such as to enrich the bottom of a planting hole for a tree or shrub.

Compost Troubleshooting

- *Pile doesn't heat up.* Conditions for heat-loving microbes are not ideal. Usually, you need more materials richer in nitrogen, such as manure. Check that the materials are damp enough, but not waterlogged, both of which conditions will inhibit the growth of microbes.
- *Ammonia or a rotten smell occurs.* The materials are not getting enough oxygen. Turn the compost more often and mix in more carbon-rich, "brown" materials.
- *Rats appear.* Check on what is being composted and make sure there is no attractive kitchen or crop waste (fruit, starchy or sweet garbage, meat scraps, etc.).

How to Make Hot Compost

Keeping in mind the general requirements given above regarding ventilation, moisture and ingredient mix, here's how to make hot compost:

1. Start with a layer of coarse stalks or small branches at the bottom of the pile to assist aeration.
2. Alternate layers of dry, brown and wet, green materials (or mix them together), using about twice as much dry material by volume as wet material. To speed up the process, shred or cut up materials. The smaller the pieces, the faster the organisms will work and the higher the temperature will be in the pile.
3. Water as you go to moisten the dry materials until they feel uniformly damp, but not soggy.
4. Turn the piles two or three times, a couple of weeks to a month apart, completely mixing material from the outside of the pile into the center. As a pile heats up, the heat drives water out of the center of the pile, so you may need to add more water when you turn the pile.
5. In warm weather, the heating phase takes about a month. But hot compost is not ready to use at the end of the heating phase; it must be given another 1–2 months to "cure" so that organisms that grow in cooler temperatures can spread throughout the compost and finish the composting process. This step is necessary to make nitrogen available to plants and to break down compounds that inhibit the germination of seeds and growth of roots.

Do You Need Compost Starter?

Nope. There are plenty of native bacteria already on the materials you compost. Not only are commercial "activators," unnecessary, but the native bacteria from your own soil are better adapted to your garden conditions than bacteria grown in a laboratory. If you want to inoculate the compost, sprinkle a little finished compost or a shovel of garden soil into the materials as you build the pile.

Using Compost

Regardless of how it was made, compost is finished when the material is dark and crumbly and has an earthy smell. The greater the variety of starting materials, the more variety of nutrients there will be in the finished product. Composted straw and manure typically has more nitrogen than leaf compost does. Generally, compost is considered to have about 0.5% up to 1% available nitrogen. The rate of release of nutrients from mature compost appears to increase over time, at least for the first eight months.

Where to use compost:

- In new soil, dig in a 4–inch (10–cm) layer of compost.
- For an established garden, dig in a 1–2 inch (2–4 cm) layer of compost once a year.
- Dig in coarse compost to aerate and improve the drainage in clay soils.
- Use screened, finished compost as an ingredient in potting soil for containers or seedlings.
- Apply coarse or half-digested compost to the soil as a mulch.

You can dig in compost between crops from spring through mid-summer, as needed. But don't apply compost (or aged manure) to the soil in the fall. Plants can't use the nutrients then and winter rains will just leach them away. Instead, keep the pile covered to shed rain and preserve nutrients until spring.

Organic Fertilizers

Fertilizers add major and minor nutrients to the soil in larger amounts than compost alone can provide. Fertilizers are necessary because vegetables and fruit need much more of these nutrients to produce good crops than they can get from unfertilized soil. Fertilizers are also necessary to replace the nutrients taken out of the soil by the crops. If you are used to maintaining landscape plants, you might be surprised at how much more fertilizer the food crops need.

The series of three numbers you see written prominently on bags of fertilizer is called the "analysis." The numbers stand for how much the fertilizer contains of the big three: nitrogen (N), phosphorus (P) and potassium (K). The numbers are always in the same order: N-P-K, so a bag of organic fertilizer with 2-4-3 on the label contains 2% available N, 4% available P, and 3% available K. (If the numbers are higher than that [e.g., 10-20-10] you are probably looking at a synthetic fertilizer, not an organic one. Since this book is about organic gardening, I won't dwell on how to use the inorganic fertilizers.) Although application guidelines are given on the fertilizer bag, don't be too concerned about the rates — they are not critical because organic fertilizers won't burn plants if too much is used. Most cost money, though, so see how things are growing before you go overboard on buying more fertilizer.

Nitrogen sources: Blood meal is far and away the best high-nitrogen fertilizer for organic gardeners. The application rate on boxes of blood meal are about 4–8 pounds per 100 square feet (2–4 kg per 10 square meters). The lower numbers would apply to root and fruit crops or for soils with good organic matter levels; the higher rate would suit leafy greens or soils low in organic matter. Alfalfa meal, fish or wood waste compost, and composted manures can also supply useful amounts of nitrogen. Now that my garden has a good supply of organic matter, I only use blood meal as a quick nitrogen boost for crops that need a lot of it.

Liquid fish fertilizer is a good source of nitrogen if plants look deficient during the growing season. Signs of nitrogen deficiency are stunted growth with leaves turning pale yellow. The yellowing usually starts with the oldest leaves and the newest leaf tips. Too much nitrogen makes soft, lush growth with large leaves — at the expense of fruiting or root growth.

Phosphorus sources: Bone meal is a good source of available phosphorus. Application rates for bone meal are usually given as 10 pounds per

FIGURE 3.3. Planting corn seedlings: I dig a heaping tablespoon of blood meal into the soil where I plant each seedling.

The Nitrogen Cycle

Nitrogen exists in different forms in the environment—in fact, air is 79% nitrogen. Microorganisms in the soil are a vital part of the natural processes that move nitrogen in a cycle through the environment. Certain kinds of soil bacteria combine nitrogen from the atmosphere with hydrogen and oxygen, "fixing" it into a form that plants can use. Other decomposers—mostly bacteria and fungi—release nitrogen from organic matter in the soil, making it available to plants.

Soluble nitrogen is leached out of the soil by heavy rain. It pollutes water bodies when it washes out of compost and manure left in uncovered piles or spread on the soil surface during the rainy season. In waterlogged conditions (called "anaerobic" conditions because of the lack of oxygen), certain microorganisms convert nitrogen from the form plants can use into a gaseous form that is lost to the atmosphere. You could look at a sodden, compacted compost pile as a tragic waste of plant food. Nitrogen in the form of ammonia is also released to the air by soil bacteria in very alkaline conditions (which is why you shouldn't put lime or wood ashes in the compost pile).

100 square feet (4–5 kg per 10 square meters). I use about half that on my garden beds. I also dig in a ½ cup of bone meal at the bottom of holes when planting fruit trees and bushes. I also use rock phosphate (a rock dust). Although it releases little phosphorus in the first year, it is a long-term, slow-release source, enhanced by the addition of organic matter to the soil.

Phosphorus-deficient plants are stunted, have less fruit than they should, and often have purplish streaks or patches on the undersides of leaves.

Potassium sources: Wood ashes are high in potassium (also called "potash"). You *can* add too much wood ash to soil, but it takes something like 20 pounds per square yard—and that is an awful lot of wood ash. So practically speaking, a sprinkling of wood ash covering the soil surface is fine.

Greensand (a type of rock mineral) is used as an ingredient in complete organic fertilizers to supply potassium.

Deficient plants don't have a clear set of symptoms, but generally plants are woodier and smaller than they should be (but there are also other reasons for this); leaves can show browning or yellowing, starting at the tips; brown spots appear along the leaf edges; there is some loss of color between leaf veins; and leaves often curl more than is characteristic for the plant.

Secondary and micronutrients: Agricultural lime (see below) adds calcium — and magnesium, if it is dolomitic limestone. Sulfur deficiency isn't a problem in coastal soils, especially garden soil with a good proportion of organic matter from compost. Compost and organic fertilizers supply sufficient micronutrients, so there is no need to specially supplement soil.

The Dose Makes the Poison

Don't try to supplement micronutrients without knowing for certain if it is necessary: most are toxic to plants in larger quantities. For example, a deficiency of boron causes brown, corky spots in apples and deformed leaves in other plants, but too much boron stunts or kills plants. In fact, boron is used in some kinds of herbicides! If you are really concerned about micronutrients, dig in kelp or seaweed meal as a source of micronutrients that doesn't risk plant toxicity.

Easy Fertilizing

Complete organic fertilizer mixes are sold at garden centers and farm supply stores. I recommend them for home gardens because they take the guesswork out of fertilizing (follow quantities per square foot on the bag). However, you can also blend your own. If you already have wood ashes from a wood stove to supply potassium and micronutrients, you could buy blood meal for nitrogen and bone meal for phosphorus and have an excellent fertilizer mix.

Table 3.1. Commonly available organic fertilizers and amendments.

	Ingredients	N-P-K	Application notes
Gaia Green All-Purpose	Alfalfa meal, bone and blood meal, glacial rock dust, potassium sulphate, natural humates, rock phosphate, greensand*, kelp meal, gypsum	4-4-4	Rates on bag
Organic fertilizer **mixed locally	Alfalfa meal, rock phosphate, langbeinite***, dolomitic lime, kelp meal, greensand*, zeolite	2-[4–5]-[3–4]	5 lbs/100 ft² (3 kg/10 m²)
Gaia Green Glacial Rock Dust	Rock dust (minerals)	0-0-1 Calcium, magnesium, trace elements	Rates on bag
Alfalfa meal	Alfalfa	2.5-1-1	Pellets are cheaper form
Kelp/Seaweed meal	Kelp	1-0-2 Micronutrients	
SeaSoil™ Earthbank™ Fish Compost Oly Mountain Fish Compost®	Composted wood and fish waste	2-1.5-0.5	Dig in 1–4 inch (2–10 cm) layer, depending on soil fertility
Fish fertilizer	Liquid fish waste	5-1-1	Instruction on container
Liquid seaweed	Seaweed extract	Micronutrients	Instruction on container
Bone meal	Ground bone	2-[11–14]-0 Source of calcium	10 lbs/100 ft² (4–5 kg/10 m²)
Blood meal	Dried blood	12-0-0	4–8 lb/100 ft² (2–4 kg/10 m²)
Compost	Mixed garden waste, leaves, etc.	1-1-1 Highly variable	Dig in 1–4 inch (2–10 cm) layer, depending on soil fertility
Rock phosphate	Rock dust	0-0-1	Little released first year, more available in later years
Wood ashes		0-1-5 25% calcium	1 lb/100 ft² (0.5 kg/10m²)

* Greensand is a natural, mined mineral containing about 7% potash plus 32 trace elements.
** All-purpose organic fertilizer mix for local soils. Look for mixes available from your local organic farm or garden supplier.
*** Langbeinite (K-Mag) is a natural, mined, mineral containing sulfur, potash and magnesium.

Our Soils Need Lime

Many soils on the West Coast are naturally acidic, though not all. Acidity is measured in terms of pH. A pH of 7 is neutral; lower numbers indicate acidic soil, and higher numbers show the soil is alkaline. Most garden plants grow best at a pH of 6.5 to 6.8, which is slightly acidic.

In the high-rainfall regions of the coast, soils have a natural pH of 5.0 to 5.5. Soils in parts of the region that are in the driest rain shadows of the Olympics and Vancouver Island mountains are less acidic and may not need much lime. If you don't know anything about the soil you plan to use for a garden, it is a good idea to have the soil pH tested (see below).

For acid soils, agricultural lime is the cheapest, most effective amendment you can buy. To compress a lot of complex soil chemistry into one short list, here is why you want to aim for a soil pH just on the slightly acid side of neutral:

- Essential nutrients in the soil become more available to plants, therefore your fertilizer is more effective.
- Naturally occurring heavy metals in the soil become less available to plants (this is usually a good thing).
- Slightly acidic soil benefits the community of soil microorganisms that fix nitrogen, break down organic matter, make nutrients available, protect roots from disease, and improve soil structure.

FIGURE 3.4. Some organic fertilizers and soil amendments available locally, including the useful bucket of wood ashes.

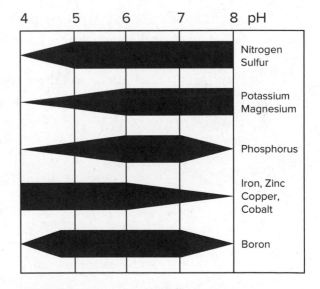

FIGURE 3.5. The relative availability of nutrients at different soil pH is shown by the thickness of the bars. Note that at a range of pH 6.5–6.8, the most nutrients and least heavy metals are available.

To make soil less acidic (i.e., to raise the pH), dig in agricultural lime, which is mainly calcium in the form of ground-up limestone. Any garden center or agricultural supplier will sell it. Dolomitic lime (from dolomite limestone) is a good choice because it also adds magnesium, which coastal soils often lack. Prilled lime, which is limestone that has been made into pellets so it can be evenly spread on lawns with a fertilizer spreader, is fine for a garden, but it costs more. Only some prilled products are acceptable for certified organic growers, so check for OMRI certification before you buy.

Unless a soil test says otherwise, add lime annually. High rainfall leaches calcium and magnesium down through the soil, and a lot of calcium is also taken up by plants. It is important not to overdo lime, but it takes a lot of lime to increase the pH significantly—and it works slowly. In average soil, it takes about 1 lb per square yard (½ kg per square meter) to raise the pH from 6.0 to 7.0. That would mean applying 100 lbs per 100 square yards (50 kg per 100 square meters).

A pound of lime is not very much—after all, it is as heavy as rock. To make a lime scoop, I take a pint cottage cheese container and weigh out a pound (about half a kilo) of lime, which half-fills the container. I draw a thick black line around the inside of the container to mark the level and then use the container as a scoop to measure out enough lime to cover a square yard (or meter).

It is a good idea to test the soil pH again after 4 or 5 years to see if you are on track.

You can skip liming the potato bed for a year if you want to. Potatoes grow fine in soils that have been limed, but they also grow well in acid soil, which suppresses the growth of the microorganism that causes scab on potatoes. This isn't really much of a problem in home garden potatoes, so if your potatoes haven't been troubled by scab, lime away.

Managing Soil Fertility Year Round

Managing the soil for all-season harvests in my garden means being generous once a year when adding amendments. After that, successive plantings and interplantings don't need much else.

Should You Have Your Soil Tested?

A soil test done by a laboratory is worth the investment when you don't know anything about the soil you are starting with. The key thing to find out is the acidity (pH) of the soil. A pH test costs $15–$20 from labs on the Canadian side of the border; US gardeners get a much better deal, with tests ranging from $3–$10. (See Resources at the end of this book for soil testing labs. And be sure to check their websites for instructions on how to collect the soil for the sample.)

If plants are not growing as well as you think they should, and pH is not the problem, it might be worth having a soil test done for all nutrients. A complete test shows levels of phosphorus, potassium, calcium and other important nutrients. It will provide an estimate of the amount of nitrogen that should be available to plants based on the organic matter in the soil.

Don't bother with pH test kits or probes sold at garden centers. *Consumer Reports* tested a range of these products—from the cheapest kits to expensive probes—and found they all gave inaccurate and inconsistent results. Save your money!

With a year-round planting schedule, the main addition of amendments happens whenever the bed is completely empty between early spring and late summer. At that time, I dig in the year's supply of fertilizer (a mix of bone and blood meal and wood ashes, or a complete organic fertilizer), the annual allotment of lime, and as much compost as I have (aiming for an inch-thick layer).

I don't usually add anything more for the next crop unless the previous plants didn't grow as well as expected. However, for hardy leafy greens for winter, which are sown in July and August, I usually do dig in some blood meal to give them a ready supply of nitrogen. There is no point in adding fertilizer or compost to the soil in the fall, because the soil bacteria that make nutrients available are dormant in cold weather, and plants can't use the

FIGURE 3.6. Spring soil preparation includes turning in lime, fertilizer and compost. I don't add any more amendments before planting successive crops during the same season unless the crops look like they need a boost.

nutrients then anyway. You could dig in lime in the fall if a bed is going to go through winter empty or before you plant garlic in October.

If overwintered plants need some extra nitrogen in the spring, you can give them liquid fertilizer or sprinkle blood meal or fish compost beside the plants and lightly scratch it in. I haven't found this necessary, perhaps because there is a natural surge in nitrogen in the spring as soil bacteria get back to work digesting organic matter.

Fertilizing during the growing season: It might be necessary to add supplementary fertilizer in mid-summer, especially for the first couple of years of a new garden that started on less-than-ideal soil. If plants seem to stop growing or are growing very slowly, it could be a lack of nutrients. If you don't know how quickly plants should be growing, ask an experienced gardener what to expect.

Nitrogen is the nutrient most likely to be in short supply, especially in the first few years of an organic garden. When leaves that should be dark green become a pale green or yellow, plants are likely deficient in nitrogen. Slow

Making Compost Tea

Put a shovelful of compost or horse, rabbit, sheep or goat manure into a 5-gallon bucket and fill the bucket with water. Let it steep for 2–5 days, until the water turns dark brown. It is too strong to use as is, so dilute it with water until it is a pale brown, like a weak tea. Water plants with the liquid every week or two or as needed. You can usually brew a couple of buckets of tea from a shovelful of manure or compost.

growth in general (if other light, watering and temperature requirements have been met) can also be a sign of nitrogen deficiency.

You can deliver a useful supply of nutrients in water for a quick boost during the growing season. If plants are low on nitrogen, they will usually respond in a week or two, with leaves becoming darker green and an increased rate of growth.

You can buy liquid fertilizer concentrates (seaweed extract, fish fertilizer) to dilute in water or make your own "tea." (For instructions, see the sidebar *Making Compost Tea*.) There are also various proprietary plant tonics for sale. These may (or may not) give good results, and some are quite expensive. Why pay, I say, when your own compost tea will do the trick?

Cultivating the Soil

It will take work to establish a new garden bed: you may need to shovel soil into raised beds or deal with sod, remove large rocks, or hack into poor, compacted soil to dig in amendments. Once the initial work of establishing new garden beds is done, there will still be work every year to fertilize and prepare seedbeds. Depending on

FIGURE 3.7. Making compost or manure "tea" is easy and cheap!

how you choose to cultivate your garden, though, this annual chore can entail a lot of hard work or a bit of light work.

Some methods are based on a "hands-off" approach: "no till," minimum tillage, deep mulching, and permaculture are examples. In contrast, some gardeners advocate annual deep digging or (worse, in this climate) double digging. Vegetables and fruit can grow under any of these systems, but some techniques are better suited to the coastal climate or are more appropriate for small gardens, than others. Having farmed and gardened over the years on a variety of soils in different climates, I have arrived at the same conclusion as many people before me: minimizing cultivation protects the soil, takes a lot less work, and gives excellent results.

The point of cultivating is to mix in fertilizer, lime and other amendments to prepare a bed for planting. Cultivation also loosens and aerates soil in the root zone, but how important this is depends on the type of soil you have and the level of organic matter in the soil. The objective in preparing a seedbed is a level soil surface free of large clods or stones. If the bed is for transplants, the surface can be left quite rough. In fact, there might be no need to cultivate if you are transplanting a second crop into a bed that has already had amend-

Does Soil Have to Be Cultivated?

It is certainly possible to garden without cultivating, as many gardeners attest. "No till" methods usually involve maintaining a thick mulch on the soil for most or all of the year. But here on the coast, such a heavy mulch keeps the soil from warming up in the spring and encourages slugs and pillbugs to have a heyday at the expense of your seedlings. On the other hand, in the summer, planting well-grown transplants directly into a deeply mulched bed can work quite well. So the answer is: it depends! In this climate, where we plant crops through both cool, wet springs and warm, dry summers, you might apply different cultivation methods to suit the seasons.

ments dug in once that year (for example, setting out cabbage plants after a spring lettuce crop is done). Just dig a hole for the transplants and put them in.

Cultivation Methods

After going through a (very short-lived!) deep-digging phase and then a rototilling phase when I had a large market garden years ago, I have arrived at a comfortable system of minimal cultivation that works fine in this climate, is easy to do, and fits into a busy life.

FIGURE 3.8. My trusty garden fork is now all I use to turn the soil.

Minimum cultivation: Spread lime, compost and other amendments over the surface of the soil. Using a garden fork, lightly fork over the top layer enough to mix amendments into the top 6–8 inches (15–20 cm) of soil. The fork easily combs through loose, open soil. If the soil stays together when you lift a forkful, turn the fork so that it slides off sideways and then mix it into the surface layer. Avoid turning forkfuls of soil completely upside down because this buries the topsoil organisms deeper than they were, away from the warmth and air circulation they need. If you want to loosen the root zone below, drive in the fork and rock it back and forth to loosen the soil, without lifting or turning the soil over.

Advantages of this method:

- It maintains a healthy topsoil community of bacteria, fungi, worms, insects and other organisms.
- It preserves soil structure.
- It drags fewer dormant weed seeds to the surface to sprout than deep digging methods (for more on the "seed bank," see Chapter 4).
- There is less interruption of the natural upward movement of moisture from the subsoil (called "capillary flow").
- Last, but certainly not least: it is less work. It takes about 20 minutes to spread amendments and lightly fork over a 40-foot square bed (if it isn't weedy).

A disadvantage of this method is that it doesn't incorporate lime deeply, which is important in the first years of a new garden with acidic soil. It is a good cultivation method, however, for small, established gardens once lime and organic amendments have been dug in more deeply for a year or two.

Double digging and deep digging: The best that can be said for these methods is they incorporate lime and other amendments deeply. But they have serious disadvantages, not the least of which is that they are a daunting amount of work. The fact that crops grow just fine without all this effort shows how unnecessary they are.

In our cool climate, any kind of deep cultivation buries the community of topsoil microorganisms down where it is cool (even cold, at times) and dark, and there is less air circulation. Because we rely on these organisms to release nutrients, protect roots from disease, and perform many other functions, it doesn't make sense to set them back this way. Deep digging also brings weed seeds from greater depths to the surface — where they will readily germinate in the light and warmth. It also disrupts the natural upward flow of moisture from the subsoil (the capillary flow) at a point well below the root zone of annual vegetable plants, at least while they are small. Because water conservation is a widespread concern in this region, it is preferable not to interrupt this natural upward movement of water to crops.

Rototilling: Tillers come in a variety of sizes, including very small models that can be used in smaller gardens. The tines of rototillers spin around, thoroughly mixing the soil to the depth of the tines. I am not a fan of rototillers because they pound apart the soil structure and are easy to over-use (plus, they make noise, use gas, and cost money); however, they are quite useful for breaking new ground. They break up sod easily and quickly compared to hand digging, and the action of the tines can incorporate large amounts of organic matter into the soil.

The disadvantages of tillers:
- They are expensive to rent or to buy and maintain.
- Even the smallest models are hard to use in very small areas, and they all require a fairly strong person to control the machine.
- The action of the tines can destroy soil structure. Some soils should not

be tilled at all, because they are too fragile, while other soils hold up pretty well to occasional rototilling — as long as a generous supply of organic matter is incorporated every time.

The bottom line: Ultimately, since plants can be grown under a wide variety of cultivation systems, how you choose to cultivate your garden depends on the time and energy you have available, the tools you want to use and size of your garden. For example, my personal objective is to harvest the largest amount of food for the least amount of work; I live where irrigation water in summer is quite limited; I have little time to garden; and I hate noisy, gas-powered machines. So my choice is to use a garden fork to disturb the soil as little as possible and use mulches to control weeds and conserve water.

CHAPTER 4

BASIC METHODS FOR GROWING VEGETABLES

Time was when most people grew up around *someone* who had a food garden, so they were more or less familiar with how to go about it. No longer. These days, many people who are interested in growing their own food are unfamiliar with even the most basic methods. So, this chapter is geared toward beginning gardeners. (You more experienced gardeners can just skip on ahead!)

How to Sow Seeds

In case you are looking at your new seed packages and wondering what's next, here is how to get going on sowing those seeds.

Preparing a seedbed: After you dig in the soil amendments (see Chapter 3), level the seedbed using a rake or the back of a garden fork. Remove stones, clods and debris from the surface, but don't go overboard working up a fine surface. In fact, depending on the soil type, over-cultivating can result in a crusty surface that is hard for seedlings to poke through. Most seedlings can pop up through surprisingly uneven soil as long as they don't have to push up stones or clods.

Remove large rocks as you come upon them. Don't be overly concerned about removing pebbles, however, unless the bed is for carrots. Carrots produce forked roots when they hit stones, so the fewer pebbles the better.

Sowing depth: The general rule is that seeds should be planted three times deeper in the soil than the width of the seed. A lettuce seed is so tiny that in practice this means covering the seeds with the thinnest possible layer of soil. Beans or corn seeds, which are much larger, should be planted about 1 inch (2 cm) deep. This is not an exact requirement, and it should be adjusted for the conditions. For example: In early spring, while the soil is still cool and moist, many tiny seeds germinate well if they are just scattered on the surface of the soil (lettuce, arugula, dill, cilantro).

In mid-summer, when the soil temperatures are higher and the surface dries out quickly after watering, seeds germinate better if they are sown a bit deeper than the three-times-the-size rule: Tiny seeds would need about ¼ inch (5 mm) of soil, and bean and corn seeds would be planted about 1.5 inches (3 cm) deep.

Seeding patterns: There are several ways to sow seeds. They all work fine, but some suit certain vegetables better than others. Seed spacing information is included under each entry in Chapter 10, A to Z Vegetables.

- **Broadcast:** Broadcast sowing is particularly suited to lettuce, other salad greens and mesclun mixes, and annual herbs, such as dill. Scatter seeds lightly over the surface of the whole bed area. "Lightly" means one or two seeds per square inch. Cover them to the right depth by sprinkling more soil over the whole bed. (Before sowing, I usually scrape back a thin layer of soil from the surface of the bed and store it to one side or in a bucket; then I use that soil to cover the seeds.) Crumble the soil between your fingers as you spread it to break up small clods, so that you deposit a fine layer over the seeds. Press seeds into good contact with moist soil by firmly patting the surface of the soil. Some seeds don't have to be covered: corn salad broadcast in late summer germinates best if you don't cover the seed.

- **Furrows:** Sowing in shallow trenches or furrows is particularly suited to bigger seeds, such as beans, peas, beets and Swiss chard, but it is really fine for all seeds. It particularly suits beds irrigated with parallel rows of soaker hoses because you can run a furrow on either side of each hose. Make the furrows with your fingers, a trowel or a hoe to a depth that fits the size of the seed. Sprinkle seeds along the bottom of the furrow or place large seeds one by one along the row. Push in the soil from the sides to cover seeds to the correct depth. Firm the soil down to ensure good contact between seeds and soil. You can fill a wide bed with closely spaced, parallel furrows.

FIGURE 4.1. Sow bean seeds in a furrow a couple of inches deep, so the seeds can be covered with more than an inch of soil.

- **Hills:** A hill is a mound of soil built up a bit above ground level to make a warmer, drier planting site. Planting in hills works well for large plants that need a lot of space, such as squash and cucumbers. These are not usually sown directly in the garden in this region as the soil warms so late there isn't much time for a crop, but you can set out seedlings in the hills. Dig in an extra supply of compost and fertilizer at the site of each hill. For squash, hills are usually spaced a yard apart.
- **Individual sites:** Large seeds, such as corn, can also be sown directly in small groups at each planting site. I like to just take a trowel, dig in a bit of blood meal and plant two or three corn seeds at each site, about a foot apart each way. When the seeds come up, the plants are thinned to the strongest seedling.

Watering: Once the seeds are planted, keep the soil damp, but not soaking wet. Seeds take up moisture from the soil and from the humid air between soil particles; so as long as the soil surface isn't allowed to dry completely, they will be fine. In the spring, when it rains frequently, it may not be necessary to water a seedbed after the initial soaking. In the summer, however, be vigilant, because a seedbed can dry out in just half a day.

The Marvel of Germination

Each seed has its own food supply inside its protective coat. When seeds are exposed to moisture and warmth (and in some cases, light) they germinate, meaning that they start to grow. The tiny developing plant uses the food stored in the seed as its energy supply. Only when it has pushed down a root and the shoot has opened its first leaves to the sun can the plant start making a new food supply through photosynthesis.

The gentle sprinkle from a watering can is ideal for watering newly seeded beds. For larger areas, use the most gentle "shower" setting on a hose nozzle. Take care not to disturb the soil by blasting a stream of water that would dislodge seeds or tear the roots of germinating seeds. Even a heavy rain can wash away small seeds, which is why I prefer a rougher seedbed — it keeps the seeds from being moved around.

When to Sow Seeds in the Spring

This is a vexing question! Some concepts useful in other climates, such as average frost-free dates (see sidebar), don't mean much for the coast. And coastal spring weather varies so much from year to year (and is likely to vary more as the climate changes) that last year's timing doesn't necessarily apply this year.

Garden books often recommend planting peas and other cold-hardy crops "when the soil can be worked." In this region, there is usually such prolonged wet weather in the spring that some soils are too wet to work until quite late. When you plant for year-round harvests, however, this isn't much of a concern because overwintered vegetables will be producing a good crop in the spring long before you can work the soil.

The key is soil temperature: For coastal gardeners, soil temperature is the best indicator of when to plant. This is the only temperature that matters to germinating seeds anyway, and it varies widely from year to year. For example, in a year with a very cold spring, the soil a few inches down in my

Forget the Average Frost-Free Date

While the average date of the last frost is used in other regions as a marker for spring planting, this concept isn't much use on the coast. Frost-free dates are calculated from many years' worth of weather records at a recording site (usually a regional airport). Because the coast is so geographically complex, even weather records from a site very near your garden may bear little relationship to the frost patterns in your garden. On the coast, there can be striking differences in frost patterns over very small areas.

Another reason the concept doesn't apply here is that spring on the coast is such a long, drawn-out affair; the "last frost" might happen anytime from February through May. In the warmest areas, there might only be one or two frosts all winter. In my garden, the last frost dates over the last 7 years have ranged from March 8 to April 30, yet a mile away, in a friend's garden, I have seen ground frosts in mid-May.

Table 4.1. Soil temperatures for germination of vegetable seeds.

Crops	Minimum °F (°C)	Better	Best
Lettuce, onion, spinach, parsnip, endive	32 (0)	60 (15)	70 (21)
Beets, broccoli, cabbage, carrots, cauliflower, celery, parsley, peas, radishes, Swiss chard	40 (5)	60 (15)	77 (25)
Tomato, turnip	50 (10)	70 (21)	77 (25)
Sweet corn (OP and normal hybrids), beans, cucumber, pepper	60 (15)	70 (21)	86 (30)
Eggplant, melons, pumpkins, squash, sweet corn (supersweet and sugar enhanced hybrids)	64 (18)	77 (25)	95 (35)

Wait until the soil reaches the temperatures in the "Better" column before sowing seeds. Temperatures in the "Best" column can only be achieved indoors, using bottom heat for seedlings.

Treated Seeds?

Treated seeds are coated with a fungicide to protect the germinating seed from fungus attack. If you plant seeds when the soil is warm enough (see Table 4.1) there is no need for chemical protection. The faster a seed can germinate and get growing in warm soil, the less time it spends vulnerable to attack by fungi or other organisms. Organic growers don't use treated seed.

garden was just above freezing on April 1st. The next year, my soil temperature was 48°F (9°C) by March 15th. It is handy to have a soil thermometer, but with a little experience you can also go by how cold the soil feels to your fingers.

Because winters are so mild here and hardy plants grow pretty well all winter, is it easy to be fooled into putting out very tender crops too early. But waiting until the soil is warm enough for seeds of heat-loving crops, such as corn and beans, could mean waiting until June. Here are some ways around this:

- Warm the soil before sowing: For at least a week before planting, lay a sheet of clear plastic flat on the soil surface and anchor it with stones or boards (black plastic is not as effective as clear). If the weather continues cloudy, it won't have much effect, but as soon as the sun comes out, the top layer of soil warms up markedly.
- After sowing, cover the beds with plastic over hoops to make a tunnel. Don't lay the plastic down on the soil after seeding, however, as the heat can literally cook the seeds.

FIGURE 4.2. Nitrogen-fixing nodules on the roots of peas. If your legumes have these pinkish lumps on the roots, they are happy and healthy.

Alternatively, bump up the temperatures by covering the beds with floating row covers or try out the new, perforated plastic film product, Gro-Therm.

- Start seeds indoors: This is more likely to ensure a higher percentage of successful plants and usually eliminates the need to re-seed poor stands of plants. Pre-sprout beans in a tray of vermiculite until they have their first true leaves. Start the first plantings of sweet corn indoors, preferably on bottom heat.

How to Sow Seeds in the Summer

The challenge for sowing seeds in the summer is keeping the soil evenly moist until germination occurs. The surface soil also needs to be below a certain temperature for some seeds. (The maximum temperature for seed germination for most crops is about 86°F [30°C]; for lettuce and spinach, it is about 75°F [24°C].) The solution to both problems is to shade the soil.

Water the soil well after sowing, then cover the beds with newspaper (anchored with a couple of stones), burlap, woven feed bags or other cloth (old beach towels work great). If you have a piece of stucco wire or chicken wire the size of the bed, lay that down first, then spread the fabric on top of the wire to give a little air circulation over the surface.

Are Legume Seed Inoculants Worth Buying?

Commercial suppliers sell cultures of nitrogen-fixing bacteria for inoculating pea and bean seeds. They usually aren't necessary, however, because most soils already have these bacteria. There is a good chance that the products in the store aren't even viable, because the bacteria don't keep for long. It *may* be worth it to buy seed inoculant the first time you plant in soil that has never had legumes grown in it, such as container mixes with a high proportion of non-soil ingredients (peat/coir, vermiculite, etc.). Follow package instructions for mixing with seeds.

FIGURE 4.3. Plastic trays protect seedlings from hot sun. Burlap in the background is shading a seedbed before the seedlings emerge.

FIGURE 4.4. Thin leafy seedlings, and eat the tender baby leaves in a salad.

The soil usually doesn't need to be watered again for several days. Lift a corner of the cover to check daily for germination and remove it the minute the first seedling shows. Seeds sprout very quickly in the summer: leafy greens may germinate in 2 or 3 days. If you need to water, remove the cover, soak the soil, and replace the cover.

If the weather is hot and sunny when they first come up, tiny seedlings will be happier if they have some mid-day shade. I like to use plastic latticework trays that hold seed flats, turned upside down and spread out over the bed. But you can use anything—branches, latticework, or strips of cloth supported on a piece of stucco wire—as long as the seedlings get *some* sun. As soon as possible, gently work in fine mulch between the seedlings to keep their roots cool and moist; you can beef up the layer of mulch as plants grow larger.

Thinning Seedlings

Whether you intentionally planted too many seeds in the row (a good strategy to make sure enough survive pests) or not, most stands of seedlings will have to be thinned once they come up. Carrots are notoriously hard to sow thinly, and no matter how carefully you place seeds of beets or Swiss chard, you still have to thin them. This is because they have several seeds inside each shriveled up "seed" (botanists call it a "seedball").

Remove crowded seedlings while the plants are tiny to avoid damaging the roots of the keepers. You can pull them or clip them off. With care, you can also transplant seedlings from crowded spots to fill in gaps. For beets, lettuce and other greens that are edible at any size, thin them in several stages and use the thinnings: first time through, thin the plants to an inch apart; next time, thin to a couple of inches and on a third pass, thin to the final spacing.

Buying Transplants

Whether you buy all of your transplants or just a few to supplement what you start from seed, here are some guidelines:

- Choose small, young plants rather than larger plants, which may have been in pots too long.
- Avoid plants that appear old, root-bound or spindly — especially those that have been held in the back of shelf units without enough light. Roots sticking out of the pot's drainage holes indicate the plant is becoming root-bound.
- Avoid plants with yellowing leaves or purplish or brown streaks on the leaves; these are likely to be nutrient deficient.
- Check for insect pests and disease; don't take home anything that looks suspicious.

A good trick for getting the best quality is to find out from your local nursery when they expect new plants to arrive (it is usually weekly); make a point of buying your plants the day they are put out for sale and try to plant immediately if the weather is suitable. If you buy transplants well before they can go outdoors, it is a good idea to move them into larger pots. This is especially important if you end up with large seedlings of leeks, onions, cabbage, Swiss chard or other plants that are easily vernalized (see Chapter 1) by a late period of cool weather.

Setting Out Transplants

First, make sure young plants are hardened off (acclimated to being in wind and direct sun. See Chapter 5).

1. In a previously prepared bed, use a trowel or your fingers to scoop a hole

a bit bigger than the root ball of the seedling. If the seedlings were growing in individual containers, you can slide the root ball out with little
disturbance. For seedlings growing in flats, gently work the roots of each
plant loose from the others with your fingers or a small tool, keeping as
much soil as possible around the roots.

2. Taking care to disturb the roots as little as possible, set the small plant
   in the hole and fill in soil around the root ball so that the seedling sits
   upright. As you fill in the soil, gently poke it around the roots to fill air
   spaces. The final level of soil around the stem should end up the same as
   it was in the original flat or just a bit higher.

3. Gently firm the soil around the roots, but don't press down hard enough
   to tear the roots. Water well.

This sounds like a slow process, but it can go quite quickly as you scoop out
the soil, plunk in the seedling, push in the soil and move on.

For squash and cucumber plants set out in hills of three or four plants,
I dig a larger hole where the group of plants will go and mix in a generous
supply of compost and ¼ cup of balanced fertilizer at the bottom of the hole.
I replace enough soil to bring the bottom of the planting hole to the right
depth for the transplants and carry on from there, planting and watering.

Nursing transplant shock: The ideal weather for transplanting is cloudy
and moist. The hotter and drier it is, the more care transplants will need to
help them recover from the shock of transplanting. Because their roots inevi-
tably suffer more damage during transplanting, seedlings that were growing
in a flat with others will take longer to recover than seedlings grown in individual pots.

Protect plants from sun and wind for 2–4 days to give them time to replace fine root hairs. You can use anything to shade the plants temporarily:
a sheet of newspaper over the seedlings, slabs of cardboard or wood shingles
pushed into the soil on the south side of the plant, or even a large plant pot
turned upside down over the seedlings. The object is to shade plants from
the midday sun until their roots recover.

If a late cool spell threatens, cover young plants with floating row covers, cloches or other covers to keep them warmer.

Irrigation

Vegetables need a lot of water, and they must be watered in dry weather. Coastal gardens on low-lying land may not need water until mid-summer because there is enough moisture in the soil. In contrast, gardens with well-drained soils might need irrigation in late May if the typical dry summer weather pattern sets in early.

How much to water: You will read in other books that intensively planted annual vegetable gardens need the equivalent of 1 inch (1–2 cm) of rainfall per week in hot weather. When it doesn't rain, you are supposed to supply the difference. Now, that is a lot of water! I do not come close to providing this much to my own garden, in part because where I live it is necessary to conserve well water. But there are other factors to consider. How much you really need to water varies tremendously, depending on the following:

- Soil characteristics: structure, drainage, and organic matter content all affect the water-holding capacity of a soil.
- Temperature and wind: both influence how much water the plants pull from the soil and transpire through their leaves.
- Plant spacing: dense plantings need more water per square yard than plants spaced farther apart (but of course, produce more per square yard too).
- Mulches: these prevent surface evaporation from the soil (which accounts for about 10–15% of water loss) and prevent weeds from growing and competing for water.
- Efficiency of the irrigation system: delivering water through drip irrigation and soaker hoses uses less water than overhead sprinkling to achieve the same harvest.
- How much water you have: what is available for gardening also depends on the water source and whether there are watering restrictions.

If your plants show wilting in mid-day, they may be water stressed. In a heat wave, though, plants wilt somewhat to protect themselves from disastrous water loss. If they don't recover by evening, that is a sign they are suffering, and fine roots have probably been injured. They will need the best of care to recover and may never produce as well as they would have if they hadn't been drought stressed.

How often to water: As a general rule, in deep soil it is better to water longer and less often because it encourages roots to grow deeply as they follow the moisture. The plants reach more nutrients and are less likely to suffer a check in growth in a period of hot weather. Gardens with deep soil probably need to be watered once a week in typical mid-summer conditions. Established fruit trees and bushes that are well mulched usually need deep watering less often (every 2–4 weeks, depending on how warm it has been).

However, gardens with "shallow soils" in raised beds over rock or gravel, won't hold much water. Gardens on sandy, well-drained soils also don't hold moisture well. In these situations, long watering *wastes* water because it drains out of the root zone. These gardens make better use of irrigation water if watered for short periods two or three times a week.

The best indication of when to water is the soil condition. Watering when the soil needs it generally uses less water than watering on a fixed schedule. Poke a finger into the soil to check: if you see darker, moist soil 2–3 inches (5–8 cm) down, the moisture in the root zone is fine. Do this in a few places and you will get a good idea whether some areas of the garden need more or less watering than others.

Irrigation Systems

There are many designs on the market. What you use and the price you pay will depend on the quality of the components, how much assembly you can do yourself, and whether or not you want a system with automatic controls. For detailed information on options, talk to local irrigation suppliers and ask other gardeners about their systems. Lee Valley Tools will send you their very helpful (and free) *Irrigation Design Guide,* or you can read it online (leevalley.com).

The following is a brief overview of the different ways to irrigate:

Hand watering: For small, urban gardens and gardens on rental property, using a hose or watering can to water the garden may be the most practical option. It takes time to hand-water, but it requires little investment in equipment (and what there is can be taken with you when you move). Sturdy plastic watering cans cost less than $10 and a garden hose costs $20–$50 (much less at garage sales). If you use a hose to hand-water, invest in a nozzle with a shut-off on it and a setting that delivers the water in a soft rain.

Overhead watering: There are many types and designs of sprinklers. They use more water than the drip irrigation or soaker hose systems described below, so are mainly useful where water shortages are not a concern or there are no municipal watering restrictions in the summer. Sprinklers can be inexpensive and they are easy to move around to water different areas. You can install a timer (several designs are available) between the hose and the tap to shut the water off automatically.

Note that watering the whole garden area will encourage weeds to grow in pathways, so it will take more work to control them. Also, be aware that overhead watering can create or worsen slug or leaf disease problems. You can lessen disease and slug problems by sprinkling early in the morning, so the leaves and soil surface dry off quickly in the morning sun.

Drip irrigation systems: These systems use much less water than overhead sprinklers because water is delivered through emitters right to the plant roots. No water is wasted on non-growing areas, which also helps control weeds in pathways. This is an excellent way to water individual perennial plants, fruit trees and bushes; it is easy to change or add drippers to the systems as the plants grow. Drip irrigation is less suitable for annual vegetable beds. Because the plant spacing differs with every crop, the drippers won't be in the right place for every crop. Some suppliers sell thin plastic piping punched with many evenly spaced drip openings that are more suitable for vegetable beds.

Soaker hoses: Parallel rows of soaker hoses laid the length of beds work very well for vegetables because they provide continuous strips of irrigation water (rather than point sources as in the emitter system above) along

FIGURE 4.5. Soaker hoses conserve water and can fit any shape of garden bed.

the length of the beds. They also save water since the water is only going to the crop and not onto pathways. Some emit water quickly, and some are much slower: whichever kind you use, make sure that all of the hoses on the system are of the same type for even distribution of water.

For my vegetables, I use a set of four, parallel, fast-rate soaker hoses (from Lee Valley Tools). They are attached to a header made up of a 4-foot length of plastic plumbing pipe with four threaded fittings for the soaker hoses and one in the middle to connect to the garden hose from the water supply (see fig 3.3). Each soaker hose is screwed onto a fitting and rolled out to run the length of the vegetable bed. The soakers stay in place permanently; I cultivate around and under them and plant along both sides of each hose so plants are right beside the water source. When the seedlings are large enough, I top off the beds with a thick mulch over everything to reduce evaporation from the soil.

Measuring Irrigation

You can easily find out how much water has been delivered by an overhead sprinkler system by setting out a rain gauge or straight-sided tin can in the middle of the sprinkler zone. Run the sprinkler and check how long it takes to rain down half an inch or an inch of water on the garden. Wait for an hour or two to let the water soak in, and then dig down to see how far that water penetrated. Then wait for a week and keep checking to see how quickly soil at 2–3inches (5–8 cm) deep dries out. Adjust your watering schedule accordingly.

With drip or soaker irrigation systems, the water spreads downward, roughly in a cone shape, with the tip of the cone at the delivery point of the water. That means that the surface soil around the nozzle or on either side

Special Case: No Spare Water for Irrigation?

In some places, such as the Gulf Islands and San Juan Islands, for example, households depend on cisterns to hold winter rain for their summer water supply and have no surplus for a summer garden. By thinking of food gardening as a fall-through-spring activity, rather than a summer activity, it is still possible to enjoy garden vegetables for much of the year.

For summer, grow a couple of tomato plants or cucumbers or other favorites in containers or keep a small bed close to the house where it will be easy to water with "light gray" kitchen water—the clean waste water you can catch in a dishpan from rinsing dishes or washing vegetables. Or, keep a bucket in the shower to catch the water while it is warming up enough for you to step in, and re-use that water for your container crops.

For overwintering crops:

- If you have a little graywater to spare, start winter lettuce and leafy greens (kales, Chinese cabbage, leaf beet, spinach, leaf mustard) in early August in a small nursery bed that you can irrigate with a minimal amount of water. Or, buy most of these as transplants from garden centers in mid-August, and put them in a small bed. Transplant your seedlings to the main garden in September. Even if it doesn't rain until October, they won't need much water because of the cooler, shorter days. Once the fall rains start, these plants will do fine.

- If you have no water to spare, sow seeds in September directly in the garden. They will sprout and grow a little in the fall, but they won't yield a crop for fall or winter harvest. They will, however, start growing again in February and produce a good crop, probably until the end of June.

- In late March, you should be able to grow an early crop of peas, potatoes, scallions from onions sets, lettuce, and possibly baby carrots before the soil becomes too dry. Without irrigation, plants will stop growing sometime in June or July. In most areas, you can grow a good crop of garlic without irrigation. Plant the cloves in October and harvest the mature crop in early July. Early garlic varieties can be out of the garden before the end of June.

of the soaker hose looks pretty dry no matter how long you water. This is an advantage because the top layer of drier soil helps to prevent moisture loss from the lower layers of soil, but it's hard to know whether you have watered enough. To check, run the system for a set time (e.g., 15 or 30 minutes). Turn off the water and wait for an hour or two for the water to penetrate. Then, in an empty section of the bed, use a trowel to dig a test hole down to the root zone to see how far the water has moved. You can back off on the watering time if the soil seems quite wet below the root zone or increase it if the water has not reached the deeper roots.

Mulching

A mulch is a material used to cover the surface of the soil. Mulches of organic material, such as leaves, straw or crop waste, benefit gardens in many ways by:

- smothering weeds and preventing seeds from germinating;
- slowing evaporation of water from the soil surface in the summer (an estimated 10-15% of water loss);
- providing stable soil temperatures: cooler in summer and warmer in winter;
- adding organic matter and nutrients to the soil as they decompose;
- protecting the soil from erosion in heavy winter rain;
- making excellent habitat for ground beetles and other beneficial insects.

There are some artificial mulches on the market made from biodegradable paper or colored plastic. Some commercial growers use these products to control weeds and warm the soil in vegetable fields. Home gardeners can use these, too, but they increase the expense of gardening. Plus, the manufacturing and disposal of these materials is a burden on the environment. None of them improve the soil like an organic mulch does — and you certainly don't need them to enjoy an excellent harvest.

Mulching a Coastal Garden

Mulches are very beneficial in coastal gardens in summer, fall and winter. The one time they have drawbacks is in spring. Mulches keep the soil cool just when we want it to warm up for seeds. Therefore, a week or two before sowing seeds in a particular bed, I rake the remaining mulch off the bed into the pathway to let the soil warm up and make it easier to dig in amendments. There usually isn't much left of winter mulches; a surprising amount will have been digested into the soil.

Removing the mulch also removes shelter for slugs from the immediate vicinity of seedlings that are too small to tolerate damage. I find that slugs are not much of a problem under mulches around well-grown plants, probably because slugs are as likely to eat the mulch as the crop. Also, slug predators (ground beetles and rove beetles) live with their prey under the mulches. If you do have a problem with slugs, safe and effective ferric (iron) phosphate slug baits are now approved for organic growers, so you can use these to control slugs around seedbeds.

After a few weeks, when seedlings are well grown and the soil is warm (and before weeds get going), I move a light layer of mulch back onto the beds. I add more material as it gets warmer and drier, especially around vegetables such as peas and broccoli that like cool soil. By late fall, summer mulches are wearing thin. This is when I start working in more mulch around winter crop plants and piling thick mulches on empty beds. In December, I top up the mulches to 6 inches (15 cm) around overwintering plants to keep their roots warmer and protect the shoulders of root crops from frost damage.

What to use for mulch depends on what you can get easily and cheaply. Most backyard gardeners don't have access to a truck or trailer to haul large amounts of bulky material, such as spoiled hay, but most urbanites have ready access to leaves in the fall.

Leaves: My favorite mulch is leaves. They are free, don't have weed seeds, and break down quickly because they have an ideal ratio of carbon to nitrogen. I use leaves as my main mulch

FIGURE 4.6. True wealth! Leaves are free, so stockpile plenty for next summer's mulch.

on all beds for winter. I stockpile leaves in big plastic bags or bins covered with plastic so I have lots for the following summer.

Contrary to what you might have heard, all kinds of leaves are fine to use as a mulch, including bigleaf maple, oak and Arbutus (Madrona) leaves. The only leaves to be wary of are black walnut, which contain a compound that inhibits growth of certain plants that are sensitive to it.

You can shred big leaves or run a mower over them, but it isn't necessary. I find that even bigleaf maple leaves used to mulch beds over winter are well broken down by May.

Straw: My other favorite mulch is slightly decomposed straw. I buy a bale or two of straw in the fall when it is least expensive, and leave it in the rain all winter, with the strings still in place. I turn the bale a couple of times over the winter to smother any seedlings that sprout from the sides. By the time I need it for early summer mulching, the straw is rotted enough to be pulled from the bale in thin, compact "sheets," almost like light sheets of cardboard.

Straw breaks down slowly as a surface mulch; I find it is good for a year or more before it disappears.

FIGURE 4.7. After a winter in the rain, straw sticks together in thin sheets that are easy to peel off the bale like tiles for mulching.

Weeding

Spring is when weeding looms large in the minds of gardeners. If you have ever wondered where all those weeds come from so quickly, the answer is: the "seed bank," the enormous collection of seeds that has been accumulating in the soil for decades. The seed bank is likely the biggest source of weeds in your garden. Many seeds lie dormant until the soil is disturbed, which brings seeds to the surface, exposes them to light and warmth, and stimulates germination. Many seeds are still able to sprout after 10 to 40 years or, in the case of curled dock, even 80 years. If you think of the soil as having been pre-planted with weeds, you can see why it is a good idea to avoid cultivation methods that bring deep soil to the surface.

Here are some ways to minimize weeding chores:

Mulches: Keep the soil in garden beds covered so that light doesn't reach weed seeds. I also keep pathways between beds well mulched to control weeds. This is a good place to use long-lasting Arbutus leaves, chipped tree branches, shredded bark, straw or any other bulky organic materials you can lay hands on.

Dense planting: Let the vegetables help with the job of controlling weeds. By planting vegetables close together, the crop shades the soil, which inhibits germination of seeds. By using small spaces intensively and all year round, the weeds don't have a chance to get ahead.

Hand weeding: If you do have to remove a few weeds here and there, do it while they are tiny and the soil is wet. This disturbs less soil than pulling large, deep-rooted weeds, and it brings fewer seeds to the surface to germinate. For larger weeds, I recommend using an old-fashioned weed fork, which has a V-shaped notch at the end of a shank. Slide the shank into the soil beside the weed at an angle to cut the roots as deeply as possible. Instead of using the tool to pry out the weed, however, withdraw the fork at exactly the same angle it went in. Then lift up the weed by the leaves. This leaves behind a small, root-sized hole, rather than a larger disturbed area. If they haven't gone to seed yet, you can leave the weeds on the soil as a mulch.

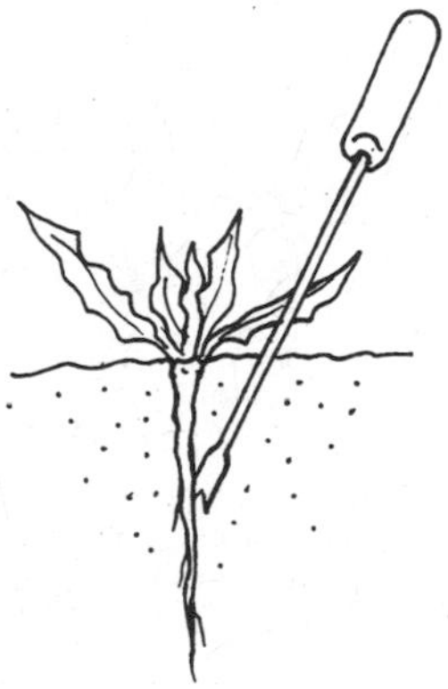

FIGURE 4.8. To use a weed fork effectively, just cut the root, but don't pry with the tool to disturb more soil.

Forget the Hoe, Bring On the Mulch

I can't think of a more tedious way to control weeds than hoeing, especially since it locks you into hoeing the same patch repeatedly. In contrast, a mulch just sits there all summer—passively keeping seeds from germinating. If you insist on hoeing, do it when weeds are tiny, use a sharp hoe, and just scuffle the surface enough to kill the seedlings. Chopping deeply injures the roots of crop plants and brings a new supply of weed seeds to the surface to germinate.

Avoid bringing in seeds: The more you can avoid adding seeds to your soil's seed bank, the better. I especially like leaves or straw for mulches and for composting because they carry few seeds. I am wary of horse manure and spoiled hay because they are full of seeds (hot composting these before using them helps). Cut off (literally) the supply of new seeds by cutting or mowing weedy area around gardens before the first flowers open.

Staking and Trellising

Some crops really have to be staked or trellised onto some kind of support system: pole beans, indeterminate varieties of tomatoes and most varieties of peas will produce well only if trellised. Trellising is optional for other vegetable such as cucumbers, melons and winter squash, but these space hogs take up less space when trained onto a trellis.

Crop supports can be made of anything, from dead branches to fancy materials that match the decor of your home. You can use heavy twine (tied to a solid support), stakes of wood, bamboo, metal, plastic, tree branches, poles, wire mesh or stucco wire. You might want to invest in tomato cages, which are useful for many years. You can also just hold plants up with strings tied to the garden fence. For annual vegetables, temporary supports, such as stick and string, work fine. But for long-lived perennials such as grape vines, invest in well-built, permanent supports.

Two rules apply here:

- Use supports strong enough to hold up the weight of the plants *and* to withstand wind. Plants in full production are heavy! A mature tomato vine loaded with fruit can easily weigh 45 pounds (20 kilograms). Now, add the force of the wind to that, and you can imagine how strong your support needs to be.
- Plan ahead. Assemble the materials and install the trellis or other supports *before* planting.

The following section describes some ways to support common crops.

Pole beans: These beans will climb on most anything, from vertical strings to wooden poles to bamboo stakes.

For a traditional bean tepee, take six to eight tall poles and securely bind the tips together with wire or string to form a tepee. Prop the base of the sticks far enough apart to make a stable structure. It is a good rule to make the width of the base at least one third of the height. When covered with beans, a tepee really catches the wind, so make sure it is anchored by pushing the legs into the soil as far as possible.

There are many variations on the bean tepee: Rather than all of the poles coming to one central point, you can lash the bean poles to a crossbar between two posts or tie them along a fence. Spacing out the poles makes it easier to pick the beans and allows the leaves to dry quickly after a rain. You can plant along a fence or at the base of a latticework trellis that has a right angle extension a couple of feet wide — like a shelf running the length of the section. The "shelf" (which can be made of latticework or stucco wire) allows the pods to hang straight down through it, making them easy to pick.

Peas: Peas vines climb best on string or wire: their tendrils don't get a good grip on smooth poles, such as bamboo garden stakes, or on supports wider than a pencil. Tall varieties need tall trellises, well anchored to

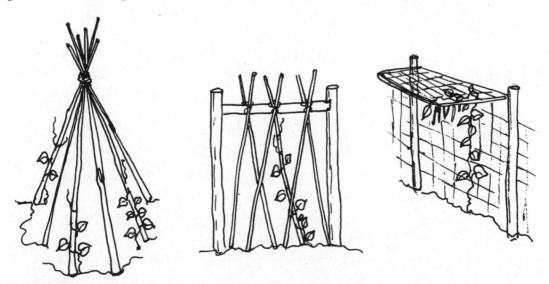

FIGURE 4.9. Variations on a bean trellis from the traditional bean "tepee" (left) to a fence with a shelf extension (right).

FIGURE 4.10. John's folding trellis supports peas and provides a perfect spot for summer lettuce underneath.

withstand wind. Short varieties, such as dwarf sugar peas, can be supported sufficiently on small branches stuck into the ground along the row. Although the shortest varieties of peas can be left to sprawl, it is much easier to pick them when they are trellised.

Beware the soft, woven string mesh sold for pea and bean supports! These are a nightmare to clean at the end of the season when the vines are all tangled up in the netting. Stiff plastic mesh, wooden latticework, woven wire fencing, or sections of stucco wire work much better. You can support sections of rigid trellis materials by tying the ends to stakes securely driven into the ground. Bamboo garden stakes are also easy to thread vertically at intervals through stucco wire or plastic lattice to hold them up. Stucco wire is galvanized, welded wire with a 2-inch square mesh, usually 4 feet wide; it is sold by the running foot at local lumber yards (or look for it at recycling depots) because many people use it to protect trees from deer. I am a great fan of stucco wire and have a collection of 4- to 6-foot long sections that I have used for years for a variety of garden uses.

John's Handy Trellis

Here is how my neighbor built a handy folding trellis: He made two frames of scrap 2 × 4 wood, with one frame fitting just inside the other. With the small frame inside the large one, he drilled a hole through the frames on either side of the top end so he could tap a wooden dowel into the hole to act as a hinge. Stucco wire is stapled over both frames. To use it, he just props the frame open as wide as desired. It is heavy enough to stand solidly, yet easy to fold together for storage.

Tomatoes: All tomatoes are much easier to manage, take up less garden space, and are less prone to leaf disease if they are staked up. If you have the space to let them sprawl, try growing determinate and small-fruited tomatoes because they do not have to be supported.

- Stakes: A strong wooden stake driven into the soil beside each plant is cheap and works fine. Keep tying the new growth to the stake as the plant grows.
- Strings: Very strong cord tied to a sturdy overhead support can make a good tomato support. Tie the bottom end of the string around the stem at base of the plant (not too tightly — the stem needs a little room to grow). As the tomato grows, wind the top of the plant around the string so that it spirals upward. For greenhouse tomatoes that grow very tall, leave a long tail on the top end of the string so you can periodically untie it from the overhead support to let down another length of string. This lowers the section of the plant where tomatoes are currently ripening, making them easy to pick.
- Tomato cages: These come in several sizes and designs, are sturdy, stable and last for years. You don't need to tie plants to the cage. These cages can be used for tomatoes grown in containers.
- Tomato spirals: If you have really deep soil without stones and can twist the spiral deeply into the ground, these might work for you. Around here, they tend to tip over once plants have a full load of fruit.

Cold Weather Protection

Most hardy crops need little, if any, protection to survive our mild coastal winter, but you might want to use some type of cover to protect overwintering crops through unusually cold weather. Covers also enable overwintered plants to grow a bit more than they would if not protected.

In the spring, with a year-round planting schedule working for you, there really isn't a need for season extension covers. Lettuce, spinach and other leafy greens, root crops, cauliflower, broccoli and cabbage overwinter just fine and will be producing until early summer. However, you might want some type of covers to protect warmth-lovers (such as tomatoes or cucumbers), to speed up growth rate in the spring, to hasten a particular delicacy to the table, or to get an early start in years when you don't have overwintered crops.

Covers for protecting plants from cold weather range from a simple sheet of plastic weighed down with rocks to high-tech greenhouses. There is considerable overlap in the designs for extending the season for warmth-loving crops and for protecting overwintering crops. This section discusses designs for both uses, with the emphasis on simple, low-cost methods. As coldframes are most useful for hardening off seedlings in the spring, rather than for season extension, they are described in Chapter 5.

Your choice of materials and design depends on what crop is being protected, the time of year, and how much you want to invest in equipment.

Floating row covers: Invented over 25 years ago, floating row covers are spun-bonded polyester or polypropylene fabrics, very lightweight and porous. They let in sunlight and rain and keep in some heat. Because they are feather-light, you can lay the fabric right on top of seedbeds and young plants without using hoops or frames as supports. Weigh the edges down with stones, boards or pegs to keep them in place.

Row covers are useful in the spring to keep plants a few degrees warmer during the day and to protect against a few degrees of frost at night. They are not sturdy enough for overwinter use.

The fabric is sold by the yard at garden centers and by mail order suppliers. It usually comes in 6- or 10-foot widths, and there are lightweight and heavier-weight fabrics. The heavier fabric holds in more heat and lasts for several years if handled carefully. The lighter fabric holds in less heat and is most useful for preventing insects from reaching crops. Kits are available that include wire hoops, clips and the fabric cut to size, with drawstring closures on the ends. When you are done with the row covers for the season, rinse out the fabric and hang it to dry before storing it.

Plastic sheets: Clear plastic is the cheapest way to cover plants for season extension or cold protection. For winter use, it has the added bonus of keeping rain off of the leaves of plants.

You can use any clear plastic sheeting you have on hand. If you are buying it, 4 or 6 mil plastic is thick enough for the purpose and lasts for years if it is stored out of the summer sun. For the longest-wearing plastic, look for UV-stabilized plastic film sold especially for cloches and tunnels.

FIGURE 4.11. An elegant plastic cover to protect spring lettuce.

- **For spring seedlings:** The weight of plastic film is too much for seedlings, so it should be supported above the seedbed on hoops or frames. If you have a piece of chicken wire or stucco wire, you can make a temporary support by arching the wire over the bed and laying the plastic on top of that. Hold down the edges of the plastic with rocks or boards. (For more elaborate tunnel frames, see next page.)

- **For winter crops:** Mature plants can hold up the plastic, so you don't necessarily have to have supports. In a cold snap, just drape the plastic temporarily over plants. Weigh down the edges to hold the plastic in winter winds. Try to keep water or snow from building up too much on the plastic and crushing the plants. Even if they are flattened, however, most leafy greens will straighten up again once the weight is removed.

FIGURE 4.12. The sheet of plastic folded to the side was laid over this bed of Swiss chard to protect it during an Arctic outbreak of unusually cold air.

Perforated transparent film (Gro-Therm): This is a very thin, transparent plastic film designed to keep seedlings warm in the spring. It has 300 tiny holes per square yard for ventilation, so the plastic doesn't have to be removed on sunny spring days. The manufacturer promises temperatures up to 10 degrees (Fahrenheit) higher than under floating row covers and better light intensity. The evenly spaced holes allow for consistent growing conditions for heat-loving crops. Remove the cover for the summer because plants can overheat under it (unless you are on the cold and foggy outer coast). This material is not designed for winter crop protection.

Cloches: Traditionally, bell-shaped glass cloches were used to cover individual plants. But these are not tools for a busy person heading out the door every morning to work! They are so efficient at trapping the sun's heat that they must be carefully managed to avoid frying seedlings in the sun. Tip them up or remove them entirely as soon as the sun comes out.

There are many variations on this idea, from dome-shaped plastic cloches with an adjustable opening in the top to recycled milk jugs with the bottom cut out. I find that 1-gallon plastic milk jug cloches gives perfectly good results. Cut the bottom out of the jug, set it over the plant and push a stick through the handle of the jug to keep it in place. Put the lid or a flat stone on the mouth of the jug at night to keep the heat in; take it off for the day to allow ventilation or just leave it off entirely. Remove the cloche as soon as the weather warms.

Cloches that extend along a whole row can be made from pairs of glass panes, pieces of rigid plastic or corrugated fiberglass. Join the rigid materials together at the top to make an A-frame cover running the length of a row. You can buy special clips to hold glass or plastic sheets together at the top edge, or make homemade supports or wooden blocks to hold the glass. Strips of corrugated fiberglass are flexible enough to be simply bent over to make row covers with rounded tops (but stake them down in case of wind). Leave ends open during the day for ventilation; at night, cover the ends with a board or plastic.

FIGURE 4.13. Milk jugs make cheap and easy cloches. Don't forget to stake them down so they won't blow away. .

Tunnels: There are many variations on the plastic tunnel, but most are constructed of some kind of hoop frame (plastic plumbing pipe, heavy wire or wood) covered with plastic. Some are temporary and designed to be moved to different beds, others are permanent and remain in place, much like a coldframe.

Tunnels are useful for season extension and for winter cold protection; they are especially useful when you want to cover the length of a garden bed. In winter they protect plants from rain, so lettuce, spinach and chard do well under them. If there is any weak sunlight at all, daytime temperatures will be higher inside than outside. However, temperature lows overnight are about the same as outdoors. In a cold snap with snow on the ground, plants outside the tunnel are often warmer than the plants inside that don't have snow cover. So be prepared to throw tarps over the tunnel during a cold snap.

Stake down tunnels or anchor them to resist wind. Heavy metal wire hoops for smaller tunnels are easy to force into the ground to a secure depth. In some soils, the ends of plastic pipe can be driven far enough into the ground to secure the tunnel (cut the pipe ends at a sharp angle). You can use pipe brackets to screw the bottom end of the pipe hoops to the sides of raised beds. Another option is to drive short sections of rebar into the ground as anchors, leaving a foot or so above ground. The ends of the plastic pipe fit down over the rebar anchors. Space the hoops about 2–3 feet apart along the length of the tunnel.

Covers for tunnels can be standard 4- or 6-mil plastic or special plastic film

FIGURE 4.14. A sturdy tunnel-coldframe design that gives easy access to plants.

FIGURE 4.15. A tunnel temporarily turns a garden bed into a greenhouse.

designed for greenhouses. Secure plastic sheeting to pipe hoops with commercially available clips or make your own from short pieces of the same plastic pipe used for the hoop. Slit them down one side and soften in hot water to make them easier to snap over the plastic on the pipe.

Ventilate and cool the tunnels during the day by opening the ends or rolling up the sides to allow air to flow. If the tunnel is going to be used all summer for tomatoes, it is essential to be able to ventilate from the sides as well as the ends to prevent condensation from forming inside and dripping onto the leaves, which promotes late blight infection.

If you have the time and skill to build a more elaborate structure, there are many plans available. Kits are also sold at garden centers and through mail order catalogs.

Things to consider in tunnel design:

- Do you want something that is easy to move to different beds, or a more permanent tunnel that stays in one place?
- Is it designed for excellent ventilation? Avoiding overheating in sunny weather is essential.

One last thing to consider — actually, it should be the first thing to consider: Do you really need a tunnel? It can be nice to have one in mid-winter to speed up the growth of leafy greens, but it is by no means necessary to achieving a good harvest in our year-round climate.

CHAPTER 5

STARTING SEEDLINGS AND SAVING SEEDS

This chapter covers how to start your own seedlings indoors for transplanting to the garden later. It also describes basic seed-saving methods for anyone interested in trying this rewarding aspect of gardening.

Starting Seedlings Indoors

There are several reasons for starting vegetables several weeks to months before they can go out in the garden:

- Heat-loving plants, such as tomatoes, peppers, winter squash and cucumbers, take too long to ripen a crop in the cool coastal climate. There really isn't enough time to sow them directly in the garden and have much of a crop.
- Some cool-season plants, such as leeks, Spanish onions, celery and celeriac, also need an especially long growing season. These are usually started indoors in February to early March.
- Summer varieties of cabbage, broccoli and cauliflower are ready to harvest much earlier if they go into the garden as transplants.
- Plants with large, starchy seeds (mainly peas and beans) are attractive to pests and prone to disease in cool soil. Pre-sprouting them indoors cuts down considerably on losses.

Should You Start Your Own Seedlings?

For beginning gardeners, I recommend starting off with transplants from garden centers or farmers markets (see *Buying Transplants* in Chapter 4 for what to look for when buying transplants). These local sources usually sell robust varieties known to do well in a range of conditions. While there are many reasons for growing your own transplants, to be successful, you have to provide good growing conditions and be prepared to give them daily care for 5 to 10 weeks. This is definitely for the advanced class!

The most compelling reason to start your own seedlings is to have the widest choice of varieties. If you are a tomato enthusiast, for example, there are many more varieties to choose from as seeds than you would be able to buy as transplants. Given the high cost of seeds, however, if you only want one or two plants of many different tomato varieties, it might make more sense to buy plants—if you can get the varieties you want. Although most garden centers now carry a large selection of tomato varieties, they rarely have more than a couple of varieties of other crops. Some vegetables may only be labeled by the crop name (e.g., "leeks" or "celeriac"). Without knowing the variety, the following year you won't know which one to look for if it was successful or avoid if it wasn't. This is particularly annoying for leeks because some varieties are much less cold hardy than others. I hate to think of an unsuspecting gardener deprived of the joy of harvesting a fine, fat leek in February!

FIGURE 5.1. Bean seedlings started in vermiculite avoid the hazards of birds, pillbugs and damping off. Every one of these seedlings grew into a sturdy plant.

Pre-sprouting Large Seeds

Unlike starting transplants, pre-sprouting peas and beans is easy. Pre-sprouting these big starchy seeds is a way to get around the fact that they are highly attractive to pests. Birds and rodents love to dig up them up, and pillbugs, wireworms, slugs, climbing cutworms and soil fungi attack them too. In typical spring weather it is often very hard to achieve a good stand of seedlings. Rather than losing time replanting over and over, I think it is well worth the effort to pre-sprout these.

Both peas and beans can be started in trays of vermiculite indoors: peas from March onward, beans starting in early May. Every seed seems to germinate, and there is little risk of root rot as the vermiculite doesn't hold excess water. The seedlings can grow for 2–3 weeks (until they are a couple of inches high) on the food stored in the seed, so they don't need soil.

How to pre-sprout seeds: I cram 30 seeds (enough for a 10-foot row or one bean tepee) into a container made from a quart (1-liter) milk carton.

- Lay the carton on one side, cut out the top side and punch drainage holes in the bottom. Fill the carton with vermiculite, and poke the seeds about an inch deep.
- Set the container somewhere warm and keep the vermiculite moist. As soon as tips of sprouts show, move the carton to a windowsill with good light and grow them for two more weeks. For better light, you could put them in a coldframe during the day and bring them in at night.
- At planting time, gently disentangle the roots in the loose vermiculite, and set them out. Plant bean seedlings so the shriveled seed leaves remain above the soil surface. These are the starchy remnants from the seed, which are so attractive to pillbugs and other pests.

Other reasons for starting your own seedlings: to make sure they are grown organically and to avoid bringing pests from nurseries to your garden (this is usually a low risk). Starting seedlings can also save cash if you need a large number of transplants, but it will cost you in terms of labor.

Requirements for Starting Seeds Indoors

The better the light, temperature and moisture conditions you provide, the healthier your seedlings will be. Providing sufficient light is usually the most challenging of the three — and it is the most critical.

Light: To grow good seedlings indoors requires the highest light levels you can manage. If you do not have an indoor grow-light set-up, you will need a greenhouse, sunroom or south-facing window that receives full sun. If you are making do with a south window, line up the individual pots or flats in a single row along the windowsill because only the seedlings right up against the window will receive adequate light. As soon as the weather permits, move seedling trays outside for the day to a coldframe or unheated greenhouse so they receive full, bright light.

If you don't have good window light and really want to grow seedlings, you will need to set up grow lights. Buy special, full-spectrum grow lights, or use four 40-watt fluorescent tubes supplemented with one or two incandescent light bulbs to balance the light spectrum. To achieve the high light

Are Your Seedlings Getting Enough Light?

Compare the stocky seedlings that come up in a bed outdoors with the seedlings grown indoors. The ones grown outdoors have hardly any distance between the soil surface and the first pair of leaves. Indoor seedlings that grow tall, lean toward the light, and have long, pale stems below the first pair of leaves are not getting enough light. They are also very susceptible to damping off because of the weak stem. Depending on how elongated the stem has become, they may or may not be salvageable. Try to get them into better light as soon as possible.

intensity required, the light tubes must be less than 6 inches (15 cm) away from the top leaves of the seedlings. If you rig the light fixture on a pair of chains, it is easy to raise it as the seedlings grow taller. This light setup is not a perfect substitute for sunlight, so as soon as possible, move the seedlings to a coldframe or greenhouse during the day.

FIGURE 5.2. Seedlings grown with plenty of light (left) have short, stocky stems, while those without enough light (right) are elongated and weak.

Temperature: Most vegetable seeds germinate well at 70–86°F (21–30°C) (see Table 4.1). The top of the refrigerator or hot water heater used to be a good place to germinate seeds, but not in this day of energy-efficient appliances. If you don't have a warm place to set seedling trays, investing in a bottom-heat unit for seedlings is well worth it. Because bottom heat is only needed for the germination period, you can cycle a lot of seedlings through one bottom-heating unit the size of a standard seedling tray (about 10 × 20 inches/25 × 50 cm).

Good air circulation over the surface is essential, so do not cover the seed trays with those plastic covers that often come with the bottom-heat units. After the seeds sprout, move the trays to cooler, bright conditions. The best temperature for growth is 60–68°F (16–20°C), which is about 10 degrees Fahrenheit lower than germination temperatures.

Moisture: The soil should be moist, but not wet. Many seeds can germinate in barely damp soil because they are able to take up enough water from the humid air between soil particles (corn, cabbage family and squash family seeds do this). More people go wrong *over*-watering rather than with *under*-watering seeds. They often lose their seedlings to damping off, which thrives in wet soil.

So, water seed trays sparingly. I soak the soil mix before sowing seeds and then don't usually have to water again for a couple of days. When the surface starts to dry out, water seed trays from the bottom by setting them in a shallow pan of water for a short time (10 minutes or so). Don't leave them so long that the soil surface becomes waterlogged.

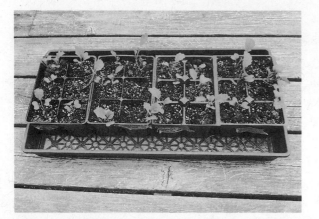

FIGURE 5.3. Seedlings grown in individual cells will be easy to transplant later.

Once the seedlings are a couple of inches tall, they take up water at an increasing rate and should be checked daily. It is fine to water sturdy, well-grown seedlings from above because they are past the high risk stage for damping off. If the soil is allowed to dry out, it kills fine root hairs and stunts future growth, but you don't want the roots to sit in waterlogged soil either.

Containers: You can use any kind of clean container for seedlings: egg cartons, milk cartons, cottage cheese containers, fast food "clam shells," etc. Just be sure to punch two or three holes in the bottom to allow water to drain.

It doesn't take long for gardeners to end up with a miscellaneous collection of pots and seedling trays. These just need to be cleaned to be reused. Soak the pots in a bucket of water to loosen the soil, then scrub with a brush to clean them. Optional step (but I highly recommend it): soak the pots in a bleach solution for 15 minutes, then rinse well. Mix 10 parts water to 1 part hydrogen peroxide (better for the environment than chlorine bleach). For best results, pots should be clean when you put them into the bleach.

New seedling trays made of recycled plastic are also available. They are inexpensive and with care last for several uses. The ones with individual cells for each seedling produce good results because roots suffer less disturbance during transplanting.

Peat pots and pellets are still sold, and since they have been on the market for decades I guess they must work for someone. I found that seedlings didn't get their roots through the pot, the pots dried out easily, and I ended up ripping off the hardened remnants of the pots to plant the seedling anyway. Reusable plastic pots for me!

Soil mixes: Back when you couldn't buy commercial organic soil mixes for seedlings, I used to make my own mix (see Table 5.1). Now, I am happy to

Table 5.1. Basic homemade seedling mix.

	Ingredient	Notes
1 part	Finished homemade compost or commercial compost	Screen it to remove large particles.
1 part	Vermiculite or perlite	
1 part	Coconut coir or peat moss	Coir is more environmentally sustainable than peat.
1 part	Good garden soil	Use the best you have.
For each gallon of mix, add:	1 T agricultural lime	For acid soils; not necessary if soil is near neutral pH.

Note: All proportions are approximate and should be adjusted according to conditions: e.g., if the soil is heavy clay, use less soil and more vermiculite and peat.

buy a bag of commercial mix, certified by OMRI (Organic Materials Review Institute) for general use by organic growers. It saves a lot of time and effort and gives consistent results.

Look for products, such as Sunshine® Organic Planting Mix or Seasoil™ Potting Mix, that state they are for seedling production. Check the labels of other commercial "potting soil" products before you buy. Some are intended as soil substitutes for use in containers and don't have nutrients. Seeds germinate in these mixes, but stop growing as soon as they run out of the food stored in the seed itself. Seedlings in such mixes need regular applications of liquid fertilizer or should be transplanted into a fertile soil mix as soon as they have two leaves.

Steps for Starting Seeds Indoors

- Fill containers with potting mix, lightly pressed down to firm the mix. I like to soak the soil mix at this point, before seeding.
- Sow the seeds. Using a pointed chopstick, open a little hole in the mix and drop in the seed and close it up. Or, don't quite fill the container

Is It Necessary to Pasteurize Soil Mix?

The purpose of heating soil to 140°F (60°C) is to kill soil-borne diseases (mainly damping off). A soil mix made with finished compost, however, contains beneficial soil fungi that help suppress damping off—and these are also killed when the soil is heated. When I used to make seedling mixes, I actually had better results when I stopped pasteurizing the soil and concentrated instead on providing warm germination temperatures and avoiding overwatering (certainly easier than trying to heat a soil mix evenly in a kitchen oven!).

with soil mix, place the seeds on the soil and cover with another layer of soil. If you are using a denser mix, such as the homemade soil mix described in Table 5.1, for good results cover the seeds with vermiculite instead of soil mix. Sow 2 or 3 seeds in individual pots or in each cell of a seedling pack. Sow 8–10 seeds in small trays where you intend to grow 4–6 seedlings.

- Set the containers on bottom heat or in a warm spot, aiming for 70–86°F (21–30°C). Don't cover the containers. Water from below when the top of the soil dries out.
- As soon as any seedlings show the tip of a shoot above the soil surface, move the tray to high intensity light and cooler temperatures (60–68°F/16–20°C).
- When seedlings are about an inch high, choose the best ones and pull out or clip off the extras.
- Grow on the seedlings. If possible, put them in a coldframe or greenhouse on sunny days. Bring them indoors at night until the minimum temperature at night stays above 54°F (12°C).
- If seedlings are growing too large for their pots and it is still too cold to put them out, repot them in bigger containers and keep them growing vigorously.

Hardening Off Seedlings

Seedlings that are grown under lights, in greenhouses, or on windowsills will have soft stems and tender leaves with thin cuticles (the thin, waxy coating on leaf surfaces). They have to gradually get used to direct sun, wind and cooler nights before they are sent out into the world. Through this process of "hardening off," their growth slows a little as food reserves build up in the roots, and the cuticle on the leaves thickens up to protect them from sunburn.

The hardening off process is simple: get seedlings used to outdoor conditions gradually, starting with an hour in the sun the first day (or longer in cloudy weather). Move them back under glass or into light shade for the rest of the day. Over about a week, expose them to direct sun for longer periods, until they are outside all day.

For hardy plants, such as onions, leafy greens and cabbage, hardening off gets seedlings used to direct sun and cooler temperatures. Small seedlings (for example, cabbage with fewer than five leaves) can get used to quite low temperatures. For seedlings larger than that, however, exposure to temperatures under 40–50°F (5–10°C) for a couple of weeks may cause them to go to seed in mid-summer (see: *Vernalization*, Chapter 1).

Hardening off tender crops, such as tomatoes, peppers, cucumber, squash and melons, mainly means getting them used to direct sun. Cucumbers, for example, can be seriously set back or even die from sunburn if they are abruptly moved from indoors into full sun for a whole day.

Coldframes are excellent tools for hardening off plants. As the weather

FIGURE 5.4. Sunburn damage on cucumbers and squash appears as biscuit-colored spots and blotches on leaves and stems.

Coldframes

A traditional coldframe is handy to have for producing good quality seedlings if you don't have a greenhouse or plastic tunnel to use. Make a simple coldframe from four boards for sides and an old window (or clear plastic) as the cover. Set it so that the glass faces south and is slanted downward at the front to allow in light. Use a stick to prop up the window to ventilate the frame during the day, because it quickly overheats inside when the sun comes out. You can build or buy much more elaborate designs, including frames made entirely of rigid clear plastic and frames with automatic openers to lift the covers. When I lived in eastern Canada, I used an extensive collection of coldframes to give seedlings a good start and to extend the growing season for various plants. When I moved to the West Coast, however, I soon found that one small coldframe was all I needed.

FIGURE 5.5. The clear sides of this coldframe provide maximum light to seedlings.

warms, plants gradually become used to the sun as the frames are opened a little more each day for ventilation. By the time plants are ready to be set out, they are used to the sun and outdoor conditions and don't need any more special treatment.

The tricky thing is that *over*-hardening plants can slow their growth so much that they may never recover, delaying and reducing the total harvest. Transplants become over-hardened if they are held too long in pots and become root-bound, or are stressed by uneven watering or lack of nutrients. Transplants for sale have usually been hardened off enough by the

How to Tell If Plants Are Root Bound

Lift the pot and look for roots coming out of the drainage holes. A few roots showing is okay, but a straggly beard of roots trailing out of each hole is a bad sign. Another way to check is to gently slide a seedling slightly out of the container: the more roots you can see wrapping around the sides of the root ball, the more root bound the plants are. If you can't get the root ball to slide out easily, it is probably extremely root bound.

time they reach the market. They risk becoming over-hardened if kept too much longer in their pots.

Ideally, you have timed seeding dates so transplants are the perfect size to plant out when the weather is right. Given the difficulty of predicting spring weather on the coast, however, that doesn't always happen. Be prepared to move seedling into larger pots to avoid over-hardening if it isn't warm enough to put them out.

Seed Saving

I think everyone should know how to save seeds—at least the easy ones. When it comes to seed saving, coastal gardeners have an enormous advantage because many vegetables are biennials and have to be kept over the winter before they will flower. This takes special management where winters are cold, but on the coast most biennials are hardy enough to stay in the garden all winter. It is just a matter of waiting until the next summer and letting them get on with flowering and setting seeds.

Saving seed cuts down on costs, of course, and with plenty of seeds on hand,

FIGURE 5.6. Saving bean seeds is dead easy. Just leave the pods on the plant until seeds harden and dry thoroughly, then pop them out of the pods.

you can sow extra to ensure a good stand despite pests. It also gives you sur-pluses to trade with other gardeners. And, when you find a variety you really like, you might be able to keep it going yourself, long after it disappears from seed catalogs.

Most seeds keep for years if stored properly (see Table 5.3), so you only need to save seeds from a few different vegetables each year to end up with a good collection of varieties. Aside from remembering not to save seeds from hybrid varieties, the main issue to be aware of is the risk of flowers being cross-pollinated by a different variety (or in some cases by related weeds).

Only Save Seeds from Open-pollinated Varieties

Don't save seed from hybrids (if a variety name has "F1" after it, it is a hybrid). Unlike hybrids, open-pollinated (OP) varieties come relatively true from seed because both parents are the same.

Basic Seed-Saving Methods

Notes specific to each type of vegetable are included under their entry in Chapter 10.

Isolate blooming plants in space or time: That sounds like science fic-tion, but all it means is this: if you want to save seeds, either put some physi-cal distance between varieties or don't allow different varieties of the same vegetable to bloom at the same time in your garden. There is also a third al-ternative for plants that are self-fertile, such as peppers and eggplants: you can cover plants with a floating row cover or screen cage to keep out bees and other pollinators (you will have to pollinate these flowers by hand).

Most vegetables have a high risk of cross-pollination (see Table 5.2). Seeds of most are quite easy to save, but you do you need to make sure the flowers don't receive pollen from other plants in your garden or nearby gardens. The best way to do this is to save only one variety at a time, and make sure no other closely related plants are flowering in the garden at the same time. Cut down flower stalks of other plants before the flowers open

Table 5.2. Risk of cross-pollination.

Cross-pollination risk	Target separation distance between varieties when in bloom	Vegetables
Low Risk	25–35 feet (8–10 meters)	Beans (except scarlet runner beans), peas, lettuce, endive, most tomatoes
Intermediate Risk	150 feet (45 meters)	Heritage tomatoes with broad leaves (their flowers are more open to pollinating insects)
High Risk	500 feet (150 meters)	Scarlet runner beans, broccoli, cabbage, Brussels sprouts, Chinese cabbage, kale, mustard, radishes, beets, Swiss chard, carrots, celery, celeriac, leeks, onions, parsnips, turnips, peppers
Extreme Risk	1 mile (1–2 kilometers)	Spinach, sweet corn

Note: The separation distance only applies to varieties that are in bloom at the same time.

or remove the plants altogether so there is no stray pollen for wind or bees to move around. Gardeners in community garden plots might not be able to save pure varieties because there may be cross-pollination from plants in other plots. Some plants with very light pollen that blows on the wind can cross with plants from gardens as far away as a mile, though the risk of that happening is pretty remote.

Vegetables that are self-fertile and have a low risk of cross-pollination (see Table 5.2), are unlikely to cross if they are grown a short distance (30 feet/ 10 meters) from related plants in bloom at the same time. In home gardens, however, where plants grow closer together, wind or bees can move pollen between these plants, so it is still best to grow out only one variety at a time, and remove flowers of related plants during the blooming period.

Saving seeds of a few vegetables is definitely for the advanced class:

- Squash, cucumber and melon: Both male and female flowers have to be bagged or taped shut so they can be hand pollinated. Squash crosses produce notoriously inferior fruit.

- Sweet corn: It takes special methods to make sure there is no chance of unwanted wind-borne pollen reaching the silks.
- Cauliflower: Heads of cauliflower have to be maintained through the winter (usually in a greenhouse), so flowers can develop the following spring.

If you are interested in learning how to save seeds from these plants, see Resources for sources of more detailed instructions.

Decide which plants to use for seed: Choose parent plants based on whether they are showing the characteristics you want. It might seem logical to save seeds from the first plants that produce seed, but for some vegetables those are the very plants you don't want to keep. For example, late seed production is a good thing in leafy greens that you want to harvest over a long period. The same goes for radishes, leeks and onions. On the other hand, you might want to save seed from bean and pea plants that produce pods earliest. Watch for plants that have other characteristics that you like, such as taste, size, vigor or color.

Save seeds from as many different plants of each variety as you can, as long as they have the characteristics you are looking for. Try to save seeds from at least three different plants at one time — from six to ten plants is even better — so you maintain a pretty good level of genetic diversity within the variety.

FIGURE 5.7. Swiss chard blooms after spending the winter in the garden.

Label everything! Mark the parent plants when they are planted, and label seed heads the moment they are harvested. Tie labels onto the stalks or label the container. Don't wait until later, because, believe me, seed pods of many plants look identical when they dry.

Allow seeds to mature on the plant: Seeds of most plants do not mature at the same time, so keep checking the plants or pods. It can take most of the summer for some seeds to ripen. You can open a test seed pod every week or two to check when seeds lose their green color and harden up. When seeds are easy to shell out of pods and look hard and dry, they are ready to harvest. Collect just the ripest pods or heads, leaving later seed to ripen on the plant. Practically, however, if you want to cut seed stalks only once, harvest them when the earliest third of seed pods have thoroughly matured. Much of the later-forming seed will still mature after the stalks are cut.

Here is when to expect seed heads to form:

- Annuals form seed their first year. Arugula, beans, summer broccoli, lettuce, peas, spinach, mustard greens, corn salad, Chinese cabbage, summer radishes, dill and cilantro are annuals. Tomatoes and pepper are perennials, but for seed-saving purposes are treated as annuals because they produce seeds the first year.
- Biennials don't form seed until the following summer. Kale, Swiss chard, winter broccoli, Brussels sprouts, cabbage, celery, endive, parsley, leeks, sweet onions, carrots, beets, parsnips, winter radishes and turnips are some of the biennials that overwinter successfully on the coast.

Dry the seeds: You can do this in a garage, basement, back porch, shed, back room, top of refrigerator, etc. The seed stalks (or entire plants of some vegetables) can be cut and hung upside down to finish drying. I hang plants inside paper bags (with holes cut in the upper part of the bag for ventilation) to catch seeds that drop. You can also pick seed heads and pods and spread them on trays to dry. Corn salad seeds, for example, shatter out of

FIGURE 5.8. Leek flowers take the whole summer to ripen their seeds.

FIGURE 5.9. One way to dry seeds and keep them from getting lost.

FIGURE 5.10. Using a pestle to crack open kale seed pods.

FIGURE 5.11. Cabbage family seeds are easy to separate from the pods once they are pounded loose.

FIGURE 5.12. Rubbing lettuce seeds through a sieve to clean off fluff.

FIGURE 5.13. Winnowing lettuce seeds in a breeze to blow away chaff.

the seed head very easily, so they should be dried on trays to avoid losing them. Never use a heat source over 90°F (32°C) to dry seed.

Shell out seeds: When seeds are thoroughly dry, shell them out of the pods or heads. Rub dry pods between your fingers to crack off shells, or pound them in a bowl with a pestle to free the seeds from pods. Shake them through a colander or a mesh screen to separate seeds from chaff. To remove finer chaff, winnow them gently in a breeze or roll the seeds down a piece of flannel, which catches the chaff. Some seed is very easy to pop out of hulls, while others, such as leeks, are tough to separate from their hulls. You do not need perfectly cleaned seed, so don't spend a lot of time getting out every particle of chaff.

How to Store Seeds

Seeds stay viable (able to germinate) longest when they are kept cool and dry. Moisture is the enemy of seeds. As soon as a seed begins to absorb moisture, it begins to wake up from dormancy.

When seeds become too old, they are no longer able to germinate. How long this takes depends on the kind of seed

Table 5.3. Approximate number of years that seed stored under cool, dry conditions should still give a high germination rate.

Seed	Years	Seed	Years	Seed	Years
Bean	3	Cucumber	5	Pea	3
Beet	3	Eggplant	5	Pepper	4
Broccoli	4	Endive	5	Pumpkin	4
Brussels sprouts	5	Fennel	4	Radish	5
Cabbage	5	Kale	5	Rutabaga	5
Carrot	3	Kohlrabi	5	Salsify	2
Cauliflower	5	Leek	3	Sea kale	1–2
Celeriac	5	Lettuce	5	Spinach	5
Celery	5	Muskmelon	5	Squash	5
Chicory	5	Mustard, leaf	4	Swiss chard	4
Chinese cabbage	5	New Zealand spinach	5	Tomato	4
Collards	5	Onion	1–2	Turnip	5
Corn	1–2	Parsley	2	Watermelon	5
Corn salad	5	Parsnip	1–2		

From: Knott, J.E. 1957. *Handbook for Vegetable Growers*. John Wiley & Sons, Co.

and how well they have been stored. Typical storage times for seeds are given in Table 5.3. If in doubt, you can always do a simple germination test to find out if the seed is still good (see page 117).

With seeds now costing $2–$5 per packet, it is well worth taking good care of your investment. If stored properly, even seeds with a short storage life can be kept a couple of years longer than the figures given in Table 5.3. Here's how:

Keep the air out: Put thoroughly dry seeds in labeled envelopes. Small paper envelopes work fine, but these should then be stored in airtight

FIGURE 5.14. The perfect seed container: What will we do now that film canisters are a thing of the past?

containers. Jars or plastic containers with tight seals work fine, as do heavy plastic zip-lock bags.

Store seed containers in a dark, cool, dry place. The ideal spot for your seeds might be in a cool cupboard in the basement or unheated back room or other place away from heat. You can store seeds in the freezer, but only if you are careful to let the contents return to room temperature before you open the container. If the container is opened while it is still cold inside, moisture in the air immediately condenses on the seed packages. This undoes the care you took to provide dry conditions. I store large quantities of seed in my freezer, but hold the quantities I want for planting this season in a cool cupboard.

The small desiccant packets that come in pill bottles, shoe boxes, etc., hold silica gel that keeps the contents of the container dry. You can reuse these or buy larger desiccant packs to put into the containers with your seeds. It is well worth the cost because it adds considerably to the life of the stored seeds. Sometimes seed suppliers include desiccant packs with seed orders or sell them separately. Lee Valley Tools (leevalley.com) sells reusable silica gel desiccant packs in a metal case for woodworkers (look up "dehumidifiers" in their catalog). One small pack (1.4 oz./40 g) is sufficient to dehumidify the interior of a closed container the size of a tool box, making it ideal for a big plastic box of seed packets. You can reuse desiccant packs for years by heating them for a couple of hours in the oven to dry out the silica gel granules.

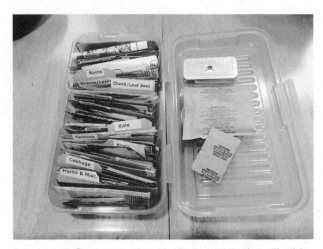

FIGURE 5.15. Storing seeds with desiccant packs will add years to their life.

A Simple Germination Test

When in doubt about the viability of old seeds, it is easy to do a quick germination test. If you do this in January, you will have time to buy fresh seed if necessary. Here's how:

- Count out 20 seeds if you have a good supply. Count out 5–10 seeds, if you don't have many left.
- Spread the seeds on the bottom half of a moist paper towel and fold the other half of the towel over the seeds to keep them moist. If you are checking several different kinds of seeds, they can be placed together in groups on the same paper towel. Be sure to label each group of seeds. Before you wet it, you can write on the paper towel with a waterproof pen or pencil. Put the moist towel with the seeds in a plastic container or plastic bag, label and cover/close loosely (not sealed closed).
- Put the container in a warm spot and check daily to make sure the paper towel doesn't dry out. Most seeds will germinate within 3–5 days (carrots, parsnips and parsley take longer).
- Count how many seeds show a tiny little root sprout and calculate the percentage of viable seeds. For example, if 15 out of 20 seeds germinate, that is a 75% germination rate.

A germination rate above 75% is fine. If the percentage is lower, sow those seeds more thickly to make up for it. If less than half germinate, it is time to buy new seed or grow out a planting to save fresh seed.

CHAPTER 6

BASIC METHODS FOR GROWING FRUIT

There are few things more delightful than sweet, juicy plums or crisp fall apples from your own tree — unless it a perfectly ripe fig or a sun-warmed bunch of grapes. And don't get me started on the delights of the many berries that grow so well here! Tree fruit can be a hit-or-miss crop on the coast because trees bloom early in the year, when rainy spring weather can keep bees from pollinating the flowers. Figs, grapes and berries don't have this problem. Even if you don't have room for fruit trees in a very small garden, you might fit in strawberries or perhaps a table grape along a fence.

The Right Size of Fruit Tree

Standard fruit trees grow up to 30 feet tall, which is way too big for home gardens. They are a lot of work to prune,

FIGURE 6.1. The August bounty in a warm summer: plums, figs and strawberries.

and when there is a crop, there is an avalanche of fruit to deal with. If you are planting new trees in a home garden, I recommend dwarf fruit trees. They don't need much pruning and you can reach the fruit without climbing a ladder. Best of all, they start producing fruit in as little as three years after planting. They can also be planted along fences or walls and kept quite small, or tied onto supporting wires or trellises (a technique called "espaliering").

Dwarf trees need more fertile soil and irrigation than standard trees, which actually makes them an *excellent* fit for a backyard garden because their needs are similar to vegetables.

Grafted vs. Genetic Dwarf Fruit Trees

Most dwarf trees are made by grafting tops from known varieties onto special dwarfing rootstocks. The rootstock constrains the top part of the tree from growing to full size, yet the tree produces normal-sized fruit. Genetic dwarf trees are not grafted to keep them small; they are just naturally very tiny trees. There are genetic dwarf varieties of peaches and nectarines, and also Meyer lemons. Most reach only 1–2 meters high and are well suited to growing in containers.

Nurseries sell dwarf apples, pears, peaches, plums and sweet cherries. Most dwarf apples stay under 8–10 feet tall; plums and other fruit grow somewhat larger. When mature, the trees can easily be as wide as they are tall, so allow enough space to work around the tree for pruning and picking.

Semi-dwarf trees (grown on a rootstock that produces a somewhat larger tree) are also available, but these do get rather large (up to 15 feet high and wide). Keep this in mind when planning. The impact of a tree on your garden is not just how much shade it casts, but also the expanse of its roots, because the roots compete with other plants for water and nutrients.

Multi-graft trees: Dwarf "multi-graft" trees are great for home gardens. Most people only have room for a couple of small fruit trees at most, which doesn't allow a wide selection of varieties. Multi-graft trees have three, four or five different varieties grafted onto a single central trunk. Not only does this give you more variety, but it can spread out the harvest. For example, my three-way plum tree has an early ripening plum (Opal), a mid-season plum (Victoria) and a later variety (Italian Prune). It provides tree-ripened plums from early August through September, much longer than a tree with one variety would. With several varieties on one tree it is also more likely that flowers will be pollinated.

Pruning multi-graft dwarf trees can be tricky because the different varieties don't always grow at the same rate. The general shape of the tree is usually already determined by how the grafted branches have been placed on the trunk. The difficulty is keeping the varieties balanced in size and vigor. Sometimes one of the grafted branches fades away. This seems to happen more on trees with four or five varieties, so I recommend trees grafted with three varieties.

Choosing Varieties

Fruit trees and bushes are a long-term investment, not only because they live for so long, but because most of them take several years before you see a crop. So choosing the variety most likely to produce a successful crop is important. Here are some things to consider when choosing fruit varieties:

Disease resistance: The coast region is a challenging one for growing tree fruit because fungus diseases thrive in the moist climate. Apple scab infections (see Chapter 9), for example, are often severe in a wet spring. You can spray sulfur (but you need to spray quite a lot!) to control apple scab, or you can sit in your lawn chair instead, enjoying the view of your *scab-resistant* apples not being infected. There are apples and grapes resistant to powdery mildew, and some pears are resistant to fireblight and other diseases.

FIGURE 6.2. Apple varieties resistant to apple scab never end up like this after a wet summer.

FIGURE 6.3. This Spartan apple is still crisp on July 1st, even though it was harvested last October.

Early or late fruit: With a mix of varieties that bear fruit early, midseason and late, you extend the length of the fresh fruit harvest. For example, there is nearly a five month spread in harvest dates between July apples, such as Yellow Transparent, and the late varieties that ripen in November.

Storage ability: You are probably familiar with long-keeping varieties of apples (what you see in the grocery store), but you may not know that winter pears and kiwi fruit also store well. Winter pears, such as Bosc or Anjou, and kiwi fruit are picked in the fall before they ripen and can be held in cold storage for 3–4 months after picking.

Cross-pollination: Flowers of apples, pears and some varieties of plums and cherries must receive pollen from another tree of a different variety for successful pollination. Before you buy, do a little research or ask at the nursery to find out whether the variety you plan to buy needs a different variety as a pollinator.

If you are planting two different apple trees, make sure they have similar bloom periods so flowers open at the same time. Varieties grafted onto multi-graft fruit trees will already have been chosen by the nursery that grafted them for compatibility and similar bloom periods.

Long production period: This mainly applies to strawberries. If you grow everbearing or day-neutral strawberries, the harvest extends from June to October, instead of just through June. To a lesser extent this applies to raspberries. There are everbearing raspberries: they don't actually produce evenly all season, but they do have two fruiting periods in one year on the same plants.

Planting Fruit Trees and Bushes

Fruit trees and bushes need well-drained soil that has good fertility, but is not overly high in nitrogen. Soil that has been previously cultivated for a garden is ideal for dwarf fruit trees and may not need much in the way of amendments if it has been a garden for a few years (see Chapter 3 for managing soil). Blueberries must grow in acid soil, so do not add lime and avoid other amendments containing calcium, such as bone meal and wood ashes.

November is a good time to plant trees and bushes on the coast, so they have all winter to establish their roots. Spring planting is also fine; there is often a larger choice of varieties at nurseries in the spring.

- When you buy fruit trees they will either have their roots in soil in a large pot or a burlap-wrapped ball, or they will be "bare-root." Bare-root trees look pitiful because they don't have many fine roots, but these will grow once the tree is planted. At the nursery, they will simply pull the tree out of the sawdust it was stored in and give it to you in a plastic bag. Such trees must be planted immediately. If the final planting site isn't ready, you should "heel them in": in a shady place with loose soil, dig enough of a shallow trench to hold the roots, lay the tree at an angle with the roots in the trench and cover them with moist soil. But this should only be a very temporary measure. Plant the tree as soon as possible.
Steps for planting a fruit tree:
- Dig out the topsoil (the darkest layer of soil) and set it aside on a tarp. Then dig a hole a hand-span larger in all directions than the root ball of the plant. Pile the subsoil separately from the topsoil.
- In acid soils, dig ½ cup of agricultural lime into the bottom and sides of the hole and mix a little lime into the soil that has been removed (skip this for blueberries).
- Depending on how fertile the soil is, dig in ½ cup of bone meal in the bottom and sides of the hole, or mix in a complete organic fertilizer. Avoid using manure or fertilizers high in nitrogen.
- Set the plant upright in the hole. If it has burlap around the root ball, ease it off the root ball after the tree is sitting in the hole. Get a helper to hold the plant straight, or brace it temporarily. Set grafted fruit trees so that the graft union (an obvious bulge at the base of the trunk) is an inch above the soil (to prevent sprouts from coming up from the rootstock). Plants that aren't grafted should sit at the same level the soil was in the container.

- Shovel the amended topsoil around the roots, taking care to work the soil into air pockets and firm the soil as you go. Once the topsoil mix is used up around the roots, use the subsoil that was set aside, mixed with amendments, to finish filling in the hole.
- When the hole is filled, build up a low mound of soil in a ring about a foot out from the trunk to make a shallow basin to hold irrigation water.
- Water well. Continue to give the tree 2 gallons of water per week until it is well-established. This will probably take all summer for a bare-rooted fruit tree planted in the spring. The recovery period is shorter for fall-planted trees and plants that were growing in containers or had their roots in a ball of soil.
- Drive in a sturdy stake about a foot away from the trunk to support the tree until the roots are well anchored. Tie the young tree to the stake with cloth strips or Velcro plant ties.
- In a year or two, install permanent posts to support dwarf fruit trees. Their root systems are not large, so trees loaded with fruit can be tipped by wind. As the branches spread, you may need to add temporary supports to keep branches from breaking when they are loaded with fruit. For a really good bracing job, space three 4-inch posts around the tree and about 2 feet away from the trunk. You can make permanent ties for trees out of heavy wire, threaded through a section of old garden hose to cushion the wire where it wraps around the trunk.

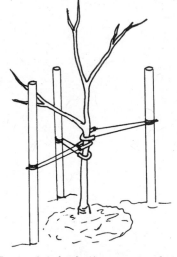

FIGURE 6.4. Anchoring a young fruit tree securely with three posts is well worth the effort. Pad the wires with pieces of old hose to protect the tender bark.

Annual Care

In following years, fruit trees and bushes need moderate amounts of fertilizer in the spring, lime in the fall, and irrigation in summer dry weather. They require at least some pruning (covered in detail, below), but the largest and most pleasant task once they mature, of course, will be picking.

Fertility: Dwarf fruit trees should be fertilized annually, but not with fertilizers high in nitrogen. Compost is an ideal fertilizer, which you might supplement with bone meal sprinkled over the soil and scratched in lightly. If your acid is soil, spreading lime in the fall (see Chapter 3) is a good idea because the lime is carried downward in the soil by fall rains; but you can also spread it in the spring. I find that since I use leaves as a mulch to keep down weeds, my trees don't need much else for good growth, other than lime and bone meal.

Irrigation: The heavier the crop of fruit, the more water a fruit tree can use in the summer. Tree roots are deep and we want to encourage them to grow even deeper, so infrequent, deep soaking is best. Generally, trees should be irrigated every 2–4 weeks in dry weather, but it can vary depending on your soil type and drainage (see Chapter 4). Fruit bushes and strawberries have much smaller roots, so they should be watered weekly, along with the vegetable garden.

If you have not watered trees much over the summer (to conserve water, or otherwise), it is a good idea to increase the irrigation as the fruit is maturing. Otherwise, a late summer or early fall rainstorm can cause fruit to split when trees that were kept short of water suddenly take up a lot of water. This is most likely to happen to soft fruit, such as plums and cherries.

Pruning Demystified

This section covers the simplest pruning methods for trees and vines. That's all most home gardeners need. Commercial orchardists need a lot of knowledge and skill to balance fruit production with plant growth for maximum yield. But for a home garden, considerations are different: it is perfectly possible to have healthy, productive plants by applying a few simple pruning methods.

There are several ways to train trees and vines, but what you choose to do depends on the space available and the look you want in your landscape. For example, tightly controlled wine grapes on a three-wire trellis look completely different from a table grape growing picturesquely over an arbor.

The following section covers tree fruit, table grapes and kiwi vines. Specific information on pruning the different kinds of berries and other fruit is included with their entries in Chapter 11. More detailed information on pruning is available online and in reference books (see Resources). Local garden clubs or garden centers may also provide pruning workshops or demonstrations.

Pruning Fruit Trees

There are only a few principles to follow. These are most important when a tree is young, because that is when you establish its shape. With dwarf trees there is not much pruning to do after the framework of the tree is established. Trees can be pruned when they are dormant (in mid-winter) and also in the summer.

Fruit trees are pruned for the following reasons:

- allow air circulation around leaves and permit sunlight to reach the center of the tree,
- select the stronger branches that are less likely to break under heavy fruit loads or wind,
- keep fruit within reach and of a good size and quality,
- maintain the dimensions so the tree fits into the space available.

If the shape of your fruit tree doesn't come out looking like a book illustration, just enjoy its idiosyncrasies and keep up the annual maintenance pruning — your tree will reward you with perfectly fine fruit.

Dormant Pruning

Pruning in the winter tends to stimulate trees to grow more vigorously in the spring. For a tree that is hardly growing, dormant pruning pushes it into a better growth rate. However, dormant pruning also encourages a rapidly growing tree, such as a rampant peach, to grow even faster.

As a rule, if you keep up with pruning every year, you should not remove more than 15% of the branches. On an established dwarf fruit tree, it could be less than that. Excessive pruning makes a tree produce soft, vertical shoots (called "watersprouts") in the summer. Extreme pruning (removing more than a third of the total branches at one time) can shock a tree badly and cause it to send up a lot of weak watersprouts. If you have a neglected tree that you want to bring back into production, reshape it gradually over three or more years, rather than all at once.

Summer Pruning

Pruning branches and removing shoots in the growing season tends to have the opposite effect from dormant pruning. It slows tree growth because it removes leaf area and reduces the amount of food the tree stores in its roots. For that rampant peach, this is exactly what is needed. Watch for watersprouts developing in June; prune them or and rub them off with your fingers while they are still small. Whether you need to cut back the tips of branches depends on how tightly you need to control the tree's size to fit the space.

Pruning Techniques

Shortening branches: When you cut off the end of a branch, growth will concentrate on the last bud, so choose a bud that will make a future branch pointing in the direction you want it to go. The ideal bud is usually on the underside of the branch, with the tip of the bud pointing away from the center of the tree. When a shoot develops from this bud, it will go outward and somewhat upward, away from the center. If the bud is on the top side of the branch, with the tip pointing up, the new branch will grow straight up, becoming a dominant, overly vigorous branch. If the bud is on the side of the

FIGURE 6.5. These upright watersprouts have been growing all summer. I should have pruned them off much earlier.

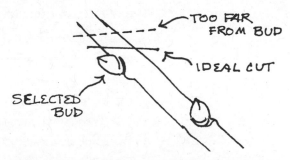

FIGURE 6.6. Where to cut in relation to the bud you have selected.

branch, the shoot may grow at a right angle from the main branch and probably cross a branch beside it.

Make the cut just past the bud you want to keep, at a slight slant. The cut should be far enough from the bud to make sure the bud isn't injured, but close enough to avoid leaving a dead stub sticking out past the bud. A cut a quarter of an inch (5 mm) past the bud is fine, but half an inch (1 cm) is too much.

Removing branches: The best branches to keep for fruit production come out and upward from the trunk at about a 45-degree angle. Branches to remove are those bending too far downward (they are more prone to sending up watersprouts) and those pointing upward at a narrower angle with the trunk. These make weak crotches and can break under a full load of fruit.

Training branches: Some trees, such as pears, naturally have narrow crotches, but when the branches are young and flexible, you can push them apart to the 45-degree angle by using spreaders. The spreader temporarily holds the branches at the wider angle until they become established. You can make spreaders from 1- or 2-inch-wide lath or scrap wood, cut just long enough to achieve the desired spread and with a notch cut at either end to hold the branch. Gently force the young branch to the wider angle and leave the spreader in place for a year.

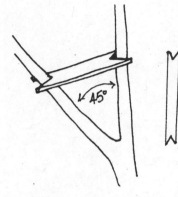

FIGURE 6.7. Use a simple spreader made from a notched piece of wood to hold a young branch at a 45-degree angle from the trunk.

Two Techniques to Avoid

Older gardening books advise cutting off branches flush with the trunk and painting the wounds with pruning paint. Research has shown that neither is good for the tree. We now know that cuts exactly flush with the branch or trunk disrupt the natural "wound collar" at the base of each branch. Wounds heal faster if cuts are made just slightly away from the trunk (see page 129), but not far enough away to leave a stub behind. It has also been found that large wounds heal better when they are *not* covered with pruning paint. There is also less risk of sealing in disease organisms when the wound is left open.

Establishing Tree Shapes

Fruit trees are usually pruned into one of two main shapes (open center or central leader), but you can prune them to any shape that fits your yard. Trees can also be trained to fit a trellis by tying young branches to the desired position while they are still flexible enough to bend. After a year tied in position, the branches will stay there.

FIGURE 6.8. The arrow points to the curve of the natural wound collar around the base of a branch. Pruning cuts should be just outside this.

Central leader: Mainly used for apples and pears, trees trained to have a central leader have an obvious central trunk with a series of strong side branches well spaced around and along the length of the trunk. To maintain this shape, keep the side branches pruned back enough so that the tip of the central trunk is always a little taller than the tips of side branches. This makes a sturdy tree, but the branch arrangement isn't suited to multi-graft trees.

To start a young tree: If the tree is a 1-year-old whip without side branches, cut it back at planting time to about 32 inches (80 cm) tall. If the tree is older, with several side branches, cut the central trunk (which will be the "leader")

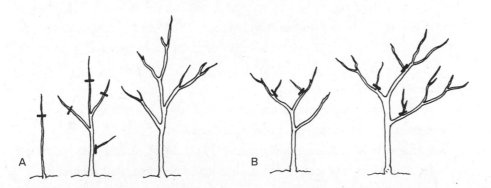

FIGURE 6.9. (A) Central leader tree in its first year, 1 year later, and as an older tree, showing location of pruning cuts. (B) Open center tree or multi-graft tree in its first year and 1 or 2 years later, showing location of pruning cuts.

back to about 8 inches (20 cm) above the topmost side branch; also remove any branches close to the ground. As the tree grows, choose branches that are more or less evenly spaced apart vertically along the trunk and around the trunk to become the main branches; remove the others. The ideal tree has a spiral of well-placed branches so no branch is right above another.

Open center: Trees pruned to this shape have several strong main branches reaching upward and outward, spaced along the main trunk. This shape allows air circulation and sunlight into the center of the tree. It particularly suits multi-graft trees because it is easier to keep the different varieties equal in size.

To start a young tree: For single-variety, 1-year-old trees, if it wasn't done at the nursery, cut back the top third of the trunk. Let the side buds develop into branches. When the buds break along the trunk, select three or four that are well spaced around and up the trunk and rub off the others. On multi-graft trees, the placement of the main scaffold branches has already been determined by the position of the grafted branches. Pruning for these mainly means keeping the dominant branches of each variety from becoming too large and overtaking the neighboring graft.

Other shapes: You can prune a tree to any shape, including flat against a wall (called "espaliering") to save space. To fit the tree into such a restricted shape, though, you really need to be vigilant for the first couple of years to select buds in the right place to become future branches. While branches are still flexible, tie them into place onto a trellis. You can buy a special tape for this purpose, but Velcro plant ties work very well, as do strips of cloth.

Annual Pruning

After the main shape is established, a little pruning is necessary each year to keep trees in good shape. Here is what to look for:

- Remove broken and crossed branches. Decide which of a pair of crossed branches is best placed and looks like it will have space all around it in future; prune out the other.
- Thin crowded branches. Look for places in the tree where a branch should be removed to open up air circulation and allow sun into the tree.

For open center trees, remove any branches and young shoots pointing "backward," into the center of the tree.

- Head back long branches. Prune back the ends of branches to keep the tree within the space or to balance the size of one grafted variety with the others on the same tree.
- For multi-graft trees, try to keep more vigorous grafts pruned back so they stay about the same size as the other grafts. If one branch isn't doing as well as the others, try to keep the tips of the other grafted branches below the tip of the weaker branch. This gives the less vigorous branch a more dominant position on the tree, which will make it more vigorous. Be prepared for the fact that sometimes one variety just gets voted off the tree by the other grafts.

Thinning Fruit

As painful as it may seem when you are looking at a tree loaded with a lot of very small fruit, you must thin them. You will harvest fewer, but much larger fruit — and the tree won't exhaust itself over-producing, which can reduce the next year's crop. Some apples varieties, such as Gravensteins, are prone to biennial bearing: if left to their own devices, they tend to have a big crop one year and hardly any apples the next year. By stringently thinning out the apples in the heavy year, you can keep the tree producing a moderate crop every year.

Do your thinning after the "June drop." This is a natural thinning process that causes trees to shed some of their immature fruit. It reduces the fruit load when the tree has set more fruit than it can handle. It may also be caused by less-than-ideal growing conditions and in some trees may be related to soil moisture (either too dry or too wet — you can't win!). In any case, wait until after the tree has dropped what it wants to, because you may not need to thin much more.

FIGURE 6.10. This tree is going to drop the smallest cherry on the right as part of the "June drop."

When you start thinning, remove damaged or deformed fruit first and then see what is left to do. Some guidelines for thinning:

- Apples and pears: If every flower cluster along the branches appears to have set fruit, thin the clusters to leave just one fruit per cluster; leave two per cluster if the branch has a light load.
- Peaches: Final spacing should be 6–8 inches (15–20 cm) between fruit.
- Plums: Space fruit so they have room to develop without touching; there should be about 3 inches (6–8 cm) between each plum.

Pruning Grapes

Grape vines have to be supported on something sturdy enough to hold a heavy vine full of ripe grapes. Commercial grapes are usually trained onto a system of two or three horizontal wires strung between strongly braced posts. You can train grapes to go anywhere you want them to: along the backyard fence, up a wall, over an arbor, or onto a trellis. The vines drop their leaves in the winter, so they can grow where you want summer shade but don't want leaves blocking light in winter. Grape vines are also very forgiving—if you don't like their form, you can reshape the vine entirely in the future.

There is one simple rule for grape pruning: prune hard. The most common reason for a poor crop is that vines were not pruned enough. You should remove 90% of the vine during the dormant pruning (I did say prune hard!).

In its first year, allow the young vine to grow without pruning. Tie it to a stake to support it temporarily.

In its second year, figure out which of the side branches to keep and which to remove, so the vine will have the shape you want. Depending on how well the plant grew, there may be 3–6 good side branches to choose from this year. Keep the ones that are spaced about 1–2 feet apart if you are following a system like the one shown on page 133. Keep up to four branches if they are where you want them; you can select more side branches next year if the vine isn't tall enough yet to reach the top wires of the trellis. These side branches will become the main "arms," or framework, of the vines. The shoots that develop all along the length of these arms are the ones that will carry the fruit.

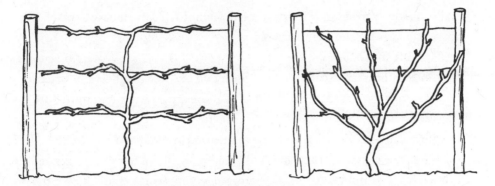

FIGURE 6.11. Basic shapes for grape vines: Parallel wires (left) or fan shaped (right).

If the vine produces flowers this year, snip them off to allow the plant to put its energy into growth.

Table grapes can be trained along, up, over, or around any structure and to fit any space — as long as there is enough room between the arms to allow the fruiting branches to develop and get full sun. While grapes over an arbor

FIGURE 6.12. A table grape vine with a confused shape halfway between a fan and parallel arms. No matter! It ripened 28 large bunches of perfect grapes last year.

really are lovely to sit under, give some thought to making it easy to reach the vines regularly for summer pruning.

Possible shapes for grapes:

- Vines along a fence can be grown with two or three parallel arms extending at right angles from the main trunk. The arms can extend from both sides or from just one side to fit the location.
- Vines can be fanned out with the main arms in a V-shape on a trellis.
- Vines can be trained over an arbor by allowing them to grow longer vertically (this could take 2 years) before selecting arms to fan out over the top of the arbor.

In the third year and thereafter, pruning is pretty straightforward because the shape of the vine is established. You can let the vines carry a couple of bunches of grapes in their third summer if they are growing well. Shoots that are as big around at the base as your little finger are doing just fine. Thinner shoots shouldn't be allowed to carry fruit this year.

Dormant pruning: In March cut back each of the side shoots that grew from the arms, leaving two buds at each joint. The first bud grows right at the base where the side shoot is attached to the arm; the second bud grows at the next obvious joint in the stem. Leaving both of these buds to grow gives you a choice of which shoot to keep once they have started to develop.

Summer pruning: After the buds have sprouted and the shoots have grown a couple of inches, choose the strongest or best-placed shoot at each joint. Rub off the rest. Also, remove any new buds that sprout on the main trunk if they are not where you want a

FIGURE 6.13. Now that the buds have sprouted, it is time to choose the strongest and rub off the smaller ones on the left.

new branch to be. To simplify pruning, you can prune to one bud instead of two in March. Most will sprout just one shoot, so you won't need to revisit them, but it is a good idea to check vines later to rub off extra shoots because sometimes a couple of buds "break" anyway.

In late June, after the grape clusters have started to develop, keep the largest one on each shoot (usually, but not always, the first one) and pinch off the rest. On vines over 5 years old, I sometimes leave a second cluster to develop on the same shoot if it is particularly vigorous. As the vines continue to grow, snap off the tips at the third to fifth leaf past the forming cluster of grapes. Also cut back the tips of branches without fruit. All summer, regularly pinch out new shoots that develop at the joints of the branches.

FIGURE 6.14. If you catch the developing shoots and tips of branches while they are soft, they are easy to snap off with your fingers.

You do have to keep on top of the summer pruning: check your vines every few weeks, or they will become a tangled mass that is very hard to deal with. If the grapes are trained over an arbor for shade, you might want to allow the vines to grow a little longer, but do remove excess bunches and head back shoots with no fruit. If you aren't happy with the harvest once the vine is 5 years old, prune it back more heavily the next year.

Protecting Grapes

Birds, raccoons, squirrels, sugar-crazy wasps and city rats love ripe grapes. There are several approaches to keeping them away (for details of all of these methods, see Chapter 9):

Netting: Cover vines with a bird netting, used fish net or a specially designed mesh for grape growers (this is quite expensive, but it doesn't snag on every little thing like plastic netting does). Use clips to secure the netting to the trellis and vines and to completely close gaps so rats and raccoons cannot get through. This works all right for severely pruned wine grapes on easy-to-reach trellises. However, it is a royal pain to cover most table grapes and next to impossible to cover vines growing on walls or other non-standard trellises.

Scarecrow™: This device sprays water when it detects motion and works very well as a temporary frightener for raccoons while fruit is ripening.

Bags: Effective against the whole range of insects and animals that might attack: Slip a lightweight cloth bag over each developing bunch of grapes, cinch up the drawstring and leave it until time to pick (instructions for making the bags are given under *Vertebrates* in Chapter 9). The bags don't interfere with summer pruning and they work for vines that are impossible to cover with netting. The bags also keep direct sun off the fruit, which is desirable (the leaves need the sun, not the fruit).

Pruning Kiwi Fruit

To grow fuzzy kiwi (the egg-sized grocery store kind), you need both a male and a female plant. Male plants can be kept much smaller than the female, so

FIGURE 6.15. One (!) mature female kiwi vine (the male is the small plant behind it) spreading on a long trellis.

the two can be trellised together on a large trellis or separately, beside each other. The shape and size of the support can be much like that for grapes: sturdy, permanent and shaped to fit whatever space you have.

Hardy kiwi is a different species with smaller fruit (for more information, see Chapter 11); some varieties are self-fertile, so you only need one plant. They are less vigorous than fuzzy kiwi, but generally follow the same pruning pattern, described below:

First year: Allow the vines to grow as tall as possible. The main stem of this new growth will eventually become the main trunk, so don't let the vines wind around the post. It will really want to do this, so keep it straight by tying it in place every foot or so as it grows.

Second year: Choose two or three well-spaced branches, which will become the main arms of the vine. Prune out the rest. The arms will run along wires or crosspieces on the trellis. Keep them from wrapping around the trellis wires by tying them straight.

Third year and thereafter: At this point, pruning instructions for the male and female vines diverge:

Male vines: After the vines flower each year, you can cut the male plant back. Prune the flowering branches back to about 2 feet (half a meter) long and keep them pinched back if they become too long later. In the winter, prune out crowded and tangled branches.

Female vines: Choose side branches spaced about a foot apart on both sides of the main arms (or to fit the trellis). These side branches are where the flowers and fruit will grow.

After the female vine starts fruiting, keep each fruiting branch for 2 or possibly 3 years, then prune that one back to one or two buds at the base of the branch. When these buds send up shoots, rub off all but the strongest shoot and let that one grow to become the next fruiting branch for a few years.

When the vine is dormant, prune out older branches to keep as much 1-year-old wood (that's what grew the previous summer) as possible. Remove crossing and crowded shoots to leave next year's fruiting arms about a foot apart.

During the growing season, starting in May, remove shoots that show no sign of flowers. Keep on top of removing watersprouts, which shoot upward from the main branches and are extremely vigorous. If you want to increase the fruiting branches for next year, cut the watersprouts back to two buds; when these sprout shoots, rub off the weakest one and keep the other. Also cut off the ends of shoots that are twisting around others and shorten up fruiting branches to fit the space.

Although this all sounds very organized, in reality, kiwi vines rapidly get out of hand, twist around each other and the trellis, and shoot vigorously off in all directions — so do the best you can to keep the vines to the basic form, and keep removing excessive growth to allow the plants to concentrate their energy in the developing fruit. A mature vine produces an awful lot of fruit no matter how it is managed. And, luckily, because kiwis are picked before they ripen, raccoons and other critters are not usually a problem.

Troubleshooting Fruit Problems

No flowers: The tree or vine may be too young to bear flowers. Dwarf trees start flowering early, usually by the time they are 3 years old, but varieties differ in how long they take to start bearing fruit. Female kiwi vines may not flower until they are 6 or 7 years old (males usually flower earlier). If a tree is old enough to flower but still doesn't produce flowers, review the growing conditions: is it receiving enough sun? too much nitrogen?

Lots of flowers, but little or no fruit: The flowers were not fertilized. Many varieties of fruit need pollen from another variety to successfully fertilize the flowers. If your tree is a self-fertile variety, it may not have been pollinated because there was too little bee activity when the flowers were open.

The main pollinating agents for fruit flowers are bees: wild bees and domestic honeybees. Although wild bees fly in cooler weather than honeybees will, no bees fly in wet weather. It is not unusual to have a complete crop failure on fruit trees that had the bad luck to bloom during a cold or rainy period in the spring. For berries, which bloom later and longer, pollination improves as the season warms. Even in good weather, however, pollination may be a problem: sadly, the number of native bees flying around our gardens is much lower than it used to be. Backyard beekeepers are also a disappearing breed, and many people never see a honeybee in their garden, because no one keeps bees in their area.

If your trees don't set fruit, even though they have plenty of flowers, you might try hand pollinating. I find that my self-fertile trees definitely set more fruit if I take a small paintbrush and dab pollen within and between the flowers. This is extremely tedious (there are a lot of individual flowers), and it doesn't take long fiddling around with a little paintbrush to appreciate the immense value of bees (and the tragedy of their loss!).

Lots of tiny fruit that fall off: If the tiny fruit don't grow at all and fall off a few weeks after the petals fall, they probably weren't pollinated. If the fruit clearly grows a little and doesn't drop off until late June or early July, then the tree is naturally thinning the crop. This is the "June drop." You should wait until after this occurs before you thin the remaining fruit.

CHAPTER 7

FOOD CROPS IN GREENHOUSES AND CONTAINERS

Containers and, to some extent, greenhouses, have traditionally been the domain of flowers and ornamental plants. Food plants, however, also grow beautifully year-round in greenhouses and for the gardener without a garden, containers are an attractive option for growing food.

Greenhouses

Sooner or later, keen gardeners end up investing in some type of greenhouse. In the cool, foggy zones near the ocean, greenhouses or tunnels are a necessity if you want to grow tomatoes, peppers or other heat-loving crops in the summer. If you already have a greenhouse of some kind, you can fix it up to produce food through the winter. It is also the ideal place to overwinter tender herbs, potted citrus trees and other plants.

A "greenhouse" can be anything from a simple plastic-covered frame to a custom-designed glass house. It can be freestanding or attached to other buildings, unheated or heated, and cost from a few dollars to thousands for a fully equipped glasshouse. I am not going into detail on all of these options, because as far as food production goes, a simple unheated greenhouse provides enough protection for summer and winter crops in this climate. Here are three important design elements to consider:

1. Site in full sun: The warmth inside a greenhouse won't make up for a shortage of the sunlight that plants need for photosynthesis. If the greenhouse will be used in the summer for tomatoes and other warm-season crops, it should receive 6–8 hours of direct sun during the growing season. For winter crops, the greenhouse should be where it will receive as much direct sun as possible in the winter. An hour or two is adequate in December, but the more light the greenhouse receives, the faster the crops will grow.

Whether the greenhouse ridge runs north–south or east–west isn't important unless it is attached to another building. In that case, the glazed (transparent) side should face south as much as possible.

2. Adequate ventilation: This is a very important feature! You will need to ventilate a greenhouse to cool it many more days of the year than you might think.

Winter ventilation: No matter how cold it is at night, in an unheated greenhouse it can easily reach temperatures over 95°F (35°C) on a sunny day in February. Such wide temperature swings from day to night are very stressful to plants. When daytime temperatures are too high, leaves grow soft, making them more susceptible to freezing and diseases. Plants do much better if daytime temperatures rise no more than 25 Fahrenheit degrees (15 Celsius degrees) above night temperatures.

Summer ventilation: Without good ventilation, temperature can easily exceed 104°F (40°C) on summer days — even with vents and doors open.

The Problem with Shading

A traditional way to cool a greenhouse in the summer is to shade it using a blind or by spattering the glass with whitewash. This is fine for ornamentals that do well in low light, but when you reduce the light levels for tomatoes and other vegetables, you also reduce the size and quality of the crop (greenhouse growers say a 1% decrease in light levels causes a 1% drop in tomato harvest). Plan to cool your greenhouse mainly through ventilation, not by shading. However, shading may still be required in mid-day in unusually hot weather.

Temperatures this high stress plants (which stop photosynthesizing) and also sterilize the pollen in tomato flowers, so they won't produce fruit.

How hot it gets inside in full sun depends on the covering material. Glass allows in the most infrared radiation, which is what heats up the inside. Greenhouse grades of fiberglass or plastics are not quite as transparent, so they don't heat up quite as much, but they still require excellent ventilation.

For adequate ventilation, the greenhouse should have at least two large openings that air can flow through. Ideally, they are at either end, with one lower and the other higher, so rising hot air draws in outside air through the lower vent. Venting along the top ridge is an efficient way to dump heat, especially if there are lower vents on either end to bring in cooler air from outside. If the openings are not big enough, you may have to use a fan to move the air. Commercial greenhouse suppliers sell electric ventilation fans. Some models are operated on batteries charged by solar cells, though these do not have the power to move large volumes of air. If you design your greenhouse with large enough vents, you won't need fans. For folks who live on the foggy ocean coast, cooling the greenhouse is much less of a problem, but there should still be provisions to ventilate well.

Manual or Automatic Vents?

If someone is around to open manual vents every day — *without fail* — you can get away with manually operated vents. But, if they aren't opened on just a single sunny spring day, it can mean serious damage or even death to the plants inside. For safety, I recommend installing at least one automatic vent that will open when temperatures inside reach a pre-set level. An economical solution is to use the heat-activated vent openers sold by garden and greenhouse suppliers. These are lifting arms that move mechanically as a wax or gas-filled cylinder heats up in the sun — no electricity needed. As the gas expands inside, it drives out a piston that lifts the vent cover. They can lift up to 15 lbs (7 kg) and are quite sturdy, lasting for years.

FIGURE 7.1. This attached greenhouse has a deep soil bed along the front, space for potted plants along the back (sweet potatoes in this case), and shelves for smaller plants on the back wall.

3. Deep soil beds: It is much easier to grow vegetables in a bed with soil at least 18 inches (45 cm) deep, than in pots or containers on benches. As well as providing more access to nutrients, deep soil doesn't heat up as much, change temperatures as rapidly, or dry out as quickly as soil in containers — all of which benefits plant roots.

The growing bed could be at ground level or in a raised bed. A dual-purpose greenhouse design has a deep, in-ground or raised bed running along the south side of the greenhouse and space for shelves or tables along the north side. For a greenhouse attached to a building, the back wall is an ideal place for shelves, with the growing bed running along the glazed side.

Managing Greenhouse Crops

There are many more exhaustive sources of information on managing specific greenhouse crops, but the following basic tips should be sufficient for gardeners growing food crops in an unheated home greenhouse.

Soil fertility: Soils in a greenhouse are not exposed to heavy winter rainfall that leaches out calcium, salts and nutrients, so it is a good idea to test the soil pH more often than for an outdoor gardens. In any case, take care not to over-use lime or other materials that raise the pH (wood ashes or bone meal). With this caveat, manage the soil like any garden bed — with yearly additions of compost and other organic amendments to maintain fertility. Use liquid fertilizer on plants in the summer if growth slows.

Mulching: In the summer, plants in a greenhouse benefit greatly from an organic mulch on the soil. It reduces water loss through evaporation and insulates the soil, keeping it cooler.

Watering: Soil in a deep bed stays moist for months in the winter, but it does have to be watered occasionally. Once the brighter and longer days of February arrive, plants grow more rapidly and start to take up more water from the soil. In the summer, watering may be required daily because plants really suck up a lot of water in hot conditions.

Cold protection: Crops in an unheated greenhouse will not have the benefit of snow cover to insulate them in a cold snap. Ironically, in the coldest weather, they may need more protection than plants growing outdoors that are covered with snow. Keep plastic sheets, old blankets or tarps handy to throw over the beds at night to protect plants if temperatures threaten to go below 14°F (−10°C). It won't be appreciably warmer inside an unheated greenhouse over a long winter night than it is outside.

Keeping the space filled: The joy of a greenhouse in this climate is a longer harvest of heat-loving vegetables. While tomatoes and cucumbers produce pretty well outdoors in a lot of coastal gardens, you can start picking them earlier and over a longer season in a greenhouse. Other crops that thrive in greenhouses include peppers, sweet basil, melons and long English cucumbers. Given their high heat requirements, you have a much better chance of harvesting large-fruited eggplants or watermelons if they are in a greenhouse (or a tunnel).

But this is only half of the equation: the other joy of having a greenhouse is that you can fill it with cool-season vegetables for the rest of the year. Unheated greenhouses are excellent for growing leafy greens (as opposed to root crops, which are better off outdoors, under mulch). I keep my small, unheated greenhouse crammed with Swiss chard and salad plants (lettuce, kale, spinach, parsley, arugula, mizuna and Komatsuna) all winter after the tomatoes, peppers and melons are done.

FIGURE 7.2. In November, the last pepper and tomato plants remain from summer. I have just transplanted lettuce, Swiss chard and other plants into the bed to fill it for winter.

To fill the greenhouse with winter crops, sow lettuce and other leafy greens under the summer crops. If there isn't space to sow winter crops, you can lift entire plants from the garden and transplant them to the greenhouse. I let melons run between the greenhouse tomatoes so the soil is covered until late in the year, but I keep the beds filled by moving good-sized Swiss chard, kale, and other greens in to take over as the summer crops finish.

Growing Food in Containers

Determined gardeners have found that it is possible to grow all kinds of crops in containers. Some food plants are more suited to container life than others, but you can grow pretty much anything if you really, really want to. Where late blight kills garden tomatoes too early for a crop, growing them in containers on a deck under the overhang of a roof (to keep the leaves dry and prevent infection) can be much more successful.

Plants with small root systems and those that produce a crop over a long season are ideal for container culture. These include tomatoes, peppers and eggplants; cut-and-come again greens such as Swiss chard, kale and perennial arugula; parsley and other herbs; strawberries; pole beans; cucumbers; and bush varieties of squash. Lettuce and other annual greens do well in containers because they have relatively short roots. They are short-lived, however, and go to seed in a few months, so plan on sowing them several times over the season.

FIGURE 7.3. Tomatoes and eggplant growing safely in pots under the overhang of the porch roof, where the leaves will stay dry, yet receive full sun.

Containers

Almost anything that holds soil and has a hole in the bottom can be used as a container, from strong plastic bags to beautifully glazed ceramic pots.

Choose lightweight materials when the weight of the container is an issue, such as on an apartment balcony, a deck or a roof. Plastic and fiberglass are the lightest;

wood weighs a bit more, but is still considerably lighter than pottery. Where containers are sitting on the ground or a patio, the weight usually doesn't matter, so you have a wider choice of materials and designs.

Hanging containers should be the lightest weight. Most on the market are 1-gallon containers or smaller, best suited to small plants with small fruit, such as cherry tomatoes or hot peppers. There are even novelty containers designed to grow tomatoes upside down (the top of the plant comes out the bottom of the container). That fad may wear off, though, because plants don't seem to produce any better or be any easier to water than those in traditional pots — and they sure look weird. For any type of hanging container, choose tomatoes with small fruit because the hanging vines break under the weight of a crop of large tomatoes. Make sure hanging containers are hooked to a strong support.

If you want to grow container plants outside over the winter, put them in frost-resistant pots of wood, plastic or fiberglass. If unglazed pottery is left where it can freeze, water absorbed into the clay freezes and expands, which chips or breaks the pot. Some glazed ceramic pots can be left outdoors in the frost because they don't absorb water, but if there is a prolonged cold snap such that the soil mass freezes solid and expands, it can crack any ceramic pot.

The larger the container, the better: The larger the volume of soil, the more room there is for roots to take up nutrients. Roots are also more insulated from temperature changes, and plants need watering less often. When it is important to keep the weight of a container low, it is better to reduce the

Pot Liners Make Light Work

I like to use slightly smaller plastic pots as liners inside large ceramic pots. It makes life easier because you can lift out the plastic pot to fill or empty it or when moving the pot. The inner plastic pot can also safely stay outdoors over the winter while the ceramic pot is stored away where it won't crack.

weight by using lightweight containers and soil mixes rather than by skimping on soil volume.

Guidelines for what to fit into a container:

- 1 gallon: four to five lettuce plants or one pepper plant
- 2 gallons: one cherry tomato, eggplant or pepper plant
- 5–7 gallons: one large-fruited tomato plant

Ensure good drainage: Every container needs drainage holes in the bottom, preferably more than one. To prevent the holes from getting clogged by roots, lay a flat rock or a piece of broken pot over the drainage hole. If the weight of the container is not a concern, spread a layer of gravel in the bottom as well.

Use pot "feet" to raise pots off of the ground to ensure that water flowing through the hole in the pot can keep on flowing away. Three small blocks of wood or similar-sized stones for each pot will do the same job as more ornamental pottery feet. Use a very large saucer under the container if water dripping from the pot will cause a problem (such as staining the surface it's on, or dripping onto a balcony below). You still need to use pot feet to elevate the bottom of the container above the saucer to ensure good drainage because the pot shouldn't ever be sitting in water.

Where to put containers: As for any vegetables, container lettuce and other greens need full sun for half a day; 6–8 hours of sun is much better for tomatoes and other crops. One advantage of container growing is that it is often possible to move pots around over the season to keep them in the best sun.

On balconies or flat roofs, set containers at least a foot away from walls or the edges of the roof to avoid stressing the flashing joint. The

FIGURE 7.4. One hot pepper growing beautifully in the right sized pot.

weight of a container pulls down on this flashing and can compromise the waterproofing at the joint and cause a leak. On decks, set heavy pots over support posts or beams. You can also spread the weight of pots over a wider area by setting them on pallets.

Provide supports: Tall plants need some type of strong, stable support. If the pot is large and heavy enough, you can fit a stake or trellis inside the pot. Tomato cages, for example, are a good way to support large tomato plants in a large pot because the four legs of the cage make it quite stable. Plants in small and lighter-weight pots can be supported on strings or trellises fastened to a frame, wall, or fence outside the pot.

Soil and Fertilizing

Soil for containers must be very fertile for vegetables because the plants have such a confined root zone. Suggested soil mixes:

FIGURE 7.5. These cucumbers won't be let down. They are supported on strings secured to a solid frame outside their pots.

- Where weight of the container is not a concern: Mix equal parts peat moss/coir, good garden soil, compost and sand. Using perlite or vermiculite instead of the sand will improve the drainage and make the mix lighter in weight.
- For containers on balconies and roofs: To make the lightest-weight mix, omit soil because it is too heavy. Mix in a generous amount of home-made or commercial compost, such as fish/wood-waste compost. You may be better off with a lightweight commercial organic planting mix.
- For all homemade mixes, mix in a cup of balanced organic fertilizer to every 5 gallons of soil. If using garden soil that usually needs lime, add about 1 tablespoon of agricultural lime to a gallon of garden soil in the mix.

Fertilizing over the season: A generous supply of homemade or commercial compost in the soil mix provides slow-release nutrients, but the heavy watering schedule and smaller soil volume in a container means that plants will usually need supplementary fertilizer. Fish fertilizer, seaweed extract, compost and manure tea are useful for organic growers. Depending on how many plants are in the pots and how they look, you may want to feed them with liquid fertilizer every 2 to 4 weeks.

Watering

Irrigation is a big challenge for container gardeners because the soil dries out so quickly in warm weather. The root zone is warmer in the summer than it would be for in-ground plants, therefore the plants transpire more water. Containers may need water every day in the summer. On hot days, a small container could easily need water twice a day. Watering is critical for container plants: a day or two of neglect can kill them.

Think about the easiest way to get water to the containers so that it won't be neglected. Watering by hand is fine, of course, but gardeners with a lot of containers often end up looking into some type of drip irrigation system to ease the chore of frequent watering.

Watering spikes: The simplest "automatic" system is a perforated plastic spike that fits into the neck of a large plastic soft drink bottle. Fill the bottle with water, screw on the plant spike and push the spike into the soil beside the plant. This releases a slow trickle of water to the roots. If you cut the bottom off the bottle so that it sits like a funnel beside the plant, it is easy to fill.

Automatic drip systems: Installing a drip irrigation system that runs on a timer takes a lot of work out of watering. Such systems give good results because the plants will be watered regularly, whether or not you are there to do it.

Inexpensive manual timers are available that you install between the tap and the hose of the watering system. Even a manual timer will reduce your watering work load considerably.

More expensive, fully automated systems are also available.

For small pots, a single dripper in a pot may be enough, but it is a good idea to put a flat stone under the dripper to help the water spread out from the single source. If the irrigation system will take the "shrubbler" type of fitting, these do a better job of watering evenly. These send out five gentle streams of water from the single fitting. It is easy to adjust the distance they sprinkle by turning the top of the fitting. You will need to experiment with how long to run a dripper/shrubbler watering system. It will usually take less than 10 minutes and possibly as little as 3 to 5 minutes to deliver sufficient water to pots.

Self-watering containers: Large containers designed with a water reservoir in the bottom are available from garden suppliers—or you can build your own. They give excellent results because they provide an even supply of water to the roots, which reach the water through a mesh in the bottom of the soil compartment. Since the filled reservoir can also last for several days in hot weather, you can get away for a few days without worrying about your plants.

The downside with these is that they are expensive and heavy. Commercial models hold up to 12 gallons of soil and 1.5 gallons of water in the reservoir, making them quite heavy when full.

FIGURE 7.6. A "shrubbler" fitting. An automatic watering system is very nice to have when there are a lot of pots to water.

If you are handy, you can make your own version of a self-watering container: Start with a large outer container to hold the water (no hole in the bottom). Fit an inner pot inside, fixed so that the bottom of that pot clears the bottom of the outer container by 6–8 inches. Replace the bottom of the inner pot with wire mesh or else punch a lot of ¼-inch holes in the bottom so that roots can reach down for water. Make a hole in the side, along the upper edge, of the outer pot so that you can pour water through this to fill the reservoir with water. You can also buy plastic inserts with integrated water reservoirs that are designed to fit several sizes of pot.

Winter Vegetables in Containers

Many hardy greens can be grown in containers over the winter: corn salad, winter lettuce, leaf mustards, Swiss chard, kales and spinach are some that I've had success with. If you have warm-season crops in pots, you can under-sow them with lettuce or corn salad in late August. By the time your tomatoes or peppers are done producing, you will have a crop of greens started in the pots.

As well as using frost-proof containers, it is a good idea to move containers to a more protected place than the open garden. In a container, roots experience colder conditions than they would growing in the ground—and plant roots don't tolerate as much cold as their above-ground parts do. It is as if they were being grown two zones colder.

For winter, move containers closer to a wall, house foundation or other shelter. For greater protection, you can group containers together and insulate between the pots with leaves, straw or other materials. Wrapping a band of burlap or plastic around the outside of the whole group of containers gives the roots even more protection from freezing.

Fruit in Containers

Strawberries do well in containers and it is possible to grow other small trees or berries in containers as well.

Strawberries: These have traditionally been grown in a strawberry jar, which is a very large pottery jar with openings around the sides that allow the plants to grow out of the sides of the pots as well as out of the top. Roots reach into the soil in the center and foliage sticks out the holes. You can make a homemade version

FIGURE 7.7. My Bearss lime in a tub carries on, providing limes summer and winter.

from a large barrel by drilling 4-inch (10-cm) holes in the sides. I recommend planting everbearing or day-neutral varieties of strawberries because they produce berries all season.

When planting a jar or barrel planter, make sure the soil is well firmed as you go — otherwise, the first time the whole thing is watered, the weight of the settling soil sucks the plants inside the barrel (trust me!). To plant, fill the soil to the first line of holes, set a plant through each hole, with the roots spread out on the soil. Cover the roots with more soil and firm it well. Continue with each tier of plants until the container is filled and then set the last couple of plants in the top opening.

Citrus: Dwarf Improved Meyer lemons and Bearss limes are now widely available in nurseries. These are naturally small trees that can grow for many years in pots. I have been pleasantly surprised at how productive these small trees are. Other citrus, such as smaller oranges, are sometimes available from nurseries as well.

FIGURE 7.8. A genetic dwarf peach isn't a big tree, but it is well-suited to life in a container.

Stone fruit: Dwarf fruit trees can be grown in large tubs, but eventually it becomes difficult to keep them in good condition. There are, however, genetic dwarf peach and nectarine trees that only grow a yard or two high that can be grown indefinitely in a tub. They produce a pretty good little crop (2–3 dozen peaches).

Other fruit: The colonnade or "stick" apple varieties are very small trees that can be grown in tubs. They fruit along the main trunk, rather than on branches, so they literally do look like a stick with leaves and apples all along the trunk. One tree doesn't produce much, though.

Figs can also be kept in tubs. Although figs will become very root bound, with sufficient water and fertilizer they continue to produce crops for about a decade. I have not grown persimmons or other small fruit such as blueberries in pots, but I've seen other people grow them successfully.

CHAPTER 8

YEAR-ROUND GARDENING CALENDAR

The crop schedule and harvest notes in this chapter are for the coastal regions of the Pacific Northwest — extending from Vancouver Island and the Lower Mainland on the south coast of British Columbia to Washington and northern Oregon, west of the Cascade Mountains. In the warmest microclimates and more southerly parts of this region, spring planting can be a couple of weeks earlier than shown here; dates for planting overwintered crops can be up to two weeks later because crops will have a longer growing period in the fall.

You will be making judgment calls every year, but over time you will fine tune these planting schedules to suit your garden's microclimate(s). The coastal spring weather is so variable that you should be prepared to handle rapid changes in weather. Be ready to cover plants in a late cool spell and to mulch and shade them in an early heat wave.

Spring (February through May)

Once you establish a year-round garden, you won't need to battle unpredictable spring weather to get an early start for many crops. There will be plenty to harvest from the garden from March through May. Overwintered lettuce, kale, spinach, Swiss chard and other greens grow new crops of leaves

TABLE 8.1. Year-round planting schedule for the south coast of British Columbia and Washington and Oregon west of the Cascades.

Dates	In the garden	Indoors or in greenhouse
February	Sow broad beans in garden.	Sow leeks, onions (from seed), celery, celeriac.
March	Sow peas. Plant onion sets, potatoes. Plant strawberries, fruit bushes & trees	Start indeterminate (tall) tomatoes, peppers, eggplants Summer broccoli, cauliflower and cabbage.
April to early May	Sow peas, lettuce and other salad greens, carrots, beets, parsnips, summer turnips, potatoes, radishes, scallions, Chinese cabbage and other leafy greens, Swiss chard, parsley. Set out summer broccoli, cauliflower and cabbage transplants and/or sow seeds. Transplant leeks, onion seedlings	Start melon, cucumber, summer and winter squash, pumpkin, sweet basil, determinate (bush) tomatoes. Start sweet corn for first planting. Pre-sprout beans.
Mid- to late May	Transplant tomatoes and zucchini. Transplant peppers, eggplant, cucumbers, other squash and pumpkin if soil is warm (or wait till early June). Sow Brussels sprouts, fall cabbage in garden beds or in seedling flats. Plant out sweet corn and bean seedlings.	Sow sweet corn, beans (outdoors if soil is warm)
Early June	Transplant melons, sweet basil to garden. Sow more sweet corn, beans. Sow summer cauliflower.	
Mid- to late June	Sow purple sprouting broccoli, winter cauliflower, quick maturing winter cabbage, parsnips.	
Early July	Sow carrots, beets, rutabagas, endive and radicchio, Swiss chard/leaf beet, kohlrabi.	
Late July to early August	Sow last of summer lettuce, radishes, summer cauliflower. Sow winter crops: arugula, fall and winter lettuce, leaf turnip/mizuna, collards, kale, daikon and winter radish, leaf mustards, Komatsuna/mustard spinach, Chinese cabbage and other hardy greens, spinach, sweet onions and scallions, broccoli raab.	
Late August to mid-September	Sow corn salad, cilantro, arugula, winter lettuce.	
October	Plant garlic. Sow broad beans.	

as the days warm and lengthen. Remaining leeks, carrots, beets, celeriac and other roots left in the garden will be in good condition until April. Purple sprouting broccoli and winter cauliflower produce heads from late February through May. Indoors, you could still have potatoes, winter squash, onions, garlic and apples if they have been stored well. In fact, I often have to make a point of using up the last of these in July.

So, go ahead and try planting early peas and potatoes in March if the weather permits, but don't worry about getting an early start for a lot of other crops. If you wait until the soil warms up, it is a lot easier to get a good stand of seedlings. It also avoids the chance that some will go to seed prematurely if there is a period of cool weather.

If you are growing your own transplants, the main planting task for spring is starting seedlings (see Chapter 4). Otherwise, plan the garden, get your supply of seeds and soil amendments, and enjoy the harvest of overwintered crops.

FIGURE 8.1. My spring planting is underway (under supervision).

Spring Planting Notes

For coastal gardeners, the best indicator of when to plant is the soil temperature. Pull back the mulch on beds where you plan to sow spring crops so the soil warms up and dries out. Wait until the soil is 50–60°F (10–15°C) to sow most seeds, even warmer for beans and corn.

To get a jump on the season, start peas, beans and corn indoors 3 weeks ahead of planting dates. Peas and bean are easy to pre-sprout in vermiculite (see Chapter 5); doing so gets the seedlings safely past the danger of pests and diseases.

Set out squash, cucumbers, tomatoes, peppers, melons and sweet basil after the weather seems to have stabilized in a warm summer pattern. Because the coastal spring is usually long and cool, this might not be until early

FIGURE 8.2. Pre-sprouted peas in vermiculite get a great head start in life.

FIGURE 8.3. After a particularly bad winter, leeks are fine under their battered exteriors.

June in some years. If you set plants out earlier, be prepared to protect them from a late cool spell, which would stop their growth.

To hasten sowing and transplanting dates, warm the soil by laying a sheet of clear plastic flat on the soil surface for a couple of weeks before planting. After planting, cover beds with floating rows covers, plastic tunnels or cover plants with cloches.

Spring Harvest Notes

Carrots, beets and parsnips: Roots still in the garden start to grow again in the spring. When they do, they begin using up the stored sugars in their roots, so quality deteriorates the longer they stay in the garden. Root crops are usually fine up to early April, but can start growing in late March in warmer years. To preserve quality, dig up any remaining roots by April 1 and store them in a refrigerator. They won't grow any larger in the spring anyway, no matter how long you leave them in the ground because they are preparing to put their energy into flowering.

Leeks: Lift remaining leeks in April and refrigerate them — or just leave them in the garden. They will grow a seed stalk as the spring progresses. The stalk is tender and edible at first, so the whole leek can still be used. Once the stalk begins to toughen up, you can simply remove it (split the leek down the middle and lift out the stalk) before using the rest of the leek.

Leafy greens: Overwintered leafy greens usually grow quickly in April. By the end of the month, there may be too much to keep up with, so pull surplus plants to make room for new crops.

You can leave spinach, kale, chard and parsley in the garden even though they begin to develop seed stalks in the spring. The leaves that grow along the seed stalk are fine to eat.

Winter broccoli and cauliflower: No matter how battered these plants were by winter winds or heavy snow, as long as the stems weren't broken, they will recover. The plants grow new leaves and then form heads. The earliest purple sprouting broccoli varieties start heading in February. Later varieties start in April and continue producing useful shoots well into June.

FIGURE 8.4. Leafy greens in March: leaf beet and namenia (leaf turnip) with Brussels sprouts underneath.

What to Do Each Month

February

- Start seeds indoors if you can provide good growing conditions: leeks, onions from seed, celeriac and celery.
- Sow broad beans outdoors if you didn't plant them last fall.
- Finish pruning fruit trees, bushes, and kiwi and grape vines (you can plan on pruning the grapes last, because they leaf out later than other plants).
- Gardeners in British Columbia: Attend your local Seedy Saturday to buy, sell and swap seeds, hear speakers, and view displays. Most communities hold them on a Saturday in February (a few are in early March).

FIGURE 8.5. This Purple Cape cauliflower lost most of its leaves in January storms, but here it is in April, ready to pick.

March

- Start seeds indoors if you can provide good growing conditions: indeterminate (tall) tomatoes, peppers and eggplants should be started now; also start summer cauliflower, cabbage and broccoli for early planting.
- Sow lettuce, spinach, arugula, leaf mustard and other salad greens in the garden if you don't have them as overwintered crops.
- Peas: Sprout seeds in vermiculite for planting outdoors in 3 weeks, or sow directly in the garden if soil has warmed to 54°F (12°C).
- Onions: Plant onion sets outdoors at the end of the month. The best sets are smaller than a dime — larger ones may bolt to seed (use them as early scallions).
- Potatoes: Set a few seed potatoes on the windowsill to develop dark green sprouts. Plant them outdoors in late March for the earliest crop of potatoes. Protect early emerging sprouts from late frosts: hill up the soil over the sprouts or cover with mulch or plastic sheets.
- Set out strawberry plants and asparagus roots.
- Plant fruit trees, grapes, blueberries, raspberries and other small fruit bushes, if you didn't do it in November.
- Finish pruning grapes.

April

- First week of April, dig any carrots, beets or celeriac roots still in the garden and refrigerate.
- If you can provide good growing conditions indoors, start seeds of summer and winter squash, pumpkins, cucumbers, melons, sweet basil and determinate (bush) tomatoes.
- Plant more peas, potatoes and onion sets.
- Plant fruit trees and bushes that have either been growing in containers or that have a good soil ball in burlap (avoid bare root stock, even if available, as it will be in poor condition by this time of year).
- By the end of April, start bean seeds in vermiculite and the first planting of sweet corn in individual small pots.

May

- The first week: plant onion and leek seedlings.
- Sow summer beets, carrots, radishes, more lettuce and other greens, Swiss chard, Chinese cabbage and kale.
- Sow parsnips for fall and winter harvests.
- Sow more peas and plant more potatoes.
- Set out cabbage, cauliflower and broccoli transplants or sow them directly in the garden.
- Plant out pre-sprouted beans and sweet corn seedlings started in April.
- Start another planting of sweet corn indoors or sow outdoors if the soil is warm.
- Last week of May, sow Brussels sprouts and winter cabbages in garden or seed flats.
- By the end of the month, if weather is stable and warm, set out tomatoes and summer and winter squash plants.

Summer (June through August)

The delicacies available in the summer harvest make this the most wonderful time of year in the garden. Fresh peas and beans, tender summer squash, tomatoes, sweet corn, artichokes, strawberries and early tree fruit add to the

FIGURE 8.6. Late June and the living is easy.

FIGURE 8.7. Pinching out tomato suckers keeps indeterminate (vining) tomatoes on track for an earlier harvest.

bounty of salad greens, cauliflower, broccoli, carrots, beets, Swiss chard, sweet onions and fresh herbs.

But it isn't all about harvesting: mid- to late summer is also the time to plant the vegetables you will feast upon next winter.

Mulch management: As the typical dry summer weather pattern along the coast starts to form in June, begin mulching the soil around the largest plants. Along the foggy, cool outer coast, wait until the end of June to allow soil to warm up before mulching.

Summer pruning: Keeping order among the fruit and vegetables is an ongoing task over the summer. Pinch out shoots of grapes and kiwi, rub off watersprouts forming on fruit tree branches, snap off tomato "suckers."

Summer Planting Notes

Succession planting: Sow vegetables that mature quickly (lettuce, radishes, salad greens, Chinese cabbage) at 3- or 4-week intervals over the summer months as spaces open up in the garden. Sowing bush beans, peas and sweet corn two or three times, 3 weeks apart, spreads out the period of prime harvest.

Sow winter crops to fill your living refrigerator: Most vegetables harvested over the winter are started in the summer. Think of the winter garden as a living refrigerator: plants don't grow, but they keep in perfect condition for months because they are still alive. Since plants grow so little from November to February, what you are going to eat then has to have grown to full size by the end of October.

Keep a planting schedule handy to remind you when to sow each crop. I also find it useful to keep all the seed packets for these later plantings together in one container. Here are main summer planting windows for winter vegetables:

• July 1st to mid-July: carrot, beets and other roots.

- Late July to mid-August: leafy greens like kale, chard, spinach, mustard and Chinese cabbage.
- Late August to early-September: winter lettuce and corn salad.

If you didn't start plants from seeds in time, you may be able to buy transplants of kale, Swiss chard, winter lettuce and other greens, as well as winter varieties of broccoli, cauliflower and cabbage. Just make sure the supplier is selling "winter hardy" varieties.

If you miss these dates and sow too late, seedlings will usually be too small by the time growth stops in the fall to provide much of a harvest. All is not lost, however, because surviving seedlings resume growing from late February onward and still produce much earlier crops than you would get from a spring sowing.

Summer Harvest Notes

New potatoes: About 10–12 weeks after planting, or when the potato plants flower, the first new potatoes are ready. (Note: not all potato plants flower.) Dig the whole plant or carefully rummage around the roots and pull off a few tubers, leaving the plant to continue growing.

Garlic and onions: Garlic planted the previous fall and onions from sets mature in July. Onions from seedlings take until

FIGURE 8.8. A bed of leafy greens for winter, sown August 1st. Note how vigorous the Komatsuna is (the tallest in the back row).

FIGURE 8.9. The onion tops have fallen over, but wait another week or two for the bulbs to finish growing.

late August or September to mature. It helps both kinds of bulbs to mature if you stop watering for 1 or 2 weeks before harvest, but it isn't mandatory. Onions and soft-neck garlic are ready to harvest when the tops have fallen over and the neck of the bulb is quite withered at the soil line. Hard-neck (Rocambole) garlic is ready to harvest when the outermost layers of the bulb are dry and papery.

For details on curing and storage, see entries in Chapter 10.

What to Do Each Month

June

- Sow succession plantings of sweet corn and bush beans up to the end of the month, indoors if it is cool, directly in the garden if the soil is warm.
- Plant more peas, lettuce and other salad greens.
- Early June, set out celery and celeriac plants (set these out when the weather is settled to avoid risk of plants going to seed).
- By June 10, sow winter cabbage varieties that mature quickly (80–100 days to harvest).
- From mid- to late June, sow winter broccoli and winter cauliflower. If you have the space, seed them directly where they will grow or start them in flats or seedling beds and transplant them in July.
- By late June, harvest earliest varieties of garlic.
- Thin tree fruit around the end of the month after the "June drop" (see Chapter 6).
- Continue pruning and training grapes and kiwi vines.

July

- First week of July: Mark the holiday by sowing a large bed of carrots for harvest all winter. Also sow beets, rutabagas and winter radish.
- Sow radicchio, kohlrabi and leaf beet.
- Plant out purple sprouting broccoli, winter cauliflower and cabbage seedlings.
- Harvest garlic and onions that grew from sets.
- Last week of July/first week of August: Sow fall lettuce, kale, Chinese

greens, spinach, sweet onions, scallions, mustards and other leafy greens to overwinter for early spring crops.
- Continue pruning and training grapes and kiwi vines; thin clusters of grapes.

August
- Finish sowing hardy leafy greens for winter and sweet onions for early spring.
- By the end of the month, sow corn salad, arugula, cilantro and winter lettuce in beds or broadcast the seeds under vines of squash and other warm-season crops.
- Continue pruning and training grapes and kiwi vines (it never stops!).

Fall (September to November)

This is the time of year to finish harvesting the main warm-season vegetables and tree fruit and to prepare the hardy vegetables for winter in the garden. If you have a greenhouse or sturdy tunnel, fill it with hardy lettuce, spinach, Swiss chard and other greens. You can transplant full-grown plants from

FIGURE 8.10. The fall garden should be crammed full of food for winter harvest by October. The only empty space in this bed has just been planted to garlic.

other parts of the garden to make the most of this protected space.

To prepare the garden for winter, cover exposed soil with leaves, straw or other mulch to protect it from erosion by heavy rain and to control weeds. However, don't spread compost or manure on the garden at this time of year. The rain leaches the nutrients away (polluting water bodies with nitrogen), and it is too cold for nutrients to be available to plants or for the plants to use them.

FIGURE 8.11. This is truly backyard bounty! Fall fruit and vegetables are rolling in.

Fall Planting Notes

Garlic: Garlic is much more productive when planted in the fall because it gives the roots time to develop over the winter. You might see small green shoots come up anytime from late fall onward; these are extremely hardy and won't be damaged by frost.

Prepare new ground: Prepare for next season's garden expansion by laying down thick layers of newspapers, cardboard, tarps or mulches to kill grass and weeds. By spring, the sod will be dead and easy to dig in, leaving valuable organic matter in place.

Fall Harvest Notes

Winter squash: Harvest mature winter squash and pie pumpkins when the vines mature (leaves begin to die back, the skin of the squash feels hard, and the stem is shriveled and drying). Winter squash and pumpkins can survive light fall frosts, but if a frost is expected, it is better to cover the plants or harvest the fruit and bring it indoors. Cure the squash for at least 10 days in warm, dry conditions to seal the skin.

Potatoes: Main crop potatoes are ready in September or when vines start to die back. Harvest on a dry day and spread the tubers in the sun for a couple of hours to dry, or spread them on newspapers on the floor of a shed. Store the unblemished tubers in cool conditions in complete darkness.

Tomatoes for later: Before a killing frost damages the fruit, pick mature green tomatoes to ripen over the next couple of months. Store them in cool conditions and bring a few at a time to room temperature to ripen. Alternatively, pull up whole plants before frost and hang them in a garage or shed to allow fruit to ripen.

Pears and kiwi fruit: Most winter pears and kiwi fruit are ready to pick from late September to early October. For the best quality and storage ability, don't let the fruit ripen on the tree. Pears are ready to pick when the stem on the fruit snaps cleanly from the branch when the fruit is lifted up. The skin of the fuzzy kiwi will be brown, without a green tinge; hardy kiwi (the one with small, grape-like fruit) remains green, but usually one or two soften on the vine, showing that all the rest are ready to pick.

Preparing for Winter

Stockpile mulches: Collect as many fall leaves as you can. Use them for mulch around plants, and stockpile more in bins to decompose over the winter to make leaf mold. While you are at it, store a supply for next summer's mulch, but keep the leaves dry in plastic bags or in covered bins so they don't decompose. Where residents put out bagged leaves on the curb for pickup, cruise the neighborhood and pick them up.

Bales of straw are usually cheaper in the fall than at other times of the year, so it is a good time to buy what you need for next summer's mulch. Leave the bale

FIGURE 8.12. The garlic bed has disappeared under leaf mulch, and more leaves are being laid around the other plants to insulate the roots.

FIGURE 8.13. Cabbage family plants are top heavy and need staking to prevent winter winds from breaking their necks.

in the rain all winter to begin to break down; turn it occasionally to smother any seedlings that sprout.

Start mulching: For winter vegetables, mulching is not optional! Mulches keep the "shoulders" of root crops from freezing (and then rotting). Mulches also insulate the soil, which prevents wet soil from turning to ice and heaving up the top layers of soil and tearing the fine roots of plants (called "frost heave"). Mulch also helps keep the soil warm, so roots are still able to take up water in cold weather.

Fluffy mulches are best for winter protection: you can use leaves, straw, bracken fern, shredded corn stalks, or any other materials you can get a hold of. Start mulching in November by working a 6-inch (20-cm) deep layer of mulch around the base of plants.

Organize crop covers: For most of the winter on the coast, above-ground vegetables will be fine in the garden without covers. In the coldest gardens and when there is the occasional cold snap, however, prepare to cover leafy greens. They will survive with less damage if they are covered at least temporarily until the weather warms up. For a quick cover, you can use sheets of plastic or tarps weighed down with rocks or boards.

Brace for wind: Fall and winter windstorms on the coast are particularly damaging to cabbage family plants. These big, top heavy plants are easily blown down, especially in the soggy, wet soil. In areas where heavy, wet snow falls, the weight of the snow also pulls over leafy plants. Drive three or four garden stakes around each stem to keep the plants from breaking during wind storms. Bamboo, wood or coated metal flower supports work fine. Tomato cages also work if you are careful not to break the plant leaves when installing the cage (you can wrap a tea towel around the leaves and gently pull the leaves inward until you work the cage down around the plant).

What to Do Each Month

September

- The first week of September is the last date you can still sow corn salad and winter lettuce in the warmest areas. It is too late to sow anything else, but if you can find transplants to buy, and it is a warm fall, you might grow a small crop of hardy leafy greens. If they don't produce much, leave them in the garden and they should give you have a head start on the spring season.
- Harvest winter squash (some may have been ready in August) and bring them indoors to cure.
- Dig potatoes when the tops begin to die down.
- Show off your produce at the local agricultural fair.

October

- In early October, pinch growing tips out of Brussels sprout plants to hasten development of sprouts.
- Sow broad beans.
- By early October, harvest winter pears and kiwi fruit.
- Dig mature plants of Swiss chard, leaf beet, kale and other greens — retaining plenty of soil around the roots — and replant under tunnels or in unheated greenhouses.
- Plant garlic by the end of the month.
- Dig agricultural lime into empty beds where vegetables will be planted next spring. This gives the lime more time to start working. (This can be done in the spring as well).
- Clear crop debris from the garden and compost it or chop it up and use as mulch to protect the soil over the winter.
- Cover compost bins and manure piles so they shed rain over the winter.
- Move potted citrus and tender herbs to protected sites. Where more than two degrees of frost is likely in the winter, move plants into an unheated greenhouse or cool sun porch. Where frosts are rare, plants can stay in a sheltered site outdoors, but be prepared to cover them or move them indoors temporarily if there is an unusual cold snap.

November

- Plant fruit trees, grapes, blueberries and other fruit so roots will become established before spring.
- Put on the first 6-inch (20-cm) layer of mulch around all overwintering plants.
- Mulch empty garden beds to control weeds and protect the soil from erosion.

Winter (December and January)

For the mid-winter months, there is no weeding, watering, sowing or planting to do, but there *is* the task of protecting crops from extreme weather. And, of course, harvesting continues for fresh salad greens, sweet and crisp carrots, cabbage, Brussels sprouts and other crops.

Protecting Crops

More mulch: In December, add another layer of mulch, especially to beds of root crops. Make sure the roots are well covered up, which means mulching right over the foliage. The foliage of celeriac is too tall to cover, so pile mulch well up over the tops of the roots; mulch kohlrabi well above the bulb.

FIGURE 8.14. Mid-winter snows aren't daunting the leeks, Brussels sprouts and carrots (under the snow in the foreground).

Temporary covers: The most damaging winter weather is the very rare extreme cold period with high winds and no snow. If temperatures are forecast to drop below 23°F (−5°C), lettuce, spinach, Swiss chard and other leafy greens will suffer less damage if they are covered. Weigh the covers down well with stones or boards because high winds usually accompany the Arctic outbreaks of polar air. Try to keep water or heavy snow from building up on the plastic for too long.

FIGURE 8.15. The final layer of mulch over the carrots keeps frost off the shoulders of the root.

If it looks like it will dip below 14°F (−10°C), cover winter broccoli and cauliflower and the less hardy varieties of leeks. The hardiest varieties of Brussels sprouts, leeks, as well as corn salad, parsley and most kales are hardy to well below this.

Effects of extreme cold: Occasionally, Arctic outbreaks bring extreme cold: below 5°F (−15°C). Such extreme cold is rare, but if there no snow on the ground, it kills the leaves of leafy greens and lettuce to the ground. This ends your mid-winter picking, but don't discard the plants. Beneath the blackened leaves, the roots are usually still alive and likely to sprout a new crop of leaves in the spring.

Effect of snow: Cooler parts of the coastal regions receive occasional snow. Snow actually *protects* plants from low temperatures, but it is usually heavy and wet, so it can break plants, especially leeks and the stems of cabbage family plants. Use broken leeks immediately, before they start to rot at the break point. Leafy greens are flattened by heavy snow, but when the snow melts, they usually spring upright.

Effects of wind: In high winds, well-staked purple sprouting broccoli and winter cauliflower can lose quite a few leaves. They can look quite ragged, but as long as the main stems aren't broken, they will grow more leaves in the spring and produce a good crop.

FIGURE 8.16. An Arctic outbreak lays low this bed of winter cauliflower and broccoli.

FIGURE 8.17. But wait! A couple of warmer weeks later, the plants have recovered. They produced a fine crop in the spring.

Winter Harvest Notes

Above-ground vegetables: The main thing to remember about harvesting above-ground vegetables is not to pick while plants are frozen. Wait until they thaw out in a warm spell. This applies to leafy greens as well as leeks, Brussels sprouts and other cabbage family plants. It may take cabbages several days to thaw completely inside. If you harvest while plants are frozen, they thaw into mush, but they will be fine if you allow the plants to thaw out in the garden and take up water again before harvesting.

To get the most from a bed of leafy greens, pick one or two outer leaves from every plant. This method of light overall harvesting allows each plant to retain the maximum leaf area to continue growth. Inner leaves are the hardiest, so continually using the outer leaves before they are damaged by frost ensures there is little waste over the season.

As leafy greens are harvested through the winter, the plants get smaller and smaller because there is hardly any replacement growth. Don't worry about nibbling them down to the smallest leaves, however, because growth begins to speed up in February with the first warm days.

Root vegetables: Even if you have to quarry through layers of snow to dig carrots, beets, celeriac and other roots, they will be in perfect condition if they were well mulched. Root vegetables keep well in the refrigerator, so choose a day with good weather and dig several weeks' supply at once (mark where to start digging next time).

What to Do Each Month

December

- Put a second, thicker layer of mulch on beds, including right over the tops of root crops.
- Be ready to cover above-ground crops if an Arctic outbreak of extremely cold air is forecast.
- It is too late to start other vegetables, but it is never too late to start planning for next winter.

January

- Yahoo! Another garden year begins, and it is time to dream over seed catalogs (see Resources for local seed suppliers). Ask other gardeners what grew well for them.
- Review your own garden notes from last year. Use them to plan the location of crops you want to rotate.
- If you will be starting your own seedlings, now is a good time to clean reusable pots and flats; buy or make your seedling soil mix.
- Starting in late January and continuing through February, prune fruit trees and bushes, grapes, and kiwi vines.
- U.S. gardeners: On January 30th, celebrate National Seed Swap Day. If you can't find a local event to participate in, organize one yourself!

FIGURE 8.18. These greens are frozen right now, so wait until they thaw before picking them.

FIGURE 8.19. A January harvest of perfect roots.

CHAPTER 9

MANAGING PESTS
AND PROBLEMS

Although you are probably concerned about pests in your garden, in my experience, more plant damage is caused by something wrong with the growing environment than by pests. Of course, that assumes your garden is well protected from deer!

The advantage of organic gardening, based as it is on building healthy soil, is that it produces healthy, resilient plants. By minimizing the use of insecticides and by planting to attract beneficial insects, organic gardeners can count on substantial help from the many insects that feed on pests. In fact, the more your food garden resembles a natural ecosystem—with mixed plantings and mulched soil—the easier gardening becomes.

Among the many possible insects and diseases that can occur, few regularly plague vegetables and fruit crops on the coast. In any one garden, you will likely see only a handful of these problems and most can be prevented, once you know what you are dealing with.

Prevention

Prevention is the key. It is the first line of defense against insect pests, diseases, weeds, mammals and other pests. Preventative methods are safe, mostly cheap, and they do a good job of avoiding damage altogether. Many provide solutions that last for the whole growing season. Here are some examples:

- Covering crops with floating row cover fabric to stop insects from laying eggs.
- Planting varieties that are resistant to diseases.
- Mulching the soil to prevent weeds from coming up.

Growing healthy plants is part of prevention because they are less susceptible to disease and more likely to survive pest attack and quickly replace damaged leaves.

Plants become stressed when they don't get enough sunlight, water or nutrients. Sometimes there is no shortage of any of these in the environment, but conditions that the gardener can control, such as acid soil or poor drainage, prevent plants from getting what they need.

Another aspect of prevention working in favor of home gardeners is the fact that we grow so many different kinds of plants in a small area. Quite the opposite of a grower with a huge field of one vegetable, which gives the pests of that crop an unlimited supply of food. Insects and disease organisms stick to their particular host plants, so the mixed plantings in a small garden limit their ability to spread. For example, even if every one of your carrots were damaged by carrot rust fly, you could still have fine beets, onions, radishes and other roots, because they are not acceptable food for that particular pest.

FIGURE 9.1. A typically mixed garden, from corn, apples, asparagus, leeks and leafy greens to flowers and herbs limits food for pests and attracts many beneficial insects.

Basics of Pest Management

Think pests are causing a problem in your garden? Here are some steps to follow that will help you decide whether or not there is a really a problem — and whether you need to (or can) do anything about it.

1. Make sure the problem is correctly identified. If you don't know what the problem is, there is no point in spraying or taking other action. You may *never* know what caused some kinds of the damage. However, because many things that go wrong with plants are caused by poor environmental conditions, you can always work on improving the growing conditions and see what happens.

Whether a problem is caused by insects, disease or other pests, the cause must first be correctly identified before you can know what controls will work and how to prevent it in future. The use of the bacterial spray BTK (*Bacillus thuringiensis kurstaki*) is a good example: it only infects caterpillars, which are the immature stage of moths and butterflies. It doesn't affect other pests, including the sawfly larvae that look just like caterpillars. So, reaching for the BTK will do you no good if your problem is sawflies.

The individual pest entries in this chapter describe the most common pests of food plants in this region, but not every problem that could possibly occur. If you need help identifying a problem, try the following (see Resources for details):

- reference books and websites (especially university cooperative extension departments);
- local Master Gardeners;
- gardener hotlines for phone queries and online forums;
- staff at local garden centers.

If you can take a picture of the problem, you can e-mail it to someone to help with identification (much better than a verbal description!). If you can't bring a specimen to a Master Gardener clinic or garden center for help in identification, bringing a photo on your cell phone is the next best thing.

2. Keep an eye on the problem. Regularly checking on a problem after you notice it can tell you whether a problem is getting worse or not and help in identification. People often notice leaf damage, for example, only after the critter that did the chewing has finished feeding and crawled away. By checking on the plants for several days, you can tell whether or not new damage is occurring. If you don't see new damage, there is no point in spraying. You can, however, note the date when you first saw the problem. Next year, start looking a few weeks earlier than that for the first signs of damage so you can track down the culprits.

Get a magnifying glass to help you see, and keep notes (sketches, photos) so you have a record for next time.

3. Decide whether treatment is needed. It is important to distinguish between the kind of damage that reduces your crop or could kill plants and damage that doesn't really affect your harvest. A parsleyworm caterpillar chewing on carrot leaves isn't really doing much damage because it isn't attacking the part of the plant you want to eat. Anyway, you might be happy to allow the caterpillar to feed, knowing it will become a beautiful Anise swallowtail butterfly. On the other hand, a codling moth caterpillar boring into the center of an apple is directly ruining the crop (though even in this worst case, the good parts of that apple can still be salvaged for applesauce or juice).

What you consider "damage" can be a matter of personal taste and practicality. This is where the home gardener has a great advantage over the commercial grower. Because produce in the commercial system is graded for perfection of appearance, growers control pests that merely do cosmetic damage. Home gardeners, on the other hand, don't need to waste food that has scars or marks, because they can simply trim off the blemished bit and use the rest. After all, how perfect does the skin of an apple need to be, if the apple's fate is to become apple pie?

The size of a pest population is another thing to consider in deciding whether you need to take action. Pests are naturally kept in check by weather

FIGURE 9.2. Blasting with water works really well to control aphids—if you repeat it a couple of days later to catch the survivors of the first spray before they reproduce.

conditions, natural enemies and other factors. In some years, some pests appear in high numbers; in other years, numbers are low or nonexistent. It is by no means certain that a small infestation of insects will grow or that a disease you see on a few leaves will spread — the problem may die out. By regularly checking, you will be able to see whether the problem is getting worse.

4. Use least toxic and non-toxic controls. There are many effective methods for managing pests that do not involve using pesticides:

- **Physical controls:** These are measures that remove pests or kill them directly. For example, blasting aphids off plants with water sprays, pruning out diseased branches, picking off leaves that have insect eggs, or mulching to smother weeds are all *physical* ways to control problems.

- **Biological controls:** Most insect pests have natural enemies that can be relied on to keep numbers down to non-damaging levels. Birds are important predators of insects, especially in the spring when they are feeding chicks, but most insects are kept in check by other insects and spiders. You can increase the number of beneficial insects to your garden by planting flowers that attract them (see page 183).

- **Pesticides:** Most pesticides are chemicals (though a few contain microorganisms). Low-risk pesticides contain low-toxicity chemicals, such as soaps or compounds extracted from plants (see table 9.1). These are only "safe" from the human point of view, of course, not for beneficial insects or other creatures. Most pesticides made from plants and other natural sources are permitted for use by certified organic growers.

  Some people make homemade mixtures on the assumption that these are safer than commercial pesticides. This is a mistake! Ingredients such as soap, oil, salt or mouthwash that don't harm people, can damage or kill the plants you spray them on. And remember that any mixture that actually works to control pests, will also work to kill beneficial organisms, such as the insects that eat the pests or the "good" fungi that control disease-causing fungi.

  The best thing you can do is avoid using pesticides of any kind. When some type of action is called for, try non-pesticidal methods first, and use pesticides as a last resort. You can minimize the harm from

Table 9.1. Pesticides acceptable for use in organic food gardens.

Active ingredient in product	Pests	Mode of action and environmental impact	Notes on use
Insects			
Bacillus thuringiensis kurstaki (BTK)	Leaf-eating caterpillars	Contains bacterial spores and protein crystals that infect and kill caterpillars. Non-toxic to other insects, animals and people. Non-persistent; breaks down in a few days in sunlight.	Spray foliage while caterpillars are small and actively feeding. Caterpillars stop feeding immediately but may not die for 2–5 days.
Horticultural (Supreme) dormant oils	Overwintering eggs of aphids and some moth species.	Contains highly refined petroleum oil or vegetable oils. Acts on contact, by suffocating, by toxicity, or by repelling insects. Sprays kill beneficial mites and insects; once residues dry, the sprayed area is safe for beneficial species.	If pests were present on trees in summer, spray deciduous trees and bushes when trees are dormant. Check label for list of plants that cannot tolerate oil sprays.
Horticultural (Supreme) summer oils	Soft brown scale, spider mites, whiteflies; also powdery mildew.	As above.	Use on shrubs and trees such as citrus, during the growing season, but not in hot weather. Check label for list of plants that cannot tolerate oil sprays.
Insecticidal soaps	Aphids and other sucking insects, caterpillars.	Contains biodegradable fatty acids. Acts on contact against insects and mites, including beneficial species. Once residues dry, the sprayed area is safe for beneficial insects.	Thorough spraying is required and repeat applications are usually necessary. Limit the number of times soap is applied to the same foliage as it can damage leaves. Check label for plants injured by soap sprays.
Pyrethrins	Flea beetles, other crawling and flying insects.	Active ingredients are extracted from pyrethrum daisies. Kills and repels beneficial insects. Toxins on sprayed leaves break down in a few days. Moderate human toxicity: avoid inhalation or contact with skin and eyes; can cause allergic reactions.	A last-resort pesticide due to toxicity to beneficial insects.
Spinosad	Leafrollers and other leaf-eating caterpillars	Natural compound extracted from a soil microorganism. Fast-acting; remains active up to 4 weeks once sprayed on leaves. Highly toxic to bees and parasitic insects at time of spraying; low risk to beneficial insects once spray residues dry.	Do not apply to squash family plants. Limit the number of applications to any one plant to 3 times per year. Avoid spray drift to water bodies.

Active ingredient in product	Pests	Mode of action and environmental impact	Notes on use
Azadirachtin, Neem oil	Powdery mildew; aphids and other sucking insects, leaf-eating caterpillars	Active ingredients derived from neem tree. Controls some plant disease fungi; repels chewing and sucking insects, also suffocates insects. Low toxicity, low environmental impact. Once dry, the sprayed area is safe for beneficial insects.	Not persistent; reapply after a couple of days. More effective on immature insects than on adults. *Not available for home garden use in Canada at this time.*
Diseases			
Sulfur	Many fungus diseases, including powdery mildew, rusts, apple scab; also controls mites.	Sulfur particles bind with fungus spores to prevent germination. Provides broad-spectrum control of fungi, also mites. Low toxicity to mammals, bees, birds, but toxic to beneficial mites. Once dry, the sprayed area is safe for beneficial insects.	Use only on plants tolerant to sulfur or extreme leaf injury may result (check label for list of plants).
Lime sulfur	Fungal diseases; also scales, mites, aphids on fruit trees.	Contains a calcium sulfur compound. Moderate toxicity to mammals, bees, birds; toxic to beneficial mites. Once dry, the sprayed area is safe for beneficial insects.	Use on deciduous fruit trees after leaves drop (can be mixed with dormant oil sprays). Will injure leaves of most plants. Use during the growing season only on plants listed on label.
Potassium or sodium bicarbonate	Powdery mildew	Acts on contact to kill fungi. Low toxicity and low environmental impact.	Start applying at first sign of disease and every 1–2 weeks thereafter.
Copper (fixed copper, copper sulfate)	Bacterial leaf spot, powdery mildew and other plant diseases.	Moderate toxicity. Can build up to toxic levels in soil if used frequently. Remains active on the leaves 1–2 weeks after spraying. Highly toxic to fish and aquatic organisms.	Many plants are sensitive to copper (read labels). Avoid spray drift or runoff to water bodies.
Slugs			
Ferric (iron) phosphate bait	Slugs and snails	Iron mixed in a granular bait attracts molluscs. Metal ions cause them to stop feeding, dry up, and die in 3–6 days. Non-toxic to people, pets, birds, insects, earthworms and other wildlife. Remains active for a week.	Broadcast small amount of bait widely over the area. Do not surround plants with a ring of bait, as it attract slugs to feed on the surrounded plant. Replace after prolonged heavy rain.

Note: There are too many products to name, therefore I have only listed the active ingredient in the pesticide, which is listed in fine print on the label. Always read and follow instructions on product labels.

pesticides by choosing the least toxic product that will do the job. For example, if insecticidal soap will work, use that instead of pyrethrins (a nerve toxin extracted from pyrethrum daisies), which are more toxic and lasts longer on leaves. If you are spraying insecticides, spray only the plants, or parts of plants, that need treatment. Spraying where it isn't required isn't just a waste of time and money; it also needlessly harms other organisms.

Many municipalities have passed by-laws restricting pesticide use within their jurisdiction. The by-laws allow gardeners to use low-risk products on their gardens but restrict more toxic chemicals. In the pest entries beginning on page 187, I have only included recommendations for pesticides that are acceptable for organic growers and people living where there are pesticide restrictions.

FIGURE 9.3. Imported currantworm eggs on the underside of leaves. Pick them off now and the currantworms won't have a chance to do any damage.

5. Follow up. Whether you take action or not, keep checking on the pest situation, and keep making notes. Your notes will tell you when problems appeared or disappeared, and how well your approach worked. If you know when to expect a particular pest, you can prepare to deal with it while the infestation is still small.

Currantworm Control by the Calendar

Because I wrote down when I first saw imported currantworms in my red currant bush in previous years, I now know when to look for them. My records show they lay eggs on my bushes during the last two weeks of April. Now that I know when to look for them, it only takes me a few minutes to pick off the leaves with eggs on them.

Attracting Beneficial Insects

There are literally thousands of species of native predatory and parasitic insects on the coast. You can benefit from these free pest control agents by attracting them to a garden that is safe (without insecticides) and hospitable (provides the adults with food).

For most beneficial insects, it is only the larvae (immature stage) that eat other insects. The adults sip nectar or feed on pollen. But when the adults have pollen and nectar to eat, they stick around, live longer, and the females lay more eggs. When these eggs hatch, the predatory larvae attack your pests. You can lure the parents of these hungry juveniles into your garden by growing flowers to attract them.

What to plant: The most attractive plants to beneficial insects are those that have a rich supply of nectar and pollen in their tiny flowers — just the right size for the tiny mouthparts. Plants in the carrot, aster, mint and cabbage families are generally the most useful. Some, such as dill, cilantro and parsley, are commonly grown in gardens anyway, so they just have to be allowed to flower (parsley will flower the year after planting). Saving seed from vegetables in these families has a great side benefit because the flowers feed the beneficial insects. Some weeds such as wild carrot, yarrow, chickweed and wild mustard, are actually good insect plants too. But you don't have to encourage weeds, of course, as there are many other plants that attract beneficial insects (see Table 9.2).

FIGURE 9.4. Tiny, bright orange aphid midge larvae are killing these aphids. The adult midges came into the garden looking for nectar flowers and stayed to lay eggs among the aphids.

FIGURE 9.5. This lady beetle is filling up on food from dill flowers.

Table 9.2. Herbs, flowers and vegetables that have particularly attractive flowers for beneficial insects.

	Annuals and biennials	Perennials
Herbs	Coriander/cilantro Dill Caraway Fennel Parsley Summer savory	Angelica Catnip Lavender Lemon balm Lovage Mints Rosemary Sage Thyme and creeping thyme
Flowers	Calendula Candytuft Coreopsis Cosmos Feverfew Heliotrope Lobelia Mignonette Schizanthus Sweet alyssum	Alyssum Basket-of-gold (*Aurinia*) Coneflower Daisies Golden marguerite (*Anthemis*) Goldenrod Rudbeckia Verbena (especially *V. bonariensis*) Yarrow
Vegetables (when allowed to flower)	Chinese greens and mustards Kale Radishes Leeks and onions	

Plant a few attractive plants among the vegetables or use them as edging plants or elsewhere in a flower border. I like to put a sweet alyssum plant or two in each long garden bed. It is important to try to have something in bloom from early spring to late summer by growing a variety of plants.

Controls for Common Insect Pests

Below are the controls I suggest for combating two main groups of pest insects found in this region: root flies and leaf-eating caterpillars. I include these here as groups rather than repeating the same information in the individual pest entries in the *A to Z Insect Pests* section that follows.

Root Fly Controls

Cabbage root maggot, carrot rust fly and onion maggot are common, widespread pests. The immature (larval) stage of these species feed on the roots of plants. Both of the barriers described below can be used to prevent the adult flies from laying eggs beside the plant stems on the soil.

Floating row covers: The most effective barriers are lightweight spun-bonded poly fabrics. These were invented to extend the growing season, but have proven useful for preventing insects from laying eggs on vegetables. The fabric lets in sunlight and water, so the covers can stay in place until harvest. You can cover seedbeds before

FIGURE 9.6. Floating row cover fabric pulled back to show the bed of carrots beneath.

Companion Planting: Myth or Reality?

Much been written about growing particular plants to repel pests, but I am afraid it is mostly wishful thinking. That's because plant-eating insects have an incredibly acute ability to "smell" their target plants, yet little ability to detect irrelevant scents. So an insect that eats cabbage can detect the mustard oil compounds in the leaves, but not necessarily the chemicals found in mint, dill, or other plants often recommended to repel pests.

But it isn't completely bunk: Some companion planting works very well—just not the way you might think. Many plants recommended as "companions" (those mint or dill plants, for example) are excellent for luring beneficial insects to the garden where they attack pests. While planting garlic is useless to repel aphids, research has shown that planting sweet alyssum works very well to attract aphid-eating insects. So forget the often contradictory companion planting lore and choose the best plants to attract beneficial insects (see Table 9.2).

seedlings germinate, making sure the edges of the fabric are held tight to the soil with sticks, boards or rocks, so adult flies can't find an opening to crawl through. Leave the covers on the crop until it is harvested or until early October (for winter carrots, daikon radishes and Chinese cabbage). Look under the cover occasionally to weed and thin the seedlings.

Exclusion fences: Few root fly adults fly more than a yard off the ground, so a high proportion of them can be kept from reaching a crop by installing a fence barrier. Although they are less effective than row covers, exclusion fences can give adequate control for a home garden. String a 40-inch-tall (1-meter) fence of nylon window screen around the bed, with the bottom edge buried in the soil. Support the fence on stakes and allow the top 12 inches (30 cm) of the screening to fold and extend outward, away from the growing bed, to make a wide overhang. When the flies reach the fence and fly upward, the overhang helps deflect them from flying over the top and into the bed. Where populations of root flies are high, exclusion fences will still allow some to get into the crop (it is thought they crawl over the fence). Fewer carrot rust flies appear to be deflected by fences than the other two species of root flies, so the wider overhang is necessary to keep their numbers down.

Having tried both methods, I have to say the floating row covers are much, much easier to put in place, though there is a "laundry-on-the-garden" look to them that isn't great. Both methods work only if you rotate crops to make sure there are no root maggots still in the soil from a previous crop.

FIGURE 9.7. Two species of caterpillars busy feeding on cabbage. Only the largest one (an imported cabbageworm) causes much damage.

Leaf-Eating Caterpillar Controls

The caterpillars (immature stage) of many species of moths and a few butterflies feed on vegetables and fruit trees. Most caterpillars eat holes in leaves, starting with tiny holes and progressing to chewing larger, ragged holes as they grow. Leafrollers are caterpillars that feed in the flower buds of fruit trees and other plants early in the spring, rolling up in the leaves at the tips of the branches.

Caterpillars have many natural enemies, including birds,

parasitic wasps and flies, and yellowjacket wasps. If they don't sufficiently control the caterpillars, however, you might need to take action.

For a small caterpillar infestation, it is usually easiest to pick them off by hand — if you can reach them — or prune them out of branches (e.g., for tent caterpillars). Squash them or drop them in a bucket of soapy water to kill them.

For larger infestations, sprays of the bacterial disease, BTK (*Bacillus thuringiensis kurstaki*) are effective. It only affects caterpillars and not their natural enemies or other insects that look like caterpillars. BTK works best when the caterpillars are large enough to bite a hole through a leaf. That way, they eat enough of the bacteria to make them sick. Make sure leaves are well covered with spray, especially on the undersides, as the bacteria only survive in the environment for a few days. Once mixed, the spray doesn't keep, so only mix what you need each time. BTK doesn't keep as long as chemicals, so there is no point in buying too much at one time, as it may not work by the time you use the last of it.

Other pesticides that control leaf-eating caterpillars are soap, spinosad and neem (which may be listed as azadirachtin on the product label) (for more information, see Table 9.1). These carry more risk of killing bees and beneficial insects than BTK, therefore I consider them last-resort pesticides.

A to Z Pests and Problems

Now, don't panic at the following list of possible disasters! Damage from most of them is preventable, and you may never see a lot of these in your garden. The worst threat to your harvest may actually come from the animals listed in the final section under *Vertebrates* (birds, deer, etc.).

Common Insects and Other Organisms
Aphids (many different species)
What to look for: Tiny, pear-shaped insects, 0.1–0.2 inch (2–4 mm long), clustered together in dense colonies on undersides of leaves or tips of young shoots. Colors range from light green to yellowish, pink, mahogany brown or powdery gray.

Biology: Aphids suck plant sap, which distorts leaves, shoots and flowers. They secrete "honeydew," which coats foliage with a sticky layer. Most species of aphids are adapted to feed on only certain host plants (e.g., rose aphids stick to roses, bean aphids to beans).

Management: Most aphids are naturally controlled by beneficial insects: lady beetles, aphid midges, hover flies, parasitic wasps and many others. Planting flowers that attract aphid predators (see Table 9.2) can make a big difference in how quickly they control aphids in your garden. If natural enemies don't act fast enough, try spraying aphids with a strong stream of water. This is quite effective if done twice, 2–4 days apart, to ensure that survivors of the first blast are knocked off before they can reproduce. Squashing aphids with your fingers or spraying them with soap or azadiractin (neem) also kill aphids, but both methods also kill beneficial insects that are nearly always present, hidden under the aphids.

FIGURE 9.8. Aphids of all ages.

E. Cronin

Cabbage Maggot (*Delia radicum*)

What to look for: Plants in the cabbage family wilt in the mid-day sun despite being well-watered. The maggots are hard to see inside the roots, but distorted roots with tunnels in them are obvious in turnips and other cabbage family root crops. Low numbers of cabbage maggots may only stunt plants; higher numbers kill plants.

Biology: The first generation of flies emerges in early spring from pupae that overwintered in the soil. They lay eggs on the soil beside the stems of plants, starting in April. Larvae feed in the roots for about 3 weeks. The next generation of adults appears in early July. There are two or three generations per year. Generations later in the summer overlap, so egg-laying is continuous.

Management: In some years, crops planted after mid-June may escape severe damage because their roots are well established by the time the summer generation of maggots appears. For plants that have been attacked but not killed, water well, and they may survive to produce a small crop.

There are no controls once the maggots reach the roots. The best approach is preventing flies from laying eggs on plants by using floating row covers or exclusion fences (see "Root Fly Controls," page 185) for the whole crop, or to protect seedlings until they are large enough for a barrier around the stem.

Protect individual plants by placing barriers around the stem at transplant time or when you remove row covers to thin seedlings to the final spacing. Make barriers from 6-inch (15-cm) squares of durable, flexible material (heavy paper, woven plastic fabric, several layers of newspaper or heavy cloth are fine to use). Cut

FIGURE 9.9. Individual barriers around the stems prevent adult flies from laying eggs.

a slit to the center of the square from one side; if the material is fairly stiff, cut a tiny X at the center to accommodate the stem. Slip the barrier around the stem of the transplant so the paper lies flat on the soil with the stem at the center X, fitting *snugly* at the base of the stem. Anchor the barrier with a stone and leave it in place all season.

Carrot Rust Fly (*Psila rosae*)

What to look for: Carrot roots have tunnels filled with crumbly, rusty brown material. Tiny white maggots, up to ¼ inch long (8 mm) may be visible in the tunnels.

Biology: Adult flies emerge from mid-April to mid-May and lay eggs on the soil beside the stems of carrot family plants. When the eggs hatch, the maggots feed on roots for 3–4 weeks. The first generation of flies emerges throughout June. The second generation emerges from mid-July to mid-August and lays eggs into the fall. In the warmest areas and in years with a long, warm fall, there can be a third generation in September–October. The maggots overwinter in the roots and the pupae overwinter in the top layer of soil.

Management: This is a serious pest of carrots on the West Coast, especially where wild carrot (Queen Anne's lace) is common. In some areas,

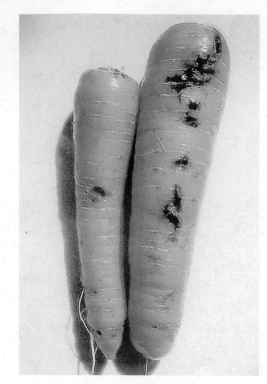

FIGURE 9.10. Typical damage from carrot root fly.

spring-planted carrots escape damage, but later plantings may be seriously injured. If the carrots sown in early July for winter harvest are allowed to be infested, the maggots will burrow in the roots all winter.

Delay sowing spring carrots until mid-May to avoid the overwintered generation. Carrots harvested before mid-July generally escape attack by maggots from second-generation flies. Barriers that prevent adult flies from laying eggs on the crop provide the most reliable control (see "Root Fly Controls," page 185). Barriers can be removed by mid-October, when flies are no longer laying eggs.

Codling Moth (*Cydia pomonella*)

What to look for: Apples and pears (sometimes walnuts, crab apples or peaches) with an obvious hole plugged with crumbly droppings. When the fruit is cut open, the track the caterpillar made boring into the core is obvious. Sometimes the pale pink or cream-colored larvae is visible inside.

Biology: Moths emerge about the time apples bloom. The moths lay eggs on the developing fruit or on leaves nearby. The caterpillars hatch in 1–3 weeks and immediately bore into the developing fruit, usually at the blossom end. They feed on the developing seeds in the core for about a month, then crawl out of the fruit and down the tree trunk to spin a cocoon. Most caterpillars pupate and emerge in 2 weeks to lay eggs for the second generation in July and August (a few caterpillars wait until the following spring to emerge). In the warmest areas and years, there may be a third generation in September.

Management: Pick up all dropped fruit immediately (same day) and destroy it. This intercepts caterpillars before they exit the fruit and produce the next generation. On the coast, unlike commercial fruit growing areas in the interior, codling moth is often a moderate to minor problem in home orchards. In this area, tree bands may provide reasonable control. Wrap a band of 6–12 inches wide (15–30 cm) corrugated cardboard around the trunk and staple in place. Put bands up in early June and check them every 7–14 days. As caterpillars make their way down the tree, about half will stop and spin their cocoons in the bands around the trunk. Destroy any co-coons or caterpillars you see in the bands or

FIGURE 9.11. Codling moth damage inside an apple.

dispose of the bands and put up fresh ones. Keep bands in place until September to catch the last generation. Bands will be more effective if you scrape off as much loose bark as much as possible to remove alternative hiding places for caterpillars.

Cutworms and Climbing Cutworms

What to look for: Overnight, young plants are chewed off at the soil line and small seedlings disappear. Climbing cutworms chew large, ragged holes in leaves, sometimes well above the ground. To distinguish cutworm damage from slug damage, look for silvery slime trails (slugs) or pellets of dark excrement caught on the leaves (cutworms). The fat, gray, brown or greenish caterpillars curl into a characteristic C-shape when disturbed.

Biology: In early spring and sometimes late fall, cutworms feed at night on plants. A recent, but now widespread invader is the Large Yellow Underwing Moth. These climbing cutworms are particularly damaging to winter vegetables because they are very cold hardy and feed during warm spells all winter through to spring. Cutworms hide in leaf litter or in the upper layers of soil during the day.

FIGURE 9.12. An adult moth and a caterpillar with typical damage from the, unfortunately, now common, Large Yellow Underwing Moth.

FIGURE 9.13. Early spring damage from climbing cutworms. Suddenly, a lot of leaf area is chewed up overnight, but there is no sign of the culprit.

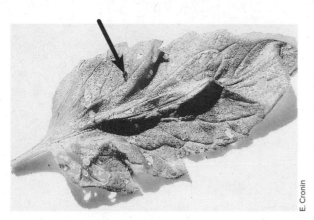

FIGURE 9.14. Leaf chewing from tuber flea beetle, (note the tiny beetle on the upper part of the leaf).

Management: Where plants show damage, look under the damaged plant for the fat caterpillar in the leaf litter or just under the soil. If damage continues, search after dark for climbing cutworms on plant leaves. Where cutworms are chewing plants off at the soil line, protect transplants with a collar around the stem. Make them of light cardboard, 4 inches (6–8 cm) wide, or use small tin cans with lid and bottom removed. Push the collar at least 1 inch (2 cm) deep into the soil (Note: this does not stop *climbing* cutworms).

Flea Beetle, Tuber (*Epitrix tuberis*)

What to look for: Tiny, round holes or pits punched in leaves of potato, tomato and related plants early in the season. Tiny, 1/16 inch long (1–2 mm), shiny black beetles that quickly jump from leaves (making them very hard to catch). Shallow, dark brown pits and marks just under the skin of potato tubers (from feeding by larvae).

Biology: Adults emerge mid-May to early June and lay eggs in the soil for a month. Larvae feed on the plant roots for 3 weeks, then pupate. There are two or three generations per year. The last generation, which feeds from mid-August onward, is most damaging to potato tubers. On large plants, leaf damage from adult feeding is merely unsightly. The main damage is from larvae in the roots.

Management: Destroy all volunteer potato plants because they give overwintered flea beetles a head start on building damaging numbers in early spring. Plant early varieties of potatoes as early in the season as possible; they escape serious injury if harvested before the largest generation of flea beetles starts feeding on tubers in late August. Where flea beetles are a common problem, cover susceptible crops with floating row covers to keep adults from feeding and laying eggs. On potatoes, do this before sprouts emerge from the soil; cover tomatoes at the time of transplanting. If there are large numbers of flea beetles attacking small plants, spray pyrethrins to control adults on leaves.

Other Flea Beetles (*Phyllotreta* spp.)

What to look for: Many tiny, round "shot-holes" in leaves of cabbage family plants, also on spinach, beets and lettuce, and occasionally on other plants.

Biology: Adults overwinter in leaf litter and soil around gardens. They lay eggs around the roots of plants from May to early July. Larvae feed in roots for another 6 weeks or more. New adults emerge from late July onward and feed on leaves until fall. Most flea beetle species that feed on cabbage family plants have a 1-year life cycle, although there may be a second generation in warm areas and years.

Management: Large numbers of beetles attacking small seedlings or leafy greens can be very damaging. Spray pyrethrins at the first sign of shot-hole damage to control adults. Next year, cover seedlings and leafy greens with floating row covers from late April to early July (make sure no cabbage family crops or weeds were growing in the bed previously).

Damage to older plants and those with waxy leaves, such as broccoli and cabbage, is usually not serious, nor is root feeding by larvae. However, larvae tunneling in roots seriously damage radishes, turnips and rutabagas. Sow root crops as late as possible to avoid attracting beetles; roots sown in July for winter harvests generally escape damage.

Where there are high numbers of cabbage flea beetles, try to break the host plant cycle by removing all cabbage

FIGURE 9.15. This leaf chewing by cabbage flea beetles is not serious, but the larvae could be damaging roots.

family plants from the garden between mid-April and late June. Also control related weeds (mustard, winter cress, etc.) in the area. This eliminates host plants during the period the overwintered beetles are searching for places to lay their eggs. Sow or transplant cabbage family crops into the garden after June. Cover these later-planted crops with floating row covers to continue depriving flea beetles of host plants.

Imported Cabbageworm (*Pieris rapae*)

What to look for: Large, ragged holes chewed in leaves of cabbage, broccoli, kale and other cabbage family plants. Velvety green caterpillars in heads of broccoli and cauliflower. Caterpillars leave dark green pellets of excrement as they feed.

Biology: Adults are white cabbage butterflies. They emerge in early spring and lay tiny conical yellow eggs on the undersides of leaves of cabbage family plants. The caterpillars feed on leaves for about 3 weeks and grow to 1 inch long (25 mm). They spin a chrysalis in debris around the plants and pupate for about 2 weeks. There are three or more overlapping generations per season, so they are present all summer.

Management: Although you may see many white butterflies and find eggs on leaves, little damage may occur because birds and wasps eat cabbageworms. Feeding damage on outer leaves of mature cabbage looks bad, but the heads inside may be fine. However, cabbageworms can destroy mid-summer seedlings, and they are a serious problem when they feed in heads of broccoli and cauliflower. Search daily to pick caterpillars off by hand or spray with BTK (*Bacillus thuringiensis kurstaki*), which is very effective. Products containing spinosad or neem (azadirachtin) also work, but carry more risk to beneficial insects. Grow plants that attract beneficial insects to your garden (such as dill, cilantro or sweet alyssum) among the vegetables.

E. Cronin

FIGURE 9.16. This cabbageworm escaped being hauled away by a wasp.

Imported Currantworm (Currant Sawfly)
(*Nematus ribesii*)

What to look for: Large, ragged holes in gooseberry or currant leaves, often with just the leaf veins left behind. The sawflies look like green caterpillars with black spots and dark heads; they grow to ¾ inch long (2 cm). Eggs laid on the undersides of leaves look like white stitches along the leaf veins (Figure 9.4 shows eggs).

Biology: Adults emerge from leaf litter under the host plants in spring, just as the leaves open. They lay eggs on leaves in the lower part of the bush. The larvae feed together in a group, chewing small holes in leaves on the interior part of the plant first, then dispersing to feed farther up. Left unchecked, they may defoliate bushes,

FIGURE 9.17. These currantworms are what you are looking for if you didn't pick off the leaves with eggs before they hatched.

causing loss of the crop. After feeding for about 3 weeks, they drop to the soil to spin cocoons. Most remain there until the following spring, but a few may emerge in July to make a small second generation.

Management: Inspect bushes every 2–3 days from mid-April, looking on undersides of leaves for eggs; continue into June looking for larvae. Start by checking leaves in the lower, center part of the bush first. Pick off leaves with eggs. When you find larvae, either pick them off or spray them with insecticidal soap or pyrethrins. Note: BTK does not have any effect on these insects.

Pea Leaf Weevil (*Sitona lineata*)

What to look for: Tiny, half-circle notches clipped out of the edges of leaves of peas and broad beans. Adults are tiny, grayish brown weevils, about ⅛ inch (4 mm) long; they feed on plants at night.

Biology: There is one generation each year. Adult weevils overwinter and become active in March. They feed on leaves and lay eggs in the soil around plants from March to May. The larvae survive best in cool, wet spring weather.

FIGURE 9.18. Small notches around the edges of pea leaves are characteristic of the pea leaf weevil.

They feed on the nitrogen-fixing nodules in roots until June. They pupate for 2–3 weeks. New adults emerge in July and feed on leaves of legumes until August, but cause little damage.

Management: Peas sown in late spring to early summer suffer less damage because roots are growing about the time egg-laying stops. In contrast, peas or broad beans sown in the fall can be seriously damaged or killed by larvae feeding in their roots in very early spring. Weevils are susceptible to pyrethrins: to control adults before they start laying eggs, check leaves of seedlings daily and start spraying as soon as the first notches appear on the leaf margins. Spray in the evening when weevils come out to feed. Ground beetle larvae and rove beetles eat the weevil larvae, so minimize the harm to them by spraying a very narrow band just along the seedling row.

FIGURE 9.19. Leafminer eggs on the underside of a Swiss chard leaf.

Spinach/Beet Leafminer (*Pegomya* spp.)

What to look for: Brown blotches on leaves of spinach, Swiss chard, beets, French sorrel and related plants. These are caused by maggots (immature stage of the leafminer flies) feeding inside the leaves.

Biology: The flies lay tiny, chalky white cylindrical eggs in small parallel groups on the underside of leaves. When the eggs hatch, the small white maggots burrow between the upper and lower surface of the leaf, leaving behind blotchy "mines." They feed for 2–3 weeks, then exit the leaf and drop to the soil to pupate. There are two or three generations each season.

Management: In light infestations, pick off the few blotchy areas on the leaves. When you see eggs laid on Swiss chard (they are not hard to see), you can harvest all of the large leaves at once and wash off the eggs. By the time the next crop of leaves grows again, that generation of flies is largely over. Don't do this on beets, because removing the leaves will stunt the roots. Lady beetles eat leafminer eggs, and birds and some predatory insects pick apart the mines and pull out the maggots.

FIGURE 9.20. Leafminer damage on a beet leaf looks like a clear blotch.

Where leafminer infestations are often severe, cover beds with floating row covers before the seeds come up to stop the flies from laying eggs on the leaves. Sprays don't work, because the insects feed within the leaves where sprays don't reach them.

Slugs and Snails

What to look for: Large, ragged holes chewed in leaves and shoots of emerging plants. You can usually see traces of their slime trails on damaged leaves. Slug eggs are perfectly round, translucent, and laid in masses in the soil.

Biology: Slugs and snails are essential decomposers of organic matter in our gardens, but they are also a West Coast scourge because they are most damaging in cool, wet weather. Snails and some slugs climb up plants and shrubs to feed on leaves.

Management: Water in the morning to allow the soil surface to dry by evening. Use drip irrigation or soaker hoses to limit the surface area of moist soil. Pull mulches well away from seedling rows until plants are well grown. Patrol the garden in the evening or early morning to kill slugs. Lay boards, slabs of damp newspaper or grapefruit halves on the soil and kill any slugs hiding underneath in the morning. Use strips of copper or zinc mesh around the edges of beds, pots and greenhouse benches to repel slugs (this only works if you are sure there are no slugs or slugs eggs already inside the area).

FIGURE 9.21. Slug eggs found under a plant.

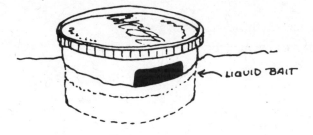

FIGURE 9.22. Homemade slug trap.

Spreading sharp materials, such as wood ashes, sharp sand or diatomaceous earth (may be listed as silicon dioxide on the label) around plants is little use in wet coastal conditions where there are a lot of slugs. Drown slugs by attracting them to containers of fermenting liquids (slugs love yeast). The bait container should have holes cut in the sides to allow slugs access and a lid to prevent ground beetles from falling in. Set the container into the soil with the holes flush with the soil surface. Fill it three-quarters full of beer or use a mixture of water, baking yeast and sugar.

Slug baits containing iron are very effective (several brands are now available); unlike the toxic slug baits containing metaldehyde, they won't harm pets or wildlife. Sprinkle the granules sparingly over the whole garden bed, and replace after heavy rain. Don't pile up large amounts of bait, because it will become moldy.

Sowbugs and Pillbugs (*Armadillidium vulgare*, *Porcellio* spp.)
What to look for: Very tiny seedlings damaged or eaten entirely. Bean seedlings with the first, starchy "seed leaves" chewed away and often the growing point destroyed as well. Stems of cucumber and melon gnawed at the soil line, and fruit with shallow scars. Pillbugs grow to ⅝ inch long (1.5 cm) and curl up into a tight ball when disturbed. Sowbugs are slightly smaller, a lighter gray, and are less damaging.
Biology: Both are land-living crustaceans that feed on fungi and decaying and living plant material. They are common in compost piles and where there is rotting wood. Their numbers are highest in the spring, especially in cool, wet years. They are very susceptible to drying out.
Management: Remove rotting wood in the landscape and replace with

stone, brick or recycled plastic "wood." Rake mulches away from seedlings and keep the soil surface bare until plants are well established. Irrigate in the morning, so the soil surface dries before evening. Wait until the soil is really warm before sowing beans, or start seeds indoors because starchy seeds rotting in cool soil are very attractive to pillbugs. This attraction to fermenting material might explain the myth that spreading cornmeal kills them; it won't, but it might re-direct their interest from your seedlings temporarily. Keep cucumber and melon fruit off of the soil. If desperate, you can spray pyrethrins along seedling rows of carrots, lettuce and other susceptible crops to protect them during the germination period; spray in the evening to minimize harm to non-target insects.

FIGURE 9.23. Pillbug scars on the large cucumber and fresh nibbles out of the tiny fruit in the foreground.

FIGURE 9.24. Pillbugs roll up when disturbed.

Wireworms (*Limonius* spp., *Agriotes* spp.)

What to look for: Narrow tunnels or small, round scars in potatoes and other roots, including onions. Golden to light brown, slender, leathery, "wireworms," up to ¾ inch long (2 cm) in the soil, in tubers, and boring into large seeds and crowns of tender plants.

Biology: Adult beetles lay eggs in the soil in April and May, especially in grasses. Wireworms can be particularly damaging for the first few years after new sod is turned for a garden. Larvae take 3–6 years to develop to adults. Damage is worst in spring and fall when wireworms feed closer to the soil surface. They burrow deeper in the soil in summer and winter and when there is nothing to eat (no plants). They can move a few yards sideways through the soil as well, attracted to roots of plants.

Management: Planting as late as possible avoids some wireworms. Don't plant fall rye as a cover crop, because it attracts adults to lay eggs. Instead of cover crops, I prefer to keep empty garden beds weed-free all winter and use compost and leaf mold to add organic matter. Sow extra seeds of peas, beans and corn to allow for losses. Lightly fork over the soil in annual beds several times before planting and pick out the wireworms; their light color makes them easy to see against the soil.

Here is a good wireworm control trick: First remove all weeds and roots from the bed. Then use chunks of potato and carrot as wireworm traps: Skewer each chunk on a short stick (to act as a marker) and bury the pieces a couple of inches deep in the soil. Pull up the traps every day or two and destroy any wireworms in the bait. For heavily infested soil, it might be worth trying "trap crops." Starting with bare soil, about 10 days before you want to plant the bed, sow rows of wheat or barley (about four seeds per inch) about a yard apart. The germinating seeds attract the wireworms if there are no other roots in the soil. After 10 days, pull the grain seedlings and destroy any wireworms found in the soil along the row and among the roots.

FIGURE 9.25. Wireworms with a dime for a size comparison.

Note: Although suppliers promote using parasitic nematodes, the only species that has been shown in lab studies to provide some control of wireworms is *Heterorhabditis bacteriophora*; whether they can provide acceptable control in the field is not clear, nor is this species widely available.

Diseases and Disorders

Plant diseases are unfortunately a fact of life for coastal gardeners. The long, wet springs and frequent cool, humid weather even in the summer are especially favorable for the development of plant diseases. Once plants are infected, diseases are very difficult to control; therefore, the best way to deal with plant diseases is prevention.

Before a plant can become diseased, the three elements of the "disease triangle" must be present: a susceptible host plant, the disease agent (called a "pathogen") and a favorable environment for the growth of the pathogen — usually, damp weather. Diseases cannot develop if any one of these elements is missing. Prevention and some control methods focus on removing one or more of these elements.

Choose disease-resistant plants. There are many resistant varieties of fruit and vegetables (see Table 2.1).

Avoid pathogens:

- Be careful about bringing potentially diseased plants into your garden, and remove any obviously infected plant as soon as you see it.
- Buy only disease-free plants or grow your own from seed to avoid bringing a new disease into your garden. Always plant certified disease-free seed potatoes.
- Destroy infected plant material. Pick off diseased leaves, prune out branches with cankers (obviously sunken or injured areas), and pull out sick plants. Burn the infected material, bury it in soil, or dispose of in the garbage. Some material, such as apples or apple leaves infected with apple scab can be safely composted.
- Remove alternate host plants for diseases (example: remove junipers because they are also hosts for pear trellis rust that infects pears).
- Disinfect pruning tools between uses (mix 1 part hydrogen peroxide to 9 parts water).

Control environmental conditions:
Although (obviously) there is nothing you can do about the weather, there are *some* things you *can* control:

- Promote rapid drying of leaves after rain. Prune, space and train plants to ensure good air circulation around branches and through foliage.
- Keep leaves dry during infection periods. Grow susceptible plants under a roof overhang. Use soaker hoses or drip irrigation systems, which don't wet the leaves, or water early in the day so leaves dry quickly.

FIGURE 9.26. This inventive cover is keeping a peach tree dry so it doesn't become infected with leaf curl disease.

- Wait until the soil is warm enough for the type of plant before sowing (see Table 4.1).
- Ventilate greenhouses and coldframes to circulate air and prevent condensation from wetting foliage.

Common Diseases

Apple Scab (*Venturia inaequalis*)

What to look for: Corky, roughly circular scabs on the skin of apples, crab apples and sometimes pears. Earliest symptom are water-soaked spots on the undersides of early leaves that turn olive green, then black. In severe infections, fruit is misshapen, cracked and covered with rough scabs.

FIGURE 9.27. Severe, early apple scab infections ruined this fruit. (See Figure 6.2 for an apple with a moderate infection.)

Biology: The disease is caused by a fungus that overwinters on old leaves beneath the trees. In the spring (about the time flower petals fall), raindrops splash the spores back up onto the tree to start another year of infection. It takes as little as 10 hours of continuously wet leaves at temperatures over 58°F (14°C) to infect tissue. Infections can continue all season if wet weather continues.

Management: In light to moderate infections, a few scabs on the skin of fruit is merely unsightly. The fruit underneath is fine, although scarred apples do not store well.

Given the likelihood of wet spring weather, coastal gardeners should choose immune or resistant apple varieties: Akane, Bramley's Seedling, Elstar, Enterprise, Fiesta, Jonafree, Liberty, Macoun, Mutsu, Prima, Priscilla, Red Free, Sunrise, Wagener, Wolf River and Yellow Transparent are good ones to try. Note: McIntosh and Cox's Orange Pippin are among the *most* susceptible.

To minimize infections, prune trees to open up the centers for good air circulation so leaves dry quickly. Use drip irrigation or soaker hoses, rather than sprinklers or overhead watering systems. In the fall, rake up fallen apple leaves and remove any leaves remaining on branches. Compost them in the center of a pile, bury them in the soil or dispose of them.

Sulfur sprays control apple scab if started early enough and re-applied repeatedly to ensure all new foliage is covered. For best results start spraying as soon as buds swell, then spray every 7–10 days until mid- to late June. Starting sprays later, immediately after the flower petals fall, can give adequate results — and means less spraying. Keep in mind that sulfur sprays kill beneficial mites that control pest mites, so only spray those trees with a history of serious infections.

Botrytis/Gray Mold (*Botrytis cinerea*)

What to look for: Brown, water-soaked spots on leaves, flowers, berries or stems, later covered with soft, fuzzy, gray spores. Often seen in the fall or after wet weather on overripe strawberries. Common on lettuce in coldframes in winter where there is little air circulation. Also occurs on stored fruit and vegetables.

Biology: The fungus is a weak colonizer, meaning that the main way it gets into plants is through bruised tissue and injuries caused by pests or other diseases. It also enters on spent blossoms and dying leaves. Once in the plant, the fungus spreads into healthy tissue. The gray fuzz that appears is a coating of zillions of spores.

Management: Botrytis thrives in damp, cool conditions, so the single most effective measure is to improve air circulation around plants. Give plants more space, prune and stake them; increase ventilation in coldframes, plastic tunnels and greenhouses. Pick off old or damaged leaves to remove infection sites. Promptly pick off infected leaves and remove all parts of infected plants.

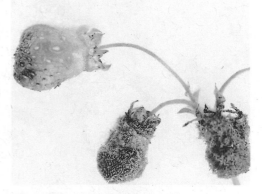

FIGURE 9.28. The progress of a Botrytis infection on strawberries, from left to right.

Brown Rot (*Monolinia fructicola*)

What to look for: Soft, rotting grayish spots on plums, peaches, nectarines, apricots or sweet cherries. Tufts of light tan or gray spores appear on the surface of infected fruit on the tree or in storage. Infections on twigs appear as oval, brownish sunken patches of dead bark (cankers) or shiny patches on the bark; tips of twigs may wilt and die.

Biology: This common fungus attacks most kinds of stone fruit on the coast. The fungus overwinters in mummified fruit on the tree or on the ground as well as in infected twigs. In the spring, spores from these mummies are spread by wind, rain and insects to fruit tree flowers. It takes as little as 3 hours of wetness at 70°F (21°C) to infect flowers, longer at lower temperatures. In warm wet weather the disease can spread quickly to all fruit on the tree. It is particularly severe when heavy rains cause ripening fruit to split before harvest or when fruit is injured by insects, hail or birds.

Management: Tart/sour cherries are less susceptible than sweet cherries; peaches are less susceptible than nectarines and apricots. Avoid over-fertilizing trees with nitrogen. Prune trees to have open centers with good air circulation, which allows fruit and twigs to dry quickly after a rain. Thin developing fruit, so it is well spaced.

Avoid irrigating with any type of equipment that wets leaves. Make sure trees receive adequate water while fruit is ripening, so fruit doesn't split if there is rain. Store only perfect fruit, handle it carefully to avoid bruising and refrigerate immediately. Thoroughly clean storage containers between uses.

When infected trees are dormant, collect and destroy mummified fruit. Knock mummies from the branches with a long stick and burn or bury them or dispose of them in the garbage. Don't compost them. Sulfur sprays can limit the infection if timed correctly: spray when blossoms first show a pink tinge and again before the petals fall. Spray again as fruit is ripening. Do not use sulfur on apricots, because it is toxic to their leaves.

FIGURE 9.29. Plums infected with brown rot and covered with tufts of spores.

Clubroot Disease (*Plasmodiophora brassicae*)

What to look for: Cabbage family plants wilt in mid-day even though they are well watered. Some die, others are stunted with yellowing leaves. When you dig up a plant, it is obvious that roots are abnormal, with thickened, whitish, tumor-like swellings. After the plants die, the decaying galls turn brown and fibrous inside.

Biology: Clubroot is caused by a parasitic microorganism. It has tough resting spores that can survive for 4 to 20 years in the soil, waiting for a crop to infect. When roots of a host plant grow nearby, the resting spores produce active spores in the spring; these swim in the soil water to the root hairs and enter the plant. They reproduce and spread through the roots, eventually forming the large tumor-like masses in the root.

Management: This is a very serious disease because the spores remain in the soil for so long. The best defense is to never bring it into your garden: grow your own cabbage family plants from seed or buy only plants grown in a soilless mix (which is usually how commercial seedlings are grown), and don't bring in cabbage family plants from other gardens. If you know your soil is infected, you must clean every tool you use in infected soil before using it elsewhere and never pass along plants from your garden to other people. Even if you stop growing cabbage family plants altogether, the soil remains infected for up to two decades. You can continue to grow reasonable crops of cabbage family plants by heavily liming the soil. The clubroot organism thrives in acid soil, so raising the soil pH to 7.0 or higher suppresses the disease. This takes a lot of lime, so test the soil pH regularly.

Damping Off

What to look for: Seedlings fall over and die, or seeds never come up. Close inspection of seedlings shows stems appear water-soaked and collapsed at the soil line.

Biology: "Damping off" can be caused by several fungi that infect germinating seeds and seedlings; it can also cause stem and root rots of older plants. Damping off can occur in the garden, but is most common in trays of seedlings. Cool, wet soil favors damping off fungi; some actually reproduce more quickly in cool conditions. Damping off usually spreads through an entire seedling tray.

Management: Damping off fungi are common in soil, so focus on making conditions unfavorable for the disease:

- Start seeds at the correct temperatures (see Table 4.1). Wait until the soil is warm before sowing outdoors.
- Avoid over-watering seedlings. Seed flats need only be kept damp, not wet.
- Make sure there is good ventilation around seedlings. Don't cover trays of germinating seeds.
- Use well-drained soil mixes with generous proportions of vermiculite, perlite or other materials that aerate the soil. Unpasteurized seedling mixes that include finely screened, well-aged compost contain beneficial fungi that suppress damping-off fungi.
- Disinfect pots and seedling trays before reusing them (soak in 1 part hydrogen peroxide to 9 parts water).
- Plant fresh (vigorous) seed at the correct depth.

Once damping off has started in a flat or row, it is usually too late to control it. Older plants sometimes survive, but their later growth may be stunted. Some gardeners recommend making a tea of horsetail (*Equisetum* spp.) or using compost teas to treat fungi in the soil; however, by wetting the soil, these remedies also risk making the problem worse. It is much better to prevent the problem in the first place!

Garlic/Allium Rust (*Puccinia allii*)

What to look for: Patches or spots of rusty orange on leaves of garlic and sometimes leeks. Infections usually show first on new growth as small, blister-like spots with a lighter yellowish ring around each spot.

Biology: Spores are spread very long distances by wind and have been blowing up the coast from California since the 1990s. This strain of rust mainly infects garlic, but other onion family plants are at risk. Cool, wet spring weather provides ideal conditions for infection. This rust grows best on leaves that are wet for at least 4 hours (from fog, rain or irrigation) and at moderate temperatures 50–75°F (10–24°C). It may overwinter on dead plant material, in soil, on infected leeks or wild alliums. It does not appear to be spread on the mature garlic cloves, so you can plant cloves from infected garlic plants.

Note: There are many different rusts, and each stays on specific host plants, so garlic rust won't spread to beans, blackberries, roses, etc.

Management: Late infections (late June) seem to have little effect on fall-planted garlic because the crop is almost done growing by the time the leaves become infected. Earlier infections weaken plants and reduce the size of bulbs. Plants over-fertilized with nitrogen or stressed by a lack of nutrients may be more susceptible.

Use drip irrigation or soaker hoses to water plants instead of overhead sprinklers. Where garlic is regularly infected, try growing early garlic varieties (e.g., Portuguese Red, which is ready about 3 weeks earlier than main crop garlic). If leeks are infected, destroy them to remove overwintering hosts for the rust. Don't put infected leaves in the compost. Sulfur sprays are registered to control rust, which might be useful if infections on leeks become widespread. European growers have rust-resistant leek varieties available, which would be worth looking into if this disease persists.

FIGURE 9.30. Allium rust on leeks. After starting out bright orange, the blisters later turn black.

Late Blight (*Phytophthora infestans*)

What to look for: Tomato plants rapidly collapse and rot. The earliest symptoms on tomatoes are dark blotches on stems and leaves, usually starting at the margins, but these are usually missed because the disease progresses very quickly. Infected fruit turns brown and leathery and quickly decays. In wet years, plants may die before any fruit ripens.

Biology: Late blight is caused by a fungus-like organism called a "water mold." In cool, damp summers, it is a widespread, destructive disease of tomatoes and, sometimes, related plants. Spores spread on the wind and in splashes of water; they rapidly infect wet leaves. The late blight organism survives mild winters on plant debris in the soil and on volunteer potatoes left in the ground. Thick-walled, dormant "spores" can also remain in the soil for years.

Management: Plant resistant potatoes varieties; although none are immune, many are resistant, such as Fundy, Kennebec and Sebago. Plant only certified disease-free seed potatoes. Destroy volunteer potato plants as these are the prime source of the next season's infection.

Grow tomatoes in the driest, sunniest place you have. Space plants out and prune and stake them to ensure good air circulation so leaves dry off quickly. Avoid splashing irrigation water on plants. Early-maturing varieties, such as cherry tomatoes, can usually produce a crop before infection strikes. The most reliable way to avoid late blight is to keep leaves entirely dry, which means growing plants in a greenhouse, under the overhang of a roof, or under a cover to keep off rain. Make a simple roof for the tomato patch from a sheet of corrugated translucent plastic (e.g., Coroplast®) screwed to sturdy posts, or cover beds with plastic tunnels that have wide, open sides and ends. It is essential to have excellent ventilation through greenhouses and tunnels to prevent condensation from dripping onto leaves and making them wet enough to allow infection. Watch seed catalogs for late blight-resistant tomato varieties, which are under development.

If late blight strikes, remove diseased plants and bury them deeply or seal them in a plastic bag and put them in the garbage. Do not compost diseased plants.

FIGURE 9.31. Late blight in tomatoes soon leads to rapid collapse of the whole plant.

Peach Leaf Curl (*Taphrina deformans*)
What to look for: Twisted, puckered and thickened leaves with reddish tinges on peaches or nectarines. Later in the season, affected leaves develop a grayish bloom and may drop. Infected fruit may be distorted or

shriveled and often drops early in the season. Leaves that grow later in the season are not infected.

Biology: Peach leaf curl is caused by a fungus that infects buds of peach and nectarines. Spores overwinter in crevices in tree bark and around buds. *Taphrina* only infects buds in February or early March as the buds begin to swell, before leaves start to open. Spores develop on the infected leaves (giving the grayish appearance) and are spread by wind and rain to trees.

FIGURE 9.32. Peach leaf curl distorts leaves.

Management: Light to moderate infections do little harm, but in a severe infection (all too common on the coast), trees can be seriously weakened and lose most of the crop.

Grow resistant varieties of peaches: Frost, Pacific Gold or Renton. Redhaven peach shows some resistance, but will still be infected. Espalier peaches and nectarines against a building where the roof overhang will keep off rain. Devise a makeshift or permanent canopy to keep trees dry for the February-to-March period when buds begin to swell (See Fig. 9.26). Lime-sulfur sprays reduce levels of infection by preventing spores from germinating. Spray in the fall after about 90% of the leaves have fallen and again in the very early spring (February) before buds swell.

Pear Trellis Rust (*Gymnosporangium fuscum*)

What to look for Bright orange, irregular spots on pear leaves in early summer that continue to grow larger. Hard, irregular structures develop on the undersides of leaves in August.

Biology: This fungus has two hosts: pears and juniper. The fungus stays dormant in juniper for most of the year, then produces masses of spores from April to early May on the branches of the juniper. These are strange, irregular, swollen growths covered with spongy, bright orange masses of spores. Spores are carried on the wind to pear leaves. Spore-producing structures develop on the undersides of pear leaves, then they release spores capable of infecting juniper from late August until leaf fall. Pear leaves are usually newly infected each spring; the rust rarely remains in the trees over the winter.

FIGURE 9.33. Late stages of pear trellis rust on the undersides of pear leaves.

E. Cronin

Management: This rust mainly occurs in the south coast areas of British Columbia and in coastal Washington. Only pears show damage; infected junipers look fine and continue to grow normally. Lightly infected pears suffer no harm either, but if the infection is severe, fruiting and growth may be reduced. Infections on pear trees vary from year to year depending on rainfall and wind patterns, so a badly infected tree one year may not be seriously infected the next year.

The best (but usually impractical) way to protect pears is to remove all susceptible junipers within a 100 foot (30 meter) radius. Finding infected junipers is a challenge — and they are usually on someone else's property. If removing junipers can be organized as a neighborhood effort, remove the junipers before they form spores; before April 1, burn, bury or dispose of them (do not chip or compost them). To prevent the disease from spreading from pears back to junipers, pick off infected pear leaves by mid-August (pear leaves can be composted because the rust dies when the leaf is picked). There is no point in spraying fungicides. If there are swollen growths on pear twigs, it shows that the infection has entered the tree; prune these out during the winter and dispose of the pruned wood.

Powdery mildew (caused by several species of fungi: *Erysiphe*, *Sphaerotheca*, *Podosphaera*)

What to look for: White powdery patches on leaves, starting as small, round, powdery white or gray spots, which quickly spread. Leaves eventually turn brown and dry up. Different species of powdery mildew fungi attack different host plants, including beans, peas, grapes, strawberries, apples and other fruit. In severe infections on fruit, the fruit becomes scarred and discolored.

Biology: Unlike other fungi, powdery mildews can infect plants in dry weather. Spores germinate more quickly in humid conditions, but water on the leaves actually *stops* spores from germinating. Infections spread rapidly in the late summer and fall (before the fall rains start), when cool night temperatures and overnight dew raises the humidity around leaves.

Management: Choose powdery mildew-resistant varieties of squash, cucumbers, grapes and apples (see Table 2.1). Rinse leaves of susceptible squash and cucumbers with water at mid-day, several times a week. This washes off spores and keeps infections to a minimum. However, this is only feasible where you can do a thorough job of spraying all the leaves, and the plants are not at risk from other fungi that thrive on wet leaves (don't try this on apples, for example). Spraying leaves with a mixture of 9 parts water to 1 part milk, twice a week, has been shown to control mildew on cucumber and squash (but not on other plants).

Pesticides containing bicarbonate ("baking soda") are registered for home gardeners to use on fruit and nut trees and many vegetables. Sprays of sulfur or neem (azadirachtin) also control powdery mildew, but they must be used frequently to keep new leaves covered with fungicide before the spores have a chance to spread to the new tissue. Note: Frequent use of sulfur sprays can damage cucumbers and squash leaves; it also kills beneficial mites on apple trees.

FIGURE 9.34. Powdery mildew on new apple leaves in the spring. (See Figure 2.7 for mildew on squash leaves.)

Disorders

Disorders are plant damage caused by nutrient deficiencies or something wrong with the growing environment. Irregular watering, for example, is at the root of several disorders, from blossom end rot in tomatoes to hollow heart in potatoes. It is essential to correct the conditions that *are* under your control (in this case, your irrigation schedule). Many disorders look like insect or disease damage, so it may take some detective work to figure out what is wrong.

FIGURE 9.35. Paste tomatoes (upper left fruit) with blossom end rot. Both older and younger fruit are fine, so a temporary lack of water is likely to blame in this case.

Blossom End Rot (tomatoes and peppers)

What to look for: Sunken tan or black areas at the blossom end of tomato or pepper fruit. On tomatoes, black spots may become quite large, taking up the bottom half of the fruit. On peppers and some paste tomatoes, the tissue is usually tan and may extend up the sides of the fruit near the blossom end.

What went wrong: Calcium deficiency in plant tissue. Your soil might have enough calcium, but it isn't available, or the plants can't take it up fast enough. This is often because the movement of calcium inside the plant has been inhibited by drought stress, possibly from irregular watering. This is often seen on tomatoes in containers that experience alternating dry and wet soil. It can also be caused when plants grow too fast as a result of too much nitrogen fertilizer.

Remedy: Maintain even soil moisture with adequate irrigation and use mulches. Use large planters for potted plants and water often enough in hot weather to keep the soil evenly moist. Amend the soil with calcium (from lime, wood ash or bone meal) and dig in more compost, which helps make calcium available to plants.

FIGURE 9.36. This potato with a hollow heart can still be eaten.

Hollow Heart/Brown Core of Potato

What to look for: Potato tubers have a cavity in the center. In extreme cases, the entire interior of the potato is affected, with dark bands in the flesh around the cavity. The dark areas are firm and not rotted.

What went wrong: Irregular watering, especially during hot weather, that allowed plants to become very dry, then very wet. Some varieties are more prone to this disorder than others.

Remedy: Potatoes with a small cavity can be salvaged for eating, although severely affected tubers are inedible. Revisit your irrigation system to ensure it provides a regular water supply, without overwatering. Even out soil moisture with the thick mulch of organic material (straw, leaves, etc.) much enjoyed by potatoes.

Sunburn (cucumbers)

What to look for: Biscuit-colored patches on leaves, from small speckles (see fig 5.4) to large areas on cucumber, melon and squash. Stems sometimes show sunken, tan areas; when they do, the plants usually die.

What went wrong: This is a sunburn injury, usually seen in transplants that were not properly hardened off (exposed to the sun gradually before they went into the garden). It can also happen to garden plants in extreme heat waves.

Remedy: There is nothing to be done after the damage occurs, but if only leaves were burned, new leaves will be fine and the plants will recover. See Chapter 5 for how to harden off and protect transplants to avoid sunburn.

FIGURE 9.37. Severely sunburned cucumbers struggling to survive.

Greenback (tomato)

What to look for: Tomatoes have a hard green area around the stem end of the fruit. Although the rest is completely ripe, the green area never ripens.

What went wrong: This can be caused by exposure to strong sunlight and intense heat, such as in a glass greenhouse in the summer. A potassium deficiency in the soil may also play a role. Some varieties are more susceptible than others.

Remedy: Make sure there isn't a potassium deficiency in the soil. If this disorder has been a big problem in the past with your greenhouse crops, consider buying only tomato varieties specifically listed for greenhouse growing.

FIGURE 9.38. Greenback is a puzzling disorder—aren't tomatoes supposed to like heat and light?

Pollination Problems

Many things can interfere with pollination and fertilization of flowers. Unfortunately, you usually don't know there is a problem until there is no fruit. For squash or tomatoes, you might have time to remedy a problem as the season goes on. For tree fruit, however, once the flowers fall, there won't be more until next spring, so a pollination failure means a crop failure. And in corn, you won't know until you open the husks that some of the kernels weren't fertilized.

Tiny squashes form, but fall off. Even if a female flower is not pollinated, the little squash behind the flower can still continue to grow a bit after the spent flower drops off (see fig 1.5). The tiny squash soon turns yellow and drops. In wet weather it may rot, making it look like disease stopped the squash from growing, but it was never fertilized to begin with. See entry for squash in Chapter 10 for information on hand pollinating squash.

Flowers appear, but no tomatoes. It might be too cold or too hot for fertilization. Most tomato pollen is damaged by temperatures below 55°F (12°C). The fruit may not form at all or it might be partially pollinated, resulting in distorted or "cat-faced" fruit. Temperatures over 30°C (86°F) also sterilize tomato pollen. It rarely happens outdoors, but it is common for tomatoes in greenhouses or tunnels without enough ventilation. Flowers that were opening when the mercury went through the roof drop off, but later flowers developing in better conditions will be fine.

Fruit flowers appear, but no fruit. There are several possibilities:
- Frost killed the flowers: A late cold snap can kill blossoms of early fruit, such as peaches and nectarines.
- Lack of pollinators: Fruit trees, strawberries and other plants need bees and other insects to transfer pollen. If the weather is cool and wet, bees won't come out. Some native bees are better pollinators in cool weather than honeybees, but even these hardy natives cannot work in wet, cold conditions. Poor weather is only a problem for plants that were in bloom during the cool weather; varieties blooming in better weather fare better.
- Lack of cross-pollination: If fruit trees flower, but don't set fruit year after year, they may be lacking a cross-pollinator. Most apples, all pears and

many plum varieties need to receive pollen from a different variety to set fruit.

- Birds ate the flowers: House finches and sometimes other birds eat fruit blossoms to get the nectar inside. They can eat all of the flowers on a small tree. Cover trees with netting (but the mesh has to be wide enough to allow bees to reach the flowers).

Corn with undeveloped kernels: Later-maturing kernels on the ear missed the boat when pollen was dropping, so they remain unfertilized and therefore undeveloped. This is common in home garden corn because the small number of plants shedding pollen at one time means than some silks can be missed (each silk is connected to a kernel and each must have a pollen grain to fertilize it).

FIGURE 9.39. It ain't pretty, but the developed kernels are just fine.

Vertebrates

Deer, raccoons, rabbits, rats and birds (not to mention the neighbor's cat or your own bouncing dog) can do more damage to a garden than all other pests put together. Deer are increasingly common in rural and suburban areas. As their numbers increase, more gardeners are finding it impossible to grow a food garden without fencing. This is an expensive investment, but if you live where deer pass through even occasionally, it will save a lot of grief if you put up a fence before you plant. A deer fence also keeps out pets, and you might as well design it to keep out rabbits while you are at it; they too are becoming a serious problem in more places.

A word of caution: Temporary measures, such as covering plants with floating row covers or plastic mesh do keep out birds, but usually end in (your) tears when the deer show up. Deer are clever at pawing away, crawling under or pulling down temporary fences or covers.

FIGURE 9.40. I'm sure this little island black-tail is thinking about my garden…

Many a gardener, convinced they had a deer-proof fence, has discovered that once their aged dog passed on, the deer soon found a way past the fence. A fence backed up with a dog inside is an excellent deer deterrent — but only if the dog isn't a digger and doesn't like to eat the crops.

Fences

I have seen a wide variety of deer fence designs and I cannot swear that any are perfectly deer proof. A motivated deer is a clever critter that will sooner or later get in; they will find a gap in the most improbable place, crawl under poorly secured fencing, or simply waltz through a gate left open. Where deer numbers are low, they are easier to keep out because they have other places to go. Where deer populations are high, there is a lot of pressure on your defenses, especially in the summer, when wild food supplies for deer are drying up.

When designing your fence, take into account the size of deer in your area. On Vancouver Island, where the deer are smaller island black-tails, fences 6–8 feet high are usually adequate. For the considerably larger white tails and mule deer on the mainland and Olympic Peninsula, however, plan on installing an 8–10-foot-high fence. Deer can jump vertical fences, but they are less inclined to try slanting fences or those with a projecting shelf at the top. These designs, however, take up more space than vertical fences and are harder to build.

Chain link: This is the ultimate defense — very expensive initially, of course, but it will outlast you and never need maintenance. Given the rigidity of chain link, deer cannot crawl under it. And, if there are no gaps between the ground and the bottom edge of the fencing, it is also effective against cottontail rabbits (though domestic rabbits may still dig under it).

Deer and rabbit wire fencing: This is a woven wire fencing with the horizontal wires closer together at the bottom of the fence to make the openings smaller. It is available in several widths. Mounted on wood or metal posts, it is moderately priced, especially if you can do some installation yourself. Wooden posts will eventually need to be replaced, but the wire can be removed and restrung onto new posts after years of service. You can extend the useful height of this fencing by stringing a higher wire or two between the posts above the top edge of the fencing. Five-foot high fencing can effectively be made 6 feet by stringing a wire a foot above the fence (tie plastic tapes to the wire so deer can see the wire).

Deer can crawl under woven wire if it is sagging or there are gaps along the bottom. One solution is to install a board or 2×2 crosspiece at ground level spanning from post to post and screwed or nailed to the post at each end. Staple the bottom edge of the fencing to this crosspiece. These crosspieces makes good supports for attaching sturdy wire mesh (such as ½-inch chicken wire or welded wire mesh) to fill gaps along the bottom of the fence to keep out rabbits. To prevent domestic rabbits from burrowing under, the bottom edge of the mesh must be buried in the soil.

Plastic mesh fences: Much cheaper "invisible fence" is sold that you are supposed to mount on lightweight posts or metal fence stakes. Deer have been known to stand on their hind legs and pull these fences right off the

FIGURE 9.41. Deer and rabbit wire fence stapled to a bottom crosspiece, with a chicken wire strip to keep out rabbits. It still didn't stop deer from reaching their noses through the fence to graze on the plants inside.

posts, so don't trust these fences unless deer are only occasional visitors to the neighborhood. People have better results with this type of fence when it encompasses a larger area, so deer don't really see the garden.

Wooden fences: You can certainly build wooden fences of latticework or boards. They are more aesthetically pleasing than the more utilitarian fences just discussed; however, they block a good deal of light. Whether this is an important consideration will depend on where your garden beds are in relation to your fence (bear in mind the long shadow a fence will cast when the sun is low in the winter).

Other Barriers and Repellents

Scarecrow: The Scarecrow™ device that sprays water when it detects motion works quite well to scare away animals. It is connected to a hose and has an internal battery to run the motion detector. When a moving animal (or person!) trips the motion sensor, it shoots a jet of water. It only shoots a cup or two of water at a time, so the tap only has to be turned on to a trickle. For the greatest startle effect, point the Scarecrow where the jet of water can hit leaves, as this amplifies the noise. The device is effective for scaring away raccoons when fruit trees or grapes are ripening and deterring cats from using garden beds as litter boxes. Animals get used to the Scarecrow if it is always in the same place, though, so keep up the element of surprise by moving it to different spots every few days. Some dogs find it hilarious to run back and forth turning it on, so to spare the battery you might want to turn it off during the day.

FIGURE 9.42. Fish nets are easy to drape over beds to keep out small animals, such as rabbits and birds.

Netting: Many mesh or netting products are sold for covering vegetables and fruit. Plastic meshes are lightweight and most useful to keep out birds. But the lightest and cheapest mesh will make you weep with frustration as it tangles and snags on everything. Stiffer plastic mesh is easier to mount on stakes or lay over beds of strawberries without tangling, but it has to be pinned down or weighted along the edges to keep animals from getting under it.

Used fishing nets are another option. Because they are soft, flexible and heavy, they drape easily over temporary supports and don't need weights along the edges. They are bulky, however, and must be perfectly dry before you put them away.

Scare tapes: As a temporary measure, while fruit is ripening, you can string shiny tapes over the top of berry plants. These are usually made of Mylar or other reflective material and are designed to turn and twist in the wind and startle birds. They work pretty well if you string enough tape back and forth, and they are certainly easier to install than trying to cover a large berry patch with mesh. Variations include tying old CDs or strips of tinfoil to cords strung over the berry bushes, so they dance and flash in the breeze.

Fruit bags: Fastening bags over individual fruit or bunches of grapes sounds tedious, but it is easy — and about as pest-proof as you can get. Growers slip paper bags over Asian pears and sometime other fruit to ensure perfection, but I use this idea in my garden for grapes. If you have ever struggled to cover a vigorously growing grape vine with mesh and tried to secure it so there are no gaps, you will appreciate how easy it is to slip a bag over each bunch, cinch up the drawstring and tie the string to the branch. Leave the bags in place until the grapes are ripe. The bags can be reused for years and provide protection from all pests, from raccoons and rats to birds and wasps. The bags don't interfere with summer pruning of the vines, and the grape leaves continue to receive full sun. They also work well for vines trained over arbors (which are impossible to screen properly), and they keep sun off the fruit, which is desirable for the best quality.

FIGURE 9.43. Old CDs can provide one last service before they become garbage.

FIGURE 9.44. My grape bags in operation. I love how easy this is!

How to Make Grape Bags

If you can use a sewing machine, you can easily make bags to protect bunches of grapes. I sew them out of tough, lightweight fabric, such as nylon or lace curtains from the local thrift shop. I use a piece of fabric 8 inches wide by 24 inches long (20 cm × 60 cm) or two pieces 8 inches × 12 inches pieces (20 cm × 30 cm). Sew them with a ½ inch (1 cm) seam allowance. Make a drawstring sleeve by turning under the top couple of inches of the (open) edge of each bag. Thread a shoelace or strong cord through the sleeve. Finished width of the bag is about 7 inches (18 cm) and length is about 10 inches (25 cm). If you sew 5–10 bags each year as the harvest increases on a growing vine, by the time the vine reaches full production, you will have accumulated all the bags you need. At the end of the season, wash the bags if they need it and store them for next year.

Metal tree collars: Animals that climb tree trunks — mainly raccoons, rats and squirrels — can be kept out of fruit trees if you wrap wide metal flashing around the trunk. It should be at least 2 feet wide to prevent their scrabbling claws from getting a grip on the trunk. For this to work, the tree has be in the open where there is no other route into the tree from other trees, buildings, shrubs, fences, etc. The metal collars will only keep out squirrels if the tree is so far away from buildings or other trees that squirrels can't make the leap. Put flashing on all of the trees in a small orchard where branches overlap.

Where these vertebrate pests are a problem, when establishing the shape of a dwarf fruit tree, branches should be kept 4 or 5 feet above the ground, so there are no branches low enough for the animals to jump up and grab.

CHAPTER 10

A TO Z
VEGETABLES

This section includes what I think is key information for growing each vegetable successfully in a home garden. Unless mentioned otherwise, assume they all should be grown in fertile soil, with a pH 6.5–6.8, and they all need irrigation in dry weather. The timing of planting and the overwintering information generally applies to the coastal regions of southern British Columbia and Washington and Oregon. Notes under "Varieties" provide examples, but is far from being an exhaustive list of all that are available. For plants noted under "Seed Saving" as being at high risk of cross-pollination, make sure there are no related vegetables or weeds blooming at the same time. For information on cross-pollination and seed saving, see Chapter 5. For more information on the most common pest problems, see Chapter 9.

Artichokes

These large, ornamental perennials with feathery gray leaves and edible flower buds grow up to 5 feet (1.5 m) high. Some plants persist for years, but most are not long-lived. They are not reliably hardy in the colder parts of the British Columbia coast or in heavy clay soils.

Culture: Plants grow readily from seed, but seedlings are quite variable. For a few plants, you might be better off buying plants from a nursery. Set plants

FIGURE 10.1. This artichoke is at just the right stage for picking.

3–4 feet (1 meter) apart in well-drained soil, rich in organic matter. Artichokes can do with less irrigation than other vegetables. Key to winter survival is protecting the crowns from heavy rain and frost. In November, cut back stalks to 6 inches (15 cm) and mulch over the crowns with dry leaves or fluffy straw. Cover each mulched crown with an overturned plastic pot (largest size) to keep the crown dry; mulch over the pot with another layer of leaves. Push a stake through a drain hole in the pot to keep it in place. As soon as the weather begins to warm in February, remove the pot and pull back some of the mulch. Be ready to re-cover if below-freezing temperatures are predicted.

Harvest and Storage: Cut flower buds at any stage, from small, tender buds until the tips of the bud scales begin to point slightly outward. The more mature the flower, the more fibrous and thistle-like the choke inside becomes.

Pests: Aphids, tended by ants, attack the flower stalks and feed between the bud scales.

Varieties: Green buds: Green Globe, Imperial Star. Purple buds: Violet Star, Violetta (purple varieties have been less hardy than Green Globe in my garden).

Asparagus

Growing your own is the only way to experience the sweetness of just-picked asparagus, but they do take up a lot of space for just a few weeks of harvest.

Culture: Best in deep soil with a 7.0 pH; plants grow poorly below pH 6.0. Set 1-yr crowns at the bottom of a trench 8 inches (20 cm) deep with crowns 1 foot (30 cm) apart in the row, rows 3–4 feet (1 meter) apart. Lightly cover crowns with soil, gradually filling in the trench with soil as the shoots grow.

Fertilize heavily and add lime in early spring every year. Wait until after two full growing seasons to begin harvest. Harvest for 2 weeks in the third year; 3–4 weeks in the fourth year; and up to 8 weeks thereafter — as long as shoots remain vigorous and a good size (finger width). You can grow plants from seed (note that they can take up to 8 week to germinate), and they will be ready for harvest after 3 years. In the summer, support the fronds, which can grow quite tall, with stakes to prevent them from breaking. Cut down fronds in late fall and mulch beds well.

Harvest and Storage: Cut or snap off spears when they reach the desired length. If cutting, take care not to injure neighboring spears.

Pests: Asparagus beetles (spray pyrethrins); slugs damage tips of emerging spears.

Varieties: Traditional open pollinated variety: Mary Washington. All-male hybrids (male plants produce up to three times more than female plants, which devote their energy to producing seeds): Jersey Knight, Larac.

Beans

Good old beans: prolific, reliable and popular! Snap beans are eaten fresh while pods are tender. Dry beans are shelled out of the pods after they mature (young soybeans can be eaten fresh, as edamame).

Culture: Beans need less soil nitrogen than other vegetables because they produce their own. Wait until the soil is at least 60°F (15°C) before sowing. Plant seeds up to 1½ inches (2–3 cm) deep, spaced 2½ inches (6 cm) apart. For an earlier start and to avoid damage from pillbugs, sprout seeds indoors in vermiculite and set out when plants have two true leaves (see Chapter 4). Provide sturdy supports for pole beans, which grow quite tall.

Harvest and Storage: Keep snap beans picked, even if you can't use them, because maturing beans stop plants from producing more flowers. For dry beans, leave pods on the plant until they are dry and yellow; finish drying indoors and shell out.

Pests: Aphids; pillbugs.

Varieties: Snap beans: Both bush and pole varieties with green, yellow and purple pods are available. Two Romano pole beans that have flat pods and exceptional quality are Musica and Goldmarie. Runner beans are a different species, also edible fresh. Dry beans: Many varieties, including soybeans, are available; the pole varieties are very productive in small areas.

Saving Seed: Easy. Flowers are self-fertile and won't cross-pollinate (except for scarlet runner beans, which are bee-pollinated). Allow pods to mature on the plant until the seeds inside are hard and the pods become papery. Finish drying indoors, then shell out.

Beets

Beets are two crops in one because the leaves are also delicious. Beets are very sensitive to acid soil, so if you have trouble growing beets, your soil pH may be too low.

Culture: Seed ½ to 1 inch (1–2 cm) deep. Each "seed" is a dried fruit containing several seeds, so plants must be thinned; space seedling 2½–3 inches (6–8 cm) apart. For a steady supply of tender beets, sow successive plantings every month, starting when soil temperature is over 50°F (10°C), usually mid- to late April. Young plants may go to seed if exposed to a cold weather for 1–2 weeks in the spring. For winter crop, sow in early July; soil must be very well-drained.

Harvest and Storage: Roots and leaves are edible any size starting with thinnings. For most varieties, the best quality roots are 2½–3 inches (6–8 cm) in diameter. Leave beets in the garden over the winter, well-mulched, and dig them as needed.

Pests: Spinach leafminer. Varieties susceptible to Cercospora leaf spot show circular spots on leaves in wet weather, but the roots are not affected.

Varieties: Dark red, round beets: Detroit Dark Red and related varieties are the gold standard for quality. Novelty yellow, orange and white varieties are available. Cylindra (elongated) types are good for summer crops, but not for overwintering because their high "shoulders" above the soil are vulnerable to frost.

Saving Seed: Easy. Overwintered beets flower in the spring and seeds ripen in mid-summer. High risk of cross-pollination because pollen is wind borne. Beets can cross with Swiss chard.

Broad Beans Or Faba/Fava Beans

Note: Broad beans are toxic to some people, causing a kind of anemia called "favism."

Broad beans grow on upright plants with large fibrous pods sticking out from a main stem.

Culture: Sow 2 inches (4–5 cm) deep, thin to 6 inches (15 cm) apart in rows. These are more tolerant of acid soil than most beans. Sow in March for summer harvest or in October for harvest early the following spring. They are very frost hardy, but plants are brittle and easily broken by heavy snow and wind. Stake them to support them in wind or grow them under a roof overhang or in a tunnel in areas where snowfall is usual in the winter.

Harvest and Storage: Shell fresh beans out of pods or allow seeds to mature and use as dry beans.

Pests: Bean aphids attack the flowers in late spring. Fall-planted beans avoid aphid damage because the beans are ready for harvest before aphids attack in the spring.

Varieties: Large seeded: Broad Windsor, Aquadulce. Small seeded: Sweet Lorane.

Saving Seed: Easy. Flowers are self-fertile and won't cross. Allow pods to mature on the plant until beans inside are hard. Finish drying indoors and shell out seeds.

Broccoli

One of the most nutritious vegetables you can grow, you can eat broccoli fresh from the garden 10 months of the year with the right choice of varieties.

Culture: Sow ½ inch (1 cm) deep, or start seedlings indoors in late March for planting out in early May. Space plants 1–2 feet (30–60 cm) apart: wider spacing is for sprouting broccoli. Keep plants well watered because even short periods of drought severely reduce the crop. A spring planting of sprouting broccoli continues to produce side shoots until December. For a steady harvest from varieties with a large central head, plant a few new plants each month until early July. Start overwintering varieties by the end of June for plants to be harvested from next February to June.

FIGURE 10.2. One of the purple sprouting broccoli plants that survived the freeze (see page 172) starts producing in late February.

FIGURE 10.3. Cardinal Late has exceptionally large heads for a purple sprouting broccoli.

Harvest and Storage: Harvest head and shoots before any individual florets begin to open or show yellow. Keep shoots cut, whether you use them or not, because plants stop producing if the flowers are allowed to bloom.

Pests: Cabbage root maggot; imported cabbageworm; cabbage aphid.

Varieties: Central head summer broccoli: Some produce a modest yield of side shoots after the large central head is harvested: Green Goliath, Green Comet F1, Packman F1. Green sprouting or Calabrese summer broccoli have a small central head followed by a large, continuous harvest of side shoots; plants grow over 3½ feet (1 meter) tall: DeCicco; Italian Green Sprouting. Purple sprouting broccoli is the main type of overwintering broccoli: Early Red Spear and Extra Early Rudolph produce heads in February and March; Cardinal Late produces a large crop April through June. There are also white sprouting winter varieties.

Saving Seed: Easy. High risk of cross-pollination. Allow the flowers to bloom and set seed pods. Harvest when pods are tan and dry.

Brussels Sprouts

A much maligned vegetable, possibly because few people have tasted the sweet, nutty flavor that develops after they have been frosted out in the garden.

Culture: Start seeds in late May to early June. Sow directly in the garden ½ inch (1 cm) deep or grow transplants. Final spacing should be 1–2 feet apart (30–60 cm) because plants are quite large. If started too early, the sprouts develop in late summer when aphids are more likely to damage them; also, sprouts that develop in cool weather are better quality. To hasten sprout development, pinch out the top cluster of leaves in late September. Stake plants in the fall to prevent stems from breaking in wind and snow.

Harvest and Storage: Leave plants in the garden all winter and snap individual sprouts off the stem as needed, leaving small sprouts to continue growing. If plants are frozen, wait until they thaw in warmer weather before harvesting.

Pests: Cabbage root maggot; imported cabbageworm; aphids feeding inside sprouts can ruin them.

Varieties: Most are hardy to 14°F (−10°C), but Roodnerf is exceptionally hardy (to 0°F/−18°C). Hybrids (Jade Cross, Bubbles, Oliver, Vancouver) often do better than open pollinated varieties in variable summer weather. Red varieties: Red Rupine, Red Bull.

Saving Seed: Leave the plants in the garden all winter without harvesting the sprouts. Flower stalks come from each sprout in the spring. High risk of cross-pollination. Harvest when pods are tan and dry, and finish drying indoors.

Cabbage

There are so many types of cabbages suited to different seasons, it is hard to know where to start: green or red, ballhead (solid, round heads), savoy (crinkly leaves) or pointed (conical) heads for summer, fall, winter or spring crops.

Culture: Be generous with irrigation to ensure heads grow rapidly. Seed directly in the garden, ½ inch (1 cm) deep or grow transplants. Spring transplants should have stems smaller than a pencil; larger plants may produce seed stalks if there is a late cold spell. Final spacing should be 1–2 feet (30–60 cm) apart. For mid- to late summer harvest, sow from March to May. For fall and winter harvest, sow from mid-May to early June. Sow

FIGURE 10.4. January King is an emperor of cabbage, with purple veins and blue-green leaves.

by early July for harvest the following spring. At the end of the summer, to stop fully mature heads from splitting in fall rains, tug or twist each head an eighth of a turn in the soil, just enough to break some fine roots and slow their growth.

Harvest and Storage: Cabbages are ready to eat as soon as heads feel solid. Hardy varieties can stand in the garden all winter and stay in excellent condition. If the heads freeze in cold weather, wait until they have thawed completely in a warm spell to harvest (it may take several days).

Pests: Cabbage root maggot; imported cabbageworm; cabbage aphid.

Varieties: Some varieties with large, solid heads need over 150 days to mature, while others take as little as 60 days. Of the hardy cabbages, January King and Danish Ballhead are classics. Savoy cabbages are also very hardy (Melissa, Embassy F1).

Saving Seed: Not easy. Leave cabbages in the garden through the winter; they will send up flower stalks in the summer. Cut an X, about an inch deep, across the top of the cabbage to help the seed stalk to emerge from the center. High risk of cross-pollination.

Carrots

Baby carrots straight from the garden are a delight you can only experience if you grow them yourself. Carrots become sweeter in early fall as the cool nights cause sugars to concentrate in their roots.

Culture: The best soil is deep, loose and without stones (stones cause forked roots). Sow thinly, ¼–½ inch (5–10 mm) deep; thin plants to 2–4 inches (5–10 cm) apart. Sow successive plantings to early July. In early July, seed a large bed of carrots for winter harvests. Carrot seeds don't tolerate deep planting, and the soil must be kept evenly moist for the germination period (10–14 days in warm weather, longer in cool conditions). To achieve a good stand of seedlings in summer, shade the beds until

FIGURE 10.5. Carrots and all the other hardy roots are a delight in mid-winter.

seeds germinate. With care, you can transplant tiny carrots to fill gaps in the bed for the winter crop (worth the effort, because there isn't time to re-seed).

Harvest and Storage: Carrot thinnings are edible in salads and roots are tasty from baby carrot-size, on up. Spring-seeded carrots usually become woody (and huge) if left to grow until September. Dig overwintered carrots by early April to preserve their flavor because they use the sugar stored in roots when they begin to grow in the spring. Store them in the refrigerator in loosely closed plastic bags or plastic bins.

Pests: Carrot rust fly; tiny seedlings can be demolished by pillbugs and slugs.

Varieties: Stump-rooted or "half-long" varieties are best for shallow soil and planters. Scarlet Nantes and related varieties have excellent flavor. Chantenay types grow long carrots. There are also purple, dark red and white novelty varieties (but I have found their flavors disappointing).

Saving Seed: Leave overwintered carrots in the garden to send up tall flower stalks in the spring. High risk of cross-pollination: if Queen Anne's Lace (wild carrot) grows in your area, don't try to save carrot seed.

Cauliflower

Tricky to grow, cauliflowers are sensitive to heat and to cold and are stressed by low fertility and uneven watering, all of which cause them to form small "button" heads. They are best when grown in cool conditions (60–65°F/15–18°C). Overwintering varieties produce the highest quality heads (in my humble opinion).

Culture: Seed beds ½ inch (1 cm) deep, or start seedlings 4–5 weeks before planting out. Final spacing in the garden is 12–16 inches (30–40 cm) apart. If spring seedlings are too large (more than five true leaves or with stems larger than a pencil), a little cool weather or any other stress will cause premature "button" heads. Sow overwintering varieties in mid- to late June for harvest the following spring.

Harvest and Storage: To produce white curds, break one or two inner leaves over the developing head to shade it; this isn't necessary for self-blanching varieties that have tightly wrapped inner leaves. Cut heads while

FIGURE 10.6. These cauliflowers were planted 12 days apart, but they were harvested the same day—after hot weather forced the later plant to produce a small head prematurely.

FIGURE 10.7. The shoulders of these celeriac will need to be well covered with mulch before winter.

the curd is fine textured and compact, before they begin to separate.

Pests: Cabbage root maggot; imported cabbageworm; cabbage aphid.

Varieties: Of the spring/summer varieties, Snowball is an old standard; there are also many hybrids. Orange and lime green varieties are also available. Overwintering varieties: Galleon (outstanding quality, heads in April to May), All the Year Round, Purple Cape, Aalsmeer.

Saving Seed: Difficult! Start summer varieties for seed in the fall and hold them over the winter in coldframes or very protected sites; winter cauliflower stands better over the winter under colder conditions. Both types eventually send up seeds stalks from the head, which take all summer to mature their seeds. High risk of cross-pollination.

Celeriac

Under the surface of this big ugly root (actually a swollen lower stem) is a creamy white, fine-textured vegetable, with a mild heart-of-celery flavor. It achieves greatness as the "cream" in cream of leek and celeriac soup.

Culture: Seeds are tiny, slow to germinate, and plants grow very slowly. Start indoors in February on bottom heat, or buy transplants in the spring. Set plants 8–12 inches (20–30 cm) apart each way in the garden. Seedlings with five true leaves or more send up seed stalks if they are exposed to temperatures below 55°F

(13°C) for a few days, so don't plant them outdoors until the soil is warm and a summer weather pattern has set in. Plants have short roots, so need very rich soil and generous water (they are descended from marsh plants).

Harvest and Storage: Mature plants are very cold hardy and can stay in the garden all winter. Mulch well to protect the shoulder of roots from freezing.

Pests: Trouble free.

Varieties: Limited selection.

Saving Seed: Leave roots in the garden over the winter; plants send up large seed stalks in the spring. Seeds ripens over a long period, so collect them several times. Risk of cross-pollination (also crosses with celery).

Celery

Grow as for celeriac. Celery tolerates only light frost; therefore, it can only stay in the garden over the winter in the warmest, frost-free parts of the coast.

Culture, pests, seed saving: As for celeriac. Don't set them out in the garden until the weather is reliably warm and stable.

Varieties: Limited selection; transplants are often available at garden centers. Most are "self-blanching," meaning that the inner stalks remain pale and tender. Cutting-leaf celery, grown for leaves to use as a flavoring, is easier to grow.

Chinese Cabbage, Leaf Mustard, Mustard Spinach, Leaf Turnip and Other Asian Greens

All of these "greens" are annuals, frost hardy to some degree, and can be grown for summer harvest or for overwintering crops. Chinese cabbage varieties are the most finicky about conditions; the other greens are robust mainstays of a salad garden all year round.

Culture: Sow ½ inch (1 cm) deep, thin to 4 inches (10 cm) apart in the row. Chinese cabbages are best sown after mid-summer for fall and winter harvest. Spring crops usually bolt to seed prematurely with the long days this far north or in response to cool weather. For a (brief) spring crop, start indoors and set plants out when conditions warm. Sow seed of all greens in mid- to late July for a fall, winter and spring crop.

FIGURE 10.8. Joi choi is a joy to grow as a late summer crop.

FIGURE 10.9. Namenia leaf turnip greens are a mainstay of my salad bowl year round.

Harvest and Storage: Use from the thinning stage on up. Cut full-grown heads of Chinese cabbage; for the other greens, pick leaves as needed and allow plants to continue growing. The Pac Choi types of Chinese cabbages are hardier than the Wong Bok types. The other greens listed are very hardy, and even small seedlings often survive the winter to produce excellent salad greens in the spring. Allow frozen overwintering greens to thaw out in a warm spell before harvesting leaves.

Pests: Cabbage root maggot; imported cabbageworm; slugs.

Varieties: There are many varieties among this large group of related plants. Chinese cabbage: Pac Choi/Bok Choy varieties have loose heads of oval leaves on wide green or white ribs; Wong Bok/Sui Choi/Napa Cabbage varieties have tightly wrapped, upright heads of pale green leaves. Leaf mustard: Osaka Purple, Green Wave. Mustard spinach: Komatsuna is extremely hardy and productive (the red variety isn't). Leaf turnip: Namenia and Mizuna have beautiful feathery leaves and mild flavor.

Saving Seed: Easy. High risk of cross-pollination. Plants produce seed in the summer from a spring planting. Allow the flowers to set seed pods and harvest when pods are tan and dry.

Corn

There is nothing like sweet corn harvested from the garden! Most heritage open pollinated

(OP) varieties won't mature in the cooler areas of the coast, but the earliest varieties of hybrids can be successful.

Culture: When the soil is warm enough for the type of corn you want to plant (see Table 10.1), sow 2–3 seeds in each spot or hill, 6–12 inches (15–30 cm) apart. Thin to one plant in each spot. Screen seedbeds against birds in the spring. For the earliest crop, start seeds indoors in late April/early May in individual pots; transplant to the garden when seedlings are 3 weeks old.

Plants are wind pollinated: the male "tassels" at the top of the plants shed pollen onto the silks that come out of the tip of the ears (the female part of the plant). To ensure good pollination, grow corn in dense blocks rather than rows. Because kernels are seeds, their characteristics depend on the genes they receive from both parents, so sweetness is affected by the

Table 10.1. Types of sweet corn			
Type of corn	Minimum germination temperature	Characteristics	Varieties (all are hybrids unless noted as OP)
Sugary normal (SU)	60°F (15°C)	Most open pollinated and common hybrids. Kernels lose sweetness quickly after picking. Isolate from SH2 types.	Golden Jubilee, Peaches & Cream, Golden Bantam OP
Sugary enhanced (SE)	64°F (17°C)	Very tender kernels easily damaged. Contains more sugar than SU, but is better adapted to cold than SH2 type. Stays sweeter longer after harvest than SU types. Isolate from SH2, but not SU.	Bodacious, Sugar Buns, Tendertreat, Miracle
Super sweet (SH2) and improved super sweet hybrids	70°F (21°C)	Twice the sugar content of SU. Sugar does not convert to starch after harvest, so kernels stay sweet longest after harvest. Isolate from SU & SE types.	Extra Early Super Sweet, Serendipity, Kandy King, Jubilee Super Sweet
Sweet gene or Tablesweet hybrids	70°F (21°C)	50% sweeter than SU types. Isolate from SH2 types.	Luscious, Brocade, Sugar Pearl
Ornamental and Popcorn	60°F (15°C)	Isolate from all types of sweet corn.	Calico Popcorn OP, Pink Popcorn OP

pollen the flowers receive. Cross-pollination between types usually causes lower-quality kernels and mixed kernels within the ear. The easiest way to ensure good results is to just grow one favorite variety of corn.

If you do want to grow more than one kind, to avoid cross-pollination, different types of corn must be isolated from each other. Grow them at least 75 yards (about 75 meters) apart or separate them in time by sowing different types at least 2 weeks apart, so pollen is not present at the same time. For a continuous harvest, plant early and mid-season varieties at the same time or make successive plantings of an early variety until late June. Don't remove the side shoots that sprout at the base of plants (the corn needs those leaves for maximum photosynthesis).

Harvest and Storage: Ears are ripe when the silks at the top of the ear have turned brown and dried up. You can open a slit in the husk with a fingernail to check whether kernels are plumped up (mature) or still a bit flat and sunken (immature). Sugary enhanced and super sweet varieties can be refrigerated for several days without losing their sweetness (see Table 10.1).

Pests: Raccoons, squirrels and rodents eat ears; birds eat seeds; wireworms attack seeds. The most destructive corn belt insects do not occur in the Pacific Northwest.

Varieties: See Table 10.1.

Saving Seed: Very difficult. Very high risk of cross pollination from any other corn growing within half a kilometer, so if you want seed, it should be hand pollinated — and that's very complicated. See reference books listed in Resources for detailed instructions.

Corn Salad

Corn salad (mache, bird lettuce) is an excellent winter salad green. It is hardier and higher in vitamins than lettuce. Leaves have a crisp texture and a mild, baby-corn flavor; they grow in a flat rosette of small leaves.

Culture: Will grow practically anywhere in any reasonable garden soil or in containers. Broadcast seeds over the surface of the soil from late August to mid-September. An ideal salad green to sow under squash vines, tomatoes and other warm-season plants in late August.

Harvest and Storage: The small rosettes are easy to handle if you cut individual plants off at the soil line, keeping the rosette of leaves together for washing. When ready to use, cut off the base of the plant and drop the bite-sized leaves into the bowl. Leaf quality is best from fall through early spring because the texture becomes soft in warm weather.

Pests: None. Even slugs don't bother it.

Varieties: Jade and Broad-leaved Dutch produce larger leaves. Vit is smaller and darker green, with slightly cupped leaves.

Saving Seed: Easy! Leave plants in the garden until the tiny white flowers turn into light tan seeds. Seeds shatter from the plants, so cut whole plants and dry on trays to avoid losses. Seeds are easy to shake from the dry plant material.

FIGURE 10.10. Corn salad is the hardiest salad green you can grow.

Cucumbers

Not easy to get started in the coastal region because both seeds and seedlings die in cool, damp spring weather. Growing varieties with mostly female flowers greatly improves the yield per vine.

Culture: Start indoors 3–4 weeks before planting out. Plants need very warm conditions, so don't try to seed directly in the garden. Plant in rows with plants 8 inches (20 cm) apart, or in hills with three plants/hill, 3½ feet (1 meter) apart. Allow vines to sprawl, or train them onto a trellis that supports the fruit. Train long English cucumbers up strings or onto a trellis and remove male flowers to prevent fertilization, which results in bulbous fruit with seeds.

Harvest and Storage: Keep all cucumbers picked, even if you don't use them, or plants will stop producing flowers. Bitterness in cucumbers depends on variety and possibly temperature (fruit grown in cool conditions can be more bitter). Most of the bitterness compounds are concentrated in and just under the skin and in the stem end, so they can be removed by peeling.

Pests: Damping off and related root rots.

Varieties: There are three main kinds. Pickling varieties are blocky, with short spines; pick them as gherkins (small) or medium size for pickling. Slicing varieties (Sweet Slice F1, Sweet Success, Straight 8) are elongated, with smooth skin. Long English cucumbers (usually grown in a greenhouse) are long and seedless, with very tender, smooth skin.

Saving Seed: Difficult. High risk of cross pollination, so flowers must be isolated in bags or taped shut so that you can hand pollinate them.

Eggplant

Mini and Asian varieties mature earliest and are most likely to ripen on the coast. Large-fruited varieties needs hotter weather than is usual for this region, so they are best grown in a greenhouse or tunnel.

Culture: Seed indoors mid-April, 8–10 weeks before setting out (mid- to late June); space 12 inches (30 cm) apart. Plants to be grown in greenhouses can be started and set out a few weeks earlier. Grow in the warmest possible conditions. All varieties do well as container plants.

Harvest and Storage: Pick fruit before it is completely mature, while the skin is glossy. Skins get quite tough if the fruit is left on the plant until the skin is dull or turns brownish.

Pests: Flea beetles; aphids.

Varieties: Some fruit are deep purple or purple streaked; there are also white varieties. "Mini" types are the smallest (Early Black Egg); Asian eggplants have long, slender fruit (Ichiban). Dusky is one of the large, oval-fruited types.

Saving Seed: Self-fertile, but there is a risk of cross-pollination by bees, so only grow one variety at a time for seed, or cover seed plants with screening. The greatest problem is having enough time for the fruit to remain on plants to ripen; in this region, a warm greenhouse is really a requirement.

Garlic

Wonderfully strong, flavorful varieties are available to gardeners: Hard-neck (Rocambole) varieties have the strongest flavor and are easy to peel; soft-neck garlic (usual grocery store type) keep longest.

Culture: Plant garlic in the fall, so it has time to grow a large root system before the increasing day lengths of May and June stimulate it to make bulbs. Separate cloves from the bulb (leave the skins on); plant them pointed end up, with the tip just covered, 8 inches (20 cm) apart each way. Mulch beds for the winter. The following June, hard-neck garlic sends up a curly central seed stalk (scape); snap these off as they appear and eat them (in stir-fries, pesto, etc.). If possible, stop irrigating about 2 weeks before harvest, which is about mid-July for most varieties.

Harvest and Storage: Hard-neck garlic is ready to harvest when about half to two-thirds of the leaves look dry, and the outermost layers of the bulb become dry and papery. Soft-neck garlic is ready after necks wither, causing the tops to fall over. Lift the bulbs and hang whole plants in bunches or braids, or spread them in trays one layer deep. Keep in a warm, dry airy place for 3 weeks to cure; don't leave bulbs in direct sun. When bulbs and leaves are thoroughly dry, rub off loose skins and any dry soil; cut off the stalks of hard-neck garlic just above the bulb. Store garlic in dry conditions, ideally just above freezing, but any cool, dry place will do.

Pests: Garlic leaf rust; White rot is a devastating root disease that stays in the soil for many years. Be sure that garlic you buy for planting shows no sign of rot. If your garlic crop is healthy, save your own bulbs for planting to avoid the risk of bringing in root diseases.

Varieties: Buy garlic from seed suppliers (not the grocery store) to ensure bulbs are disease-free. There are many varieties with either white or purplish cloves. Portuguese Red is a very early, hard-neck variety.

FIGURE 10.11. Just harvested hard-neck garlic (left) and soft-neck garlic (right).

Saving Seed After harvested bulbs are cured and cleaned, select the best ones and reserve them to plant for the next crop.

Kales and Collards

The reliable, productive kales are champions in the winter garden, when their leaves are so tender they can be used as salad greens. Collards have a distinctly different flavor, but are grown like kale.

Culture: Seed ½ inch (1 cm) deep; thin to a final spacing of 6–12 inches (15–30 cm) between plants. Plants sown earlier for summer harvests can remain in the garden through the winter or they can be sown in early August for winter harvest. Both tolerate low temperatures of 14°F (−10°C), but cover plants if temperatures threaten to drop lower in an extreme cold snap.

Harvest and Storage: Frost improves flavor; winter crop leaves are tender, sweet and mild. Wait to harvest frozen leaves until the plants have thawed out in a warm spell.

Pests: Cabbage root maggot; imported cabbageworm; cabbage aphid.

Varieties: Few varieties of collards are available. There are many kale varieties: Winterbor has dark green, frilly, leaves; Siberian has flatter, tender leaves. Red Russian, Winter Red and Redbor add color to salads. Lacinato varieties (Tuscan, Nero di Toscana) have nearly black, plume-shaped leaves. Ornamental kales are also edible.

Saving Seed: Easy. High risk of cross-pollination. Allow overwintered plants to flower in spring; harvest seed pods when they are tan and dry, usually by late July.

Leeks

Leeks grow beautifully in the coastal climate, and the hardy varieties are outstanding vegetables for winter harvests.

Culture: Start seeds indoors in February (or plan to buy seedlings later). Plant out seedlings in late April or early May, spaced 8 inches (20 cm) each way. Seeds sown in the garden in May will produce baby leeks for fall. Leeks need rich soil because their roots are short. Don't bother planting in trenches—this is one of the most widespread garden myths I know of.

Seedlings planted at a normal depth grow long, straight (and clean!) white stalks. If seedlings are too large when set out (more than half the width of a pencil) they may go to seed later in response to a cold spell. In late fall, mulch around the plants as far up the stalks as possible. If temperatures below 14°F (−10°C) are predicted, cover beds with a tarp.

FIGURE 10.12. No need to plant leeks in trenches—and these Unique leeks have the ribbon to prove it!

Harvest and Storage: Harvest as soon as leeks are big enough to be useable. If leeks freeze solid in a cold snap, wait until plants thaw out in a warm spell before harvesting.

By spring, leeks still in the garden have a ragged outer layer of leaves, but the stalks are fine underneath. Overwintered leeks develop seed stalks in early spring, but remain edible through June (cut leeks lengthwise and strip out the center stalk).

Pests: Trouble-free.

Varieties: Summer/fall varieties: Varna and Elephant are not very hardy. Winter varieties: Unique (outstanding quality and cold tolerance), Durabel, Siegfried Frost, Bandit and Saint Victor (a beautiful purplish color).

Saving Seed: Easy. Allow overwintered leeks to flower; it takes the whole summer to mature seeds. High risk of cross-pollination, including with onions. When seeds turn hard and black inside the florets, cut the heads and finish drying indoors. It is difficult to separate seeds from chaff.

Lettuce

This favorite salad green comes in an amazing variety of leaf textures and colors. With the right choice of varieties, it thrives in coastal gardens all year round.

Culture: Sow ¼ inch (5 mm) deep or, in early spring, broadcast seed on the soil surface (cover with screen if birds are a problem). Thin plants to

3–4 inches (8–10 cm) apart. Sow small amounts at 2–4 week intervals from early spring to late July. Plants produce harvestable leaves in 3–4 weeks, and grow to full-size heads in 1½ to 2 months. After that, they go to seed and leaves become increasingly bitter. Sow frost-hardy varieties in August for winter and early spring harvest. Lettuce survives winter in better condition when it is protected from heavy rain under a tunnel or building overhang. Overwintered plants crushed by their winter experience often sprout beautiful heads in the spring, though, so don't be in a hurry to pull damaged plants.

Harvest and Storage: Useable from thinning stage on up. Pick individual leaves or harvest whole plants at any size.

Pests: Slugs; Botrytis.

Varieties: There are thousands of varieties among butterhead, romaine/cos, loose leaf, oakleaf and iceberg types. Choose varieties adapted to the season. Summer: Red Sails is heat-tolerant. Winter: Winter Density, Rouge d'Hiver, Arctic King and Bakito. A few grow well in all seasons: Continuity, All the Year Round.

Saving Seed: Easy annuals. Allow the best plants to go to seed. Little risk of cross-pollination, but best to save only one variety at a time. Seeds ripen unevenly, so collect them over a month. Shake flower heads vigorously over a bucket or bag to knock loose ripe seeds.

Melons

A challenge for even experienced gardeners, melons are delicate, need a lot of heat and are often disappointing in coastal gardens. But when they work out, they are wonderful!

Culture: Start seeds indoors 5–6 weeks before planting out. Plant in rows or in hills, three plants/hill, 3½ feet (1 meter) apart. Set plants outdoors only after the soil is very warm and the weather is stable, which may take to mid-June. Most varieties need warmer weather than the coastal climate provides, so they are best grown in a greenhouse or plastic tunnel. Hand pollinate flowers of plants growing under covers or where bees are scarce.

Harvest and Storage: Melons don't continue to ripen off the vine, so wait to pick them until the fruit slips easily from the stem.

Pests: Pillbugs; powdery mildew.
Varieties: Only the earliest varieties have a good chance of maturing outdoors in most areas: Passport F1, Earlidew F1 and Fastbreak F1. Later varieties can ripen in greenhouses or tunnels.
Saving Seed: As for cucumbers.

Onions

If you are only familiar with grocery store onions, you might be amazed at the range you can grow: from small shallots to huge Kelsea Giants, in colors of magenta, dark red, yellow and white, and with flavors ranging from sweet and mild to extremely pungent.
Culture: Onions have short roots, so they need steady moisture; they grow best in soils with a high pH (7.5–7.8). Start seeds indoors 6–12 weeks before planting out in late April to mid-May, or buy seedlings or sets (tiny onions that grow again when planted). Space plants 5–6 inches (10–15 cm) each way. Seedlings larger than half the width of a pencil or sets larger than a dime may go to seed in response to a cold spell in the spring.

Onions are sensitive to increasing day length. Most varieties suitable to the Pacific Northwest need 13- to 16-hour day lengths to start forming bulbs. Plant by late April/early May, so they have time to grow before the long days of June stimulate them to form bulbs. Sow bunching onions any time from April through August; some are quite hardy and stand all winter. Sweet onions can also be sown in late July; if they overwinter successfully, they produce early onions the following June; however, snow and cold take their toll, and sometimes few survive. Plant perennial onions any time from seed, sets or bulbils (tiny bulbs that form on the top of stalk) and harvest as needed.
Harvest and Storage: Pull onions of any size for immediate use. Onions from sets mature in July, those grown from seeds usually mature in August or September. Harvest mature onions after the neck withers and the tops fall over, but don't be in a hurry: bulbs put on substantial weight after the tops start to wither.

It helps cure onions to stop watering a week or two before you expect to harvest. Don't bend tops down artificially, because damaged tissue may

FIGURE 10.13. Curing Italian red torpedo onions and Walla Walla sweet onions.

become diseased. Pull mature bulbs and spread them in trays or hang them in bunches in warm, dry conditions (out of the sun) for 3–4 weeks. When bulbs are thoroughly dry, rub off dry leaves, soil and loose skins, and store them in cool, dry conditions. The ideal temperature is just above freezing, but under 46°F (8°C) will do. Well-cured storage varieties keep for 6–12 months. Sweet onions keep 2–4 months.

Pests: Onion maggot (biology and control similar to cabbage root maggot); root rot diseases can be a problem in wet years or if onions are overwatered.

Varieties: Storage varieties: Redwing F1 is an outstanding red onion. Yellow onion sets are usually unnamed, but seeds of many excellent varieties are available. Sweet onions: Riverside Sweet Spanish, Walla Walla (both are large, white and sweet); Tropeana Lunga (magenta, Italian red torpedo type). Bunching onions/scallions: Kincho Japanese Bunching (also winter hardy). Perennials: Egyptian walking onion, shallots, perennial bunching onions (a.k.a. Welsh onions).

Saving Seed: Hold the best bulbs until spring and

Onion Seedlings: To Trim or Not to Trim?

Leaves of onion seedlings started indoors can be floppy and tangled, so clipping them back every few weeks to 4 inches (10 cm) is often recommended to make sturdier plants. However, removing leaf area can also slow their growth and reduce the size of the later bulbs. Some gardeners never trim the tops, others always do—and everyone seems happy with their results. Whether or not you trim seedlings (I never bother), at planting time do cut tops back to 6 inches (15 cm) to reduce the leaf area while roots recover.

replant them in the garden. They will send up tall stalks with the ball of florets at the top. High risk of cross pollination, so ensure no other onions or leeks are flowering at the same time. Cut seed heads after the seeds have turned black and hard; spread in trays to dry because the ripe seeds drop easily.

Parsnips

I don't like parsnips, so reader alert: the following information lacks the benefit of personal experience.

Culture: In early spring, seed ½ inch (1 cm) deep, thin to 3 inches (8 cm) apart (crowding is said by some to promote tender roots, though I can't imagine why this would work). Use fresh seed every year because seed is only viable 1–2 years. Some people sow in May for their winter crop, others wait until mid-June to avoid roots becoming woody. Hill the soil over the shoulders of the roots to prevent greening. Protect roots with a thick layer of mulch for the winter.

Harvest and Storage: Leave them in the garden for the winter and dig as needed. Aficionados claim the flavor is best after several weeks of frosty weather.

Pests: As for carrots.

Varieties: Limited choice: Hollow Crow and Harris Model are common; a few hybrids are also available from British seedhouses.

Saving Seed: As for carrots.

Peas

It is an enormous pleasure to eat raw peas straight from the vine (in the interest of researching the optimum time to pick, of course). Peas grow well in coastal summers and can be grown here from spring through fall in most regions.

Culture: Sow up to 1½ inch (2–3 cm) deep, space plants 2½ to 3 inches (6–8 cm) apart. Very early plantings (in March) often have high losses to pests with little gain in harvest time.

Peas can germinate in soils at 39°F (4°C), but they germinate better at 46°F (8°C) (optimum is actually 75°F/24°C). For heavy, wet soils that can't be worked until late spring, prepare the seedbed the fall before, and mulch to control weeds over winter. In the spring, pull back the mulch for a couple of weeks to warm the soil, then poke the seeds into the soil. For an early start and to avoid damage from pests, pre-sprout seeds indoors and set out when plants are 3–4 weeks old. Pea roots grow their own nitrogen, so there is usually no need to provide extra nitrogen fertilizers. Tall varieties need tall trellises because some grow 2 yards or more; short varieties can be allowed to sprawl but are easier to pick if trellised. Plant two or three crops in succession from early spring to late June for fresh peas through October. Choose varieties resistant to the pea enation virus for summer crops.

FIGURE 10.14. Symptoms of pea enation mosaic virus, which is spread by aphids, usually to mid-summer crops of peas.

Harvest and Storage: Pick shelling peas when the pods have filled out. Snap peas can be eaten pod and all at any size, but are at their maximum crunchy sweetness when pods are plump rather than flat. Snow peas (also called "sugar peas") are meant to be harvested while the pods are flat; if they become overgrown, shell the peas out of pods.

Pests: Powdery mildew, aphids and pea leaf weevil; pea enation mosaic virus is spread by aphids and is best managed by choosing resistant varieties. Birds and rodents dig up seeds, so you may have to screen seedbeds until plants are several inches high.

Varieties: Shelling peas: Green Arrow and many others. Snap peas: Cascadia and Sugar Ann are enation virus resistant; Sugar Snap and Sugar Daddy are not. Snow peas: Oregon Giant (enation resistant), Dwarf Gray Sugar. Snow peas are more tolerant of hot weather than shelling or snap peas.

Saving Seed: Easy. Flowers are self-fertile. Leave pods on the vine until they have become dry and leathery. Pick and dry further indoors, then shell seeds out of pods.

Peppers

It takes a longer, warmer season to ripen large sweet bell peppers than coastal gardens usually experience. Smaller fruited, sweet ramshorn types and hot peppers are quicker to ripen.

Culture: Seed indoors in late March to early April. Plant out in early to mid-June after the soil is very warm, spacing plants 1 foot (30 cm) apart. Plants need as much warmth as possible, so are better under cloches at the beginning of the season. Poor fruit production is usually due to low temperatures. All peppers ripen earlier and produce larger crops in greenhouses or tunnels; they also do well as container plants. Support plants by staking or use tomato cages. Pinching the tips of branches makes plants bushier and produce more flowers, but delays ripening of fruit.

Harvest and Storage: Sweet peppers are edible green and become quite sweet when fully ripe. Sweet peppers freeze well, while hot peppers are traditionally dried for long-term storage. Pull whole plants and hang up in a shed to ripen the last immature fruit; spread the fruit on trays or thread them onto a string and hang up to dry.

Pests: Aphids are common on seedlings, but are usually controlled by beneficial insects when plants are set outdoors.

Varieties: Hot or chile peppers: many varieties, mostly small to medium sized, slender, red, green or yellow elongated fruit. Habanero is many times hotter than Jalapeno. Sweet peppers: California Wonder (block, bell type); Gypsy F1 (vigorous ramshorn type); pimento peppers and purple, brown and orange varieties also available.

Saving Seed: Flowers are self-fertile, but there is a high risk of cross-pollination. Grow only one variety or screen plants from bees. Leave fruit to mature to the point of over-ripeness. Cut open fruit and spread seeds on a plate to dry. Wear rubber gloves when handling hot peppers.

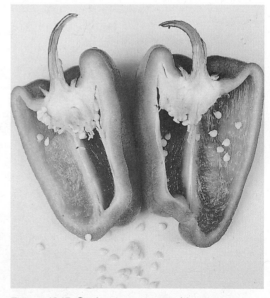

FIGURE 10.15. Saving pepper seed is easy as long as you prevent bees from moving the pollen around.

Potatoes

Potatoes grow well in the coastal climate and are very productive in a small space, even producing good crops in bags of soil. A yard-square bed can yield 20–40 pounds (10–20 kg per square meter).

Culture: Plant seed potatoes (small potatoes that are planted whole, not cut up) from March through May. Set them 2–3 inches (5–8 cm) deep, 8 inches (20 cm) apart in rows or hills 12–18 feet (30–45 cm) apart each way. Plant only certified seed potatoes (organic seed potatoes are available); there is a high risk of importing soil-borne diseases on uncertified stock, which can spread to tomatoes and related plants. Though often stated that spuds must be grown in acid soils, that is only to prevent infection by scab, an organism that doesn't tolerate acid soil. Scab is usually not a problem in home gardens unless infected potatoes were planted. Apply a thick mulch to keep soil cool and moist, or keep the soil well hilled up around plants to prevent tubers from being exposed to light and turning green (green areas are toxic). Tuber growth is determined by day length; they grow faster as days get shorter at the end of the summer.

Harvest and Storage: New potatoes are ready about 10–12 weeks after planting or when the flowers bloom (some don't flower). To harvest new potatoes, dig the whole plant or gently feel down around the roots to remove a few tubers, leaving the plant to grow. Harvest main crop potatoes in September or when vines start to die back. On a dry day, leave them in the sun for a couple of hours to dry, or spread them to dry on newspapers on the floor of the garage. When dry, brush off the soil and store them in opaque containers (burlap bags, cardboard boxes) in cool (50°F/10°C is ideal), completely dark conditions. In cold storage, stored tubers become sweeter and the texture changes; to restore flavor and texture, leave them at room temperature for a week before using them. Po-

FIGURE 10.16. Pre-sprouting seed potatoes on a windowsill gives them an early start.

tatoes have a natural dormancy, so they won't sprout for several months no matter what the storage conditions. Some people leave potatoes in the garden to dig through the winter; however, this also allows diseases, such as late blight to overwinter (it is the main source of infections the following year in garden tomatoes).

Pests: Flea beetles, aphids; late blight. Disorder: hollow heart.

Varieties: Early varieties: Warba, Yukon Gold, Seiglinde. Late varieties for storage: Red Pontiac, Russet. There are many white-, and yellow-, and also red- and blue-skinned potatoes; different varieties are suited for different uses (baking, chips, new potatoes).

Radishes

Radishes are the fastest vegetable to mature (and the fastest to become overmature!). For a steady supply of prime summer radishes, sow small amounts every week or two and don't hesitate to discard overgrown ones.

Culture: Sow ½ inch (1 cm) deep, thin to 1 inch (2 cm) apart, any time from March through August. Interplant them with slower-growing vegetables or sow a few seeds in the rows with carrots and parsnips; radishes break the crust on clay soils and will be half grown by the time the other plants germinate. The key to mild radishes is growing them fast (well-fertilized and watered) in the spring and late summer. Radishes become strong flavored in hot weather or when stressed by lack of water. Sow winter radishes or daikon in late July to early August for large, overwintering roots.

Harvest and Storage: Harvest summer radishes starting when they are the size of a nickel. They keep well in the refrigerator. Leave the much larger winter radishes in the garden, well mulched, for winter harvests. Green pods that form on flower stalks are also edible.

Pests: Cabbage flea beetle; cabbage root maggot can be very destructive.

Varieties: Summer radishes: Many varieties of round red, long red or white radishes; White Icicle; French Breakfast (elongated heirloom variety). Winter radishes: Daikon, Black Spanish.

Saving Seed: Easy. Leave roots in the garden to send up seed stalks later in the season (winter radishes go to seed in the spring). Allow seed pods to dry, and harvest. High risk of cross-pollination with turnips, Chinese cabbage, leaf mustard and wild mustards.

Spinach

If you have been frustrated by how quickly spinach bolts to seed, try planting it in August. You can pick leaves all fall and winter and right on through May because the same plants grow a whole new crop of leaves in the spring.

Culture: Spinach is sensitive to acid soil. Sow seeds ½ inch (1 cm) deep; thin plants to up to 1½ inches (2–4 cm) apart each way. Seeds germinate best in cool soil; in warm soil, sow extra seeds to compensate for lower germination rates. Rapidly increasing day lengths in spring cause spinach to go to seed, as does heat stress, so spring- and summer-sown plants don't produce much. Sow in early to mid-August for the overwintering crop. Shade the seedbed during the germination period. Seedlings stand up to late summer heat well, with only a few going to seed prematurely. Spinach does better in winter when it is protected from low temperatures and heavy rain in a greenhouse or plastic tunnel or under a roof overhang.

Harvest and Storage: Pick leaves from August-sown plants over the fall and winter. No matter how battered plants look by February, from March through the end of May they will produce a large crop of new leaves before going to seed.

Pests: Spinach leafminer.

Varieties: Long Standing Bloomsdale and related varieties are reliable, hardy and resistant to bolting; many disease-resistant hybrids are also available.

Saving Seed: High risk of cross-pollination. Pollen can travel a long way on the wind. If there is no other spinach going to flower in the area, allow your plants to set seed and leave them until seeds ripen. Save seed from the last plants to bolt, not the first.

FIGURE 10.17. Planted last August, growth is really taking off in March. By early June, I have had enough spinach and am happy to see it going to seed!

Squash and Pumpkins

Summer squash are very large, productive plants, so don't plant too many! Many winter squash and pumpkins need quite a lot of space because they have sprawling vines.

Culture: Start seeds indoors 5–6 weeks before planting out. Theoretically, summer squash can be sown directly in the garden in early to mid-June if the soil temperature is over 61°F/16°C (higher than 77°F/25°C is better), but the crop will be late. Plant in rows or hills with three plants per hill, 3½ feet (1 meter) apart for bush varieties, somewhat wider for vine types. Dig in a generous supply of compost and high-nitrogen fertilizer before planting.

Open-pollinated varieties usually produce male flowers for several weeks before female flowers appear. In poor soil they may never produce female flowers. Some hybrids produce only female flowers for the first few weeks; for such plants, pick off the early female flowers because premature fruit set stunts the plant. Be prepared to hand pollinate flowers (see sidebar for instructions), at least in early summer, before bees are numerous. Pollen must be transferred to flowers within the same *Cucurbita* species (see Table 10.2). Large-fruited winter squash take all summer to mature; keep the first two fruit that form on each vine, and pinch off later fruit because they won't have time to mature.

FIGURE 10.18. Keep summer squash, like this zucchini, picked to ensure plants continue to flower; if you planted too many, pull a few plants.

Harvest and Storage: Summer squash: Usable at any size, but best when small (e.g., 6 inches/15 cm long for zucchini). Winter squash: Harvest when the vines mature (leaves begin to die back), the skin of the squash feels hard, and the stem is shriveled and drying. Winter squash and pumpkins can survive light fall frosts, but if a frost is expected, cover the plants or harvest the fruit and bring it indoors. To harden and seal the skin against rot organisms, cure fruit for at least 10 days in a warm (80–86°F/27–30°C), dry location with good air circulation. When fully cured, the stem is dry and gray (and as hard

Hand Pollinating Squash

We can't rely on bees to pollinate flowers reliably, both because their numbers are lower than they used to be and because they don't fly in the spells of cool weather that are common on the coast. The most important plants to routinely hand pollinate are the squash family plants. To make sure you get a crop, you should count on hand pollinating squash, pumpkins, melons and gourds. Here's how:

- First, find an open female flower: they have a miniature squash forming on the stem, just behind the flower.
- Then find an open male flower: they don't have the miniature fruit below the flower, and you can also see pollen, like yellow dust, on the center structure of the flower.
- Pick the male flower, peel back the petals, and dab some of the bright yellow pollen dust onto the center structure of all the open female flowers. You can dust several female flowers with the pollen from one male flower.

Do this in the morning, before the blossoms wilt later in the day. I detour past my squash bed on the way to work every morning and quickly pollinate any open flowers on my way out the gate.

There is, however, one complication to keep in mind: Three different species of squash are grown in this region, and pollen from one species won't pollinate flowers of a different species (for typical varieties in each group, see Table 10.2). As long as you stay within the species group, you can use pollen from one plant to fertilize the flowers of another variety. If you don't know which group your squash or pumpkins belong to, just stick to transferring pollen from male flowers to female flowers within plants of the same variety.

FIGURE 10.19. Male squash flower (top) and female flower (bottom). Note the small squash below the female flower.

FIGURE 10.20. Transferring the pollen to the female flower.

as wood). Gently brush soil off of cured squash and store them in cool (60°F/15°C), dry conditions. Most keep at least 3 months and some for 9 months or more. Some people wipe the skins with bleach solution (1 part hydrogen peroxide to 9 parts water) before storing them, but I haven't found this necessary. Banana and acorn squash do not need to be cured; they keep 2–3 months in cool, dry conditions. Check stored squash at least monthly for signs of rot.

Pumpkins: For Jack-o-lanterns or Thanksgiving pies, the fruit is fine even if frost has killed the vines. To store sweet pumpkins over the winter, harvest them before frost and cure and store as for winter squash.

Pests: Powdery mildew; grow resistant varieties of zucchini to produce a longer crop.

Varieties: Summer squash: zucchini (dark green, yellow and round varieties), vegetable marrows, yellow crooknecks, pattypans (like little flying saucers), vegetable spaghetti, Italian tromboncino (long and narrow). Radiant F1 zucchini is powdery mildew resistant. Winter squash: Many colors and shapes, most are vining; a few are bushes better suited to small areas. Varieties with large fruit (hubbards, large buttercups) take longest to mature. Small-fruited varieties ripen more reliably in cooler regions: Gold Nugget, Delicata, Sweet Dumpling, Acorn and crosses, such as Festival F1 (sweet flesh, exceptionally long keeper).

Saving Seed: Difficult. For advanced seed savers only. Flowers must be isolated in bags

FIGURE 10.21. This squash is dark orange and looks ready to pick, but the stem is still soft—so give it more time.

FIGURE 10.22. Butternuts are the one type of squash you might be able to save seeds from without a high risk of crossing, because there are so few other varieties in the same species group.

Table 10.2. Common squash varieties within each species group.	
Cucurbita pepo (Most summer squash)	Zucchini Yellow crookneck Acorns Vegetable spaghetti Delicata Stripetti Scallopini/Pattypan Sugar pumpkin, most pie pumpkins* Vegetable marrow
Cucurbita maxima (Most winter squash)	Buttercups Bananas Hubbards Turbans Rouge Vif d'Etampes pumpkin Most mammoths Sweet meat
Cucurbita moschata	Butternuts Tromboncino

*There are some pumpkin varieties within each species group.
Note: When hand pollinating, transfer pollen only between flowers within the same *Cucurbita* species group.

or taped shut for hand pollination. Don't save seed from squash if flowers weren't isolated because the resulting fruit is usually poor quality.

Swiss Chard, Leaf Beet

These vigorous leafy greens with large upright leaves yield an outstanding amount in a small space —for a full year, from one planting in May.

Culture: Chard grows best at a high soil pH of 6.5–7.5. Seed ½ to 1 inch (1–2 cm) deep; thin seedlings to 2½–3 inches (6–8 cm) apart. Each "seed" is a seed ball containing several seeds, so seedlings must be thinned. Spring-sown plants carry through the following winter and spring. Sow more plants by late July for winter harvest, especially leaf beet varieties, which are generally hardier than Swiss Chard.

Harvest and Storage: Chard does better under some type of cover in the coldest weather. Allow frozen leaves to thaw out in a warm spell before harvesting. In a severe cold snap, leaves of chard can freeze to the ground, but don't hurry to discard plants, because the roots usually sprout new leaves in spring.

Pests: Spinach leafminer; some varieties (e.g., Rhubarb chard) are susceptible to Cercospora leaf spot (which shows as many tiny round leaf spots) in wet weather and are best avoided if leaf spots are often a problem.

Varieties: Swiss chard: Bright Lights has red, yellow, purple and white stems; it stands well all winter; Fordhook has heavily savoyed dark green leaves and wide, white ribs. Leaf beet: Perpetual Spinach and Bietina (these may be the same variety) have narrow, light green stems and smooth leaves.

Saving Seed: Easy. Overwintered plants send up a seed stalk in late May; flowers appear in June, and seeds mature in July. Strip the seeds from the stalks and dry the seeds thoroughly. High risk of cross-pollination because pollen is wind borne; can cross with beets.

Tomatoes

Probably the food crop grown by more people than any other. Tomato varieties are generally one of two types: determinate or indeterminate. Determinate, or bush varieties, are shorter plants. They stop producing new shoots and flowers after reaching full size. Their fruit ripens early, over a short period. Indeterminate, or vine tomatoes, continue to grow new shoots and flowers until the weather is too cold or they are pulled out; vines can grow over 8 feet (2 meters) long.

Culture Start bush tomatoes indoors in early April, 6–8 weeks before setting out (usually late May to mid-June, after the soil is warm). Start vine varieties up to 12 weeks before setting out. Or, buy transplants, which are widely available. Space bush varieties 2 foot (60 cm) apart; vine varieties may need up to 3½ feet (1 meter) spacing, depending on the staking system. Let bush tomatoes sprawl on the ground (mulch the soil to keep fruit clean), or stake them to save space. Vine tomatoes should be staked. To speed ripening, pinch out shoots ("suckers") that form between a leaf stem and a main stem. To help the remaining fruit ripen at the end of the summer, reduce irrigation and cut back the growing tips of vines. Do this after mid-August for outdoor plants or mid-October for greenhouse plants. Big beefsteak varieties won't ripen to full flavor outdoors in cool regions, so are better grown in a greenhouse. To improve air circulation around greenhouse tomatoes, remove lower leaves up to the currently ripening truss of fruit. Because of the high risk of late blight infection, it is essential to keep leaves of tomatoes dry. Bush tomatoes grow well in containers and small-fruited varieties can be grown in hanging baskets. Bring container plants indoors to a sun porch or greenhouse to extend the season. Because tomatoes are perennials, it is possible to cut back container plants and overwinter them indoors to produce a crop next year.

Harvest and Storage: Before killing frost damages the fruit, pick mature green tomatoes (these are full size and light green). Some people wrap each tomato in newspaper; others spread them out in shallow boxes or trays. Stored at 50–60°F (10–15°C), they will hold for several months. To finish ripening, bring tomatoes to room temperature; exposure to light increases their color somewhat, but is not required for ripening. You can also pull whole vines and hang them in a shed to allow fruit to ripen (spread newspapers below!). Check stored tomatoes often to remove ripening or rotting fruit.

Pests: Flea beetles; late blight. Disorders: blossom end rot; greenback. Pollination problems: Most varieties can't set fruit at temperatures below 50°F (10°C) or above 86°F (30°C) (heat sterilizes pollen). While flowers open during a heat wave may fail, flowers that develop in cooler weather will be fine.

Varieties: Too numerous to mention! Zillions of red varieties, also green, yellow, orange, brown and striped varieties. Parthenocarpic varieties (Oregon Spring, Siletz) set fruit in cool weather without

FIGURE 10.23. Fermenting tomato seeds for a few days removes the coating.

fertilization, so are good for earliest fruit and cool areas. Paste tomatoes contain less juice and make excellent sauces.

Saving Seed: Easy. Plants are self pollinating, and there is low risk of crossing. Squeeze pulp and seeds from a completely ripe fruit into a glass of water. Allow to ferment for 2 days to break down the gel coating on the seeds, then pour off the water and rinse the seeds well in a sieve. Spread the clean seed on a plate to dry (not on a towel because they stick). Some people skip the fermenting stage and just dry the seeds with good results.

Turnips and Rutabagas

Turnips grow quickly, and both the root and leaves are edible. Rutabagas (also called "Swedes") are larger, yellow roots, with a distinctively different flavor, usually grown for winter harvests.

Culture: Sow ½ inch (1 cm) deep, thin to 2 inches (5 cm) apart (up to 6 inches/15 cm for rutabaga). Sow small amounts of turnips at 2–3 week intervals from March to mid-July. Sow enough for fall and winter harvest by end of July. Sow rutabagas for winter harvest by July 10th. The best roots grow in deep soil without stones.

Harvest and Storage: For best flavor, harvest summer turnips when they have a diameter of 2 inches (5 cm). Overgrown turnips become woody. Rutabagas grow much larger; leave them in the garden for the winter, well mulched, and dig as needed.

Pests: Cabbage root maggots are particularly destructive; imported cabbageworm.

Varieties: Turnips: Purple Top, White Globe, Tokyo Cross. Rutabagas: Laurentian, Marian (resistant to clubroot).

Saving Seed: Easy. Overwintered roots send up flower stalks in the spring. Harvest when seed pods are tan and dry. High risk of cross-pollination; will cross with radishes, Chinese cabbage, leaf mustard and wild mustards.

CHAPTER 11

A TO Z FRUIT

All of the fruit described below grow best in full sun and well-drained, fertile soil. Unless stated otherwise (blueberries are the main exception), grow them in slightly acid soil (pH 6.5–6.8). To produce a good crop, fruit should be irrigated during summer dry periods. If possible, avoid using overhead sprinklers, which prolongs the length of time leaves are wet and thus susceptible to fungal diseases. Details on planting and pruning tree fruit, table grapes and kiwi are given in Chapter 6.

Apples

There are many apples varieties (thousands?), from favorite heritage varieties to recent selections. All apple trees are grafted because apples don't come true from seed. Dwarf apples grow to 8–10 feet (2.5–3 meters) high and about as wide. Semi-dwarf tree grow to about 12–15 feet (3.5 to 4.5 meters). Multi-graft trees have three or more varieties grafted onto one trunk. Columnar apples bear their fruit along the single trunk, so they can be planted closely together along a fence.

Culture: Space dwarf trees 10–12 feet (3–3.5 meters) apart or allow that diameter of growing zone around each tree. Allow 15 feet (4.5 meters) around semi-dwarf trees. Install a permanent support post for each dwarf tree or

FIGURE 11.1. Spartan apples on a multi-graft dwarf tree.

espalier them against a wall or fence. When trees branches are heavy with fruit, they may need temporary props to prevent them from breaking.

Pruning: If you see shoots coming from the base of the tree below the graft, cut them off and pull away a layer of soil to make sure the graft union stays above ground. After the "June drop," thin to one to two apples per cluster. In years with poor pollination, this won't be necessary, but when there is a heavy crop, it is important to do the thinning to ensure a crop next year.

Harvest and Storage: Ripe apples part easily from the twig with a gentle tug. When apples start to drop, it shows the crop is maturing. Good storage varieties keep until May or even longer in good conditions: 35–41°F (2–5°C) with high relative humidity. Store them in loosely closed plastic bags or containers to keep humidity high, but allow a little air exchange. Don't store apples with other fruit or potatoes because apples give off ethylene gas, which speeds up ripening (or sprouting) of the other produce. Check regularly for signs of rot in stored apples.

Pollination: Apples must to be cross-pollinated by another variety. If you don't have space for two trees, grow a multi-graft tree. Gravenstein, Mutsu and Jonagold varieties won't pollinate each other or other apples. Varieties on multi-graft trees will have been chosen to be compatible for pollination and blooming time.

Pests: Codling moth; leafrollers; apple scab.

Varieties: By choosing well, you can extend the harvest of fresh apples from late July to November if desired (see Table 11.1 for approximate harvest dates). Apples that store well include: Elstar, Gala, Libery, Macoun, Melrose, Criterion, Spartan, Empire, Golden Russet, Bramley's Seedling, Belle de

Table 11.1. Approximate harvest period for common varieties of apples growing on southern Vancouver Island.

Harvest period	Cultivars
Early August	Yellow Transparent* (late July in warm sites)
Late August	Sunrise, Summer Red, Red Free*
Early September	Paula Red, Akane*
Mid-September	Gravenstein (ripens for a month), Prima,* Greensleeves, Queen Cox, Sunrise,* Golden Delicious
Late September	Elstar,* Gala, Macspur, Fiesta,* Liberty,* Jonagold, Jonafree,* Spartan
Early October	Empire, Macoun,* Bramley's Seedling,* Belle de Boskoop,* Priscilla,* Honeycrisp
Mid-October	Ambrosia, Melrose, Criterion, Golden Russet, Enterprise*
Late October	Cox's Orange Pippin, Mutsu,* Northern Spy, Idared
Early November	Fuji (needs a very long growing season; not for cool coastal gardens)

* = Resistant or immune to apple scab

Boskoop, Mutsu, Idared, Fiesta, and Fuji. Harvest dates can vary by a couple of weeks either way from year to year. Some varieties, such as Gravenstein, ripen over a month or more.

Blueberries

Blueberries thrive on the coast. Highbush blueberries and half-high hybrids (highbush crossed with eastern native lowbush blueberries) are most commonly grown. The bushes have beautiful red or yellow leaves in the fall.

Culture: Blueberries grow best in cool, moist, well-drained acidic soil (pH 4.5–5.5 is ideal). Don't lime the soil or use bone meal, wood ashes or other fertilizers containing calcium. If your soil is not acidic, amend with sulfur and leaf compost or grow bushes in containers with an acid soil mix. Mulch with a thick layer of leaves, pine needles or shredded bark mulch to control weeds and acidify the soil.

Pruning: Prune while bushes are dormant, up to late February. Remove crossed, broken and weak branches. Shape the bush to be narrower at the base with a wider top. Thin out crowded branches to make an open center. Plants begin to decline after 8–10 years, so starting when the bush is 7 years old, remove one or two of the oldest canes each year and allow new ones to take their place.

Harvest and Storage: Blueberries look ripe long before they are — wait until they turn deep blue-black under the bluish bloom. With their waxy skins, blueberries keep in the refrigerator longer than other berries. They freeze well and are excellent dried.

Pests: Birds and sometimes other vertebrates cause the greatest losses.

Varieties: Grow a mix of early to late varieties to ensure good pollination and provide a longer harvest (late July to early September). Most varieties are partially self-fertile, but fruit set is improved by cross-pollination. Early: Earliblue, Duke, Spartan, Reka, Patriot (adapted to heavy, wet soils). Mid-season: Bluecrop, Northland, Hardyblue, Blueray. Late: Brigitta (a tall, productive hybrid). Half-high hybrids: Northland (early), Northsky (mid-season), Northblue (late). Some nurseries sell native huckleberries and low-bush blueberries.

Blackberries

When Himalayan blackberries already grow wildly on the coast, you might wonder why anyone would plant more. But there are other domestic blackberries with unique flavors that are well worth growing.

Culture: All blackberries thrive in deep soil as long as it is well-drained in winter. These are vigorous, large plants that produce large crops when grown in good soil with summer irrigation. Spread a layer of compost around the base of plants each year and mulch well to control weeds. Keep on top of the task of removing weak canes and any shoots that come up in pathways and away from the main crowns because blackberries can quickly get out of hand.

Pruning: Each cane is biennial: it grows the first year and fruit the second year. After that it should be pruned out entirely. One system to keep trailing types (most varieties) well organized is to grow them supported on some type of trellis with four to six parallel wires or rails. The first year, allow new canes to grow unchecked, but train half of them to grow to the left, tied to the lower wires and the other half tied to the lower wires on the right. Next year these become fruiting canes. In the spring, untie them, shorten them to 6–8 feet long and fan them out and tie them to the upper part of the trellis. Allow this year's new canes to grow in either direction along the lower part of the trellis. At the end of the second season, cut off at the ground the canes that have just finished fruiting. Every year, thin the canes to leave a total of 12–15 per plant (half would be first year and half would be second year, fruiting canes).

Harvest and Storage: Good frozen and as jam, jelly or juice.

Pests: Generally healthy. Powdery mildew or leaf rusts sometimes occur.

Varieties: Thornless blackberries, Marion berries, loganberries and boysenberries are all types of blackberries. Tayberries are raspberry-blackberry hybrids, with large, early berries.

Cherry, Sweet

A standard sweet cherry can grow 30 feet (9 meters) high, but now that you can buy sweet cherries on Gisela dwarfing rootstocks (growing about 10 feet, or 3 meters, high) it is possible to grow them in a home garden.

Culture: Give the dwarf tree a 10-foot (3-meter) diameter growing space all around the tree.

Pruning: When you plant the tree, also plan how you intend to protect the fruit from birds when it reaches full size, so you can shape it accordingly. Key to harvesting a crop is controlling the spread of branches, so you can throw bird netting over them or keep them inside a frame covered with netting.

Harvest and Storage: Some varieties are almost black when ripe, others are lighter red, so the taste test is the best way to determine when to pick. Cherries don't keep very long: eat them fresh or freeze or preserve them immediately.

Pests: Birds and raccoons. Disease: Brown rot.

Varieties: Sour cherries (pie cherries) are self-fertile. Sweet cherries: Some varieties need cross-pollinators: Bing, Lambert and Van. If you only want one tree, choose self-fertile varieties: Glacier, Lapins, Stella or Sweetheart. Multi-graft trees with three varieties of cherries on Gisela rootstock ensure good pollination and a longer fresh harvest period.

Currants and Gooseberries

Depending on your passion for these, you may only need one bush to meet your needs for jelly or pies. You will need several blackcurrant bushes to make a reasonable quantity of juice.

Culture: Avoid wet soils and hot, dry sites. Space plants about 3–4 feet (1 meter) apart (farther apart for black currants, which are larger). Mulch to keep soil cool and moist. Most varieties have self-fertile flowers and do fine as a single bush, but they may produce larger fruit if cross-pollinated by another variety.

Pruning: For gooseberries, red and white currants: Prune to keep an open center, and remove canes low to the ground. Fruit is produced at the base of 1-year old branches and on spurs (small side shoots) of 2- and 3-year-old branches. Branches 4 years and older produce very little. At the end of the first year, remove all but six to eight of the most vigorous canes. In years two and three, leave three to four new canes and keep six to eight of the older ones. At the end of the fourth year and for the following years, remove the oldest canes, and continue to keep three or four new, 1-year-old canes each year.

Black currants: Plants produce most fruit on the last year's canes, therefore once plants start fruiting, annual pruning consists of cutting out most of the old canes that fruited the previous year. If growth was good, remove most of the old wood that fruited (old stems are darker, with loose or peeling bark; new stems are light brown, with smoother bark). If there aren't many new canes, cut out about a third of the old branches at a time.

Harvest and Storage: Strip ripe currants from bushes by hand or clip off trusses of berries. To pick gooseberries, wear gloves and long sleeves to protect yourself from thorns.

Pests: Imported currantworm and currant fruit fly, which leaves tiny marks on developing currant fruit. These are eggs scars; when they develop, there will be a white maggot inside each berry. Eggs are laid early May to end of June. Cover plants during this period with floating row cover fabric tied at the top and around the base to prevent flies from laying eggs.

Varieties: Red currant: Red Lake (late crop, widely considered the best red currant); Viking (late crop, resistant to white pine blister rust). Mid-season: Wilder (some resistance to powdery mildew); Perfection (susceptible to powdery mildew); Stephens (vigorous). Black currant hybrids immune to white pine blister rust: Consort, Crusader, Mina Smyriou and Titania. Gooseberries: both green- and pink-fruited varieties are available. Jostaberries are disease-resistant hybrid crosses of black currant and gooseberry.

FIGURE 11.2. The marks on these developing currants show that a fruit fly egg has been laid inside.

Citrus, Lemons and Limes

Citrus trees can tolerate a degree or two of frost when hardened off for winter. Limes and dwarf Meyer lemons do well in containers and ripen good quality fruit in the coastal climate. Some gardeners grow oranges and other citrus; these are generally larger trees and need a longer warm period to ripen than lemons and limes. Experimenting with them is for gardeners who can provide especially warm growing conditions and winter shelter.

Culture: Soil pH 6.0 is ideal; too much lime in the soil causes iron and zinc deficiency. Leaves turn yellow with green along the leaf veins and take a long time to turn green. Because citrus nutrition is very tricky, I recommend supplementing additions of compost with a complete citrus fertilizer available from nurseries. Avoid overwatering citrus. For winter, move containers to a very protected site where temperatures won't dip lower than 30°F (−1°C) over the winter (an unheated greenhouse or glassed-in porch, for example).

The trees are much better off in the cool, humid, bright conditions typical in an unheated greenhouse than inside the house because they tend to drop leaves when brought indoors to warm, dry, low-light conditions.

Pruning: Little to do except for thinning crowded branches or pinching back tips to keep plants compact. They regularly set too many fruit for the size of the tree, so thin the developing fruit to 6 inches (5 cm) apart on the branches.

Harvest and Storage: Fruit color isn't a reliable indicator because ripe limes may be yellowish and ripe lemons may still be light green on one side. Citrus are ripe when the seeds turn brown; however, some have only a few seeds. Ripe fruit can stay on the tree for long periods without deteriorating, so the picking time is not critical.

Pests: Soft brown scale is common on citrus. These are sucking insects that look like tiny brown bumps on the stems and the undersides of leaves. The most noticeable symptom of a scale infestation is that leaves have sticky patches of honeydew. In the fall, spray trees with horticultural oil mixed according to package directions for a growing season spray. Make sure to thoroughly cover the undersides of *all* leaves.

Varieties: Two widely available varieties are Improved Dwarf Meyer lemon and Seedless Bearss lime.

Figs

Figs are beautiful, tropical looking trees with smooth gray bark. The key to harvesting figs in the Pacific Northwest is planting the right variety. Most fig varieties have two crops over a season, but only the figs from the first crop will ripen. Second crop figs are still too immature when fall weather arrives, so you want a variety with a good first crop.

Culture: Figs grow fine in any well-drained soil, but prefer a higher pH (6.0–7.8) than many garden plants. Plant them in the warmest site in the yard, such as against a building or rock wall where reflected heat will help ripen fruit. Avoid fertilizers high in nitrogen, which cause trees to produce more leaves than fruit. Mulch to protect roots for winter. Unpruned trees grow to up to 30 feet (9 meters) tall, but they can be pruned to smaller dimensions and still produce a good crop. You can grow them in large containers and keep them to about 10 feet (3 meters) in height.

Pruning First crop figs are produced on the new growth from last summer, so pruning to cut back the ends of branches when trees are dormant can remove the next crop. Pruning to shape trees should be limited to pinching back tips of branches during the growing season. Do this after five or six leaves have appeared on this season's new growth at the end of the branch. When trees are dormant, remove crowded and crossed branches. Every year, remove a few whole branches older than two years old to keep the height of the tree down. Winter temperatures below 14°F(−10°C) can damage tips of branches, but most of the tree will be fine. Figs are always the last trees to leaf out in the spring (so don't panic if they are late).

Harvest and Storage: Figs don't ripen further once they are picked, so they must be left on the tree until they are perfectly ripe. When the neck of a ripe fig is so soft that it collapses and the fruit droops over, then it is ripe. Figs don't keep at all, but are delightful fresh, frozen or dried.

Pests: Birds and raccoons; yellowjacket wasps feed on juice from cracks in ripening fruit.

Varieties: Brown Turkey; Peter's Honey (a type of Italian honey fig that bears a good first crop of very sweet, straw-colored fruit); Desert King (bears a single, late summer crop of reliable, large green fruit that is pink inside).

FIGURE 11.3. The neck on the fig in the middle has collapsed, showing the fruit is ready to pick. The other two figs are not yet ripe.

Grapes, Table

American grapes (*Vitis labrusca*) and American grape hybrids need less heat to ripen than European table grapes, and the early varieties ripen pretty reliably on the coast. They are also hardy to at least 0°F(−18°C), so can be grown in northern coastal areas where there are Arctic outbreaks in winter. Note: Wine grapes are mostly European grapes (*Vitis vinifera*), which need a long warm season.

Culture: Grapes do best in deep soil, but garden vines manage in shallower soils as long as it is fertile and well-drained. Grow grapes in the warmest part of the garden where they can be supported on a trellis, along a fence or over an arbor. Space plants 8 feet (2 meters) apart or leave that diameter of growing area around a single vine. Dig in generous amounts of bone meal when setting out young plants.

Pruning: See Chapter 6.

Harvest and Storage: Leave grapes on the vines until fully ripe for maximum sweetness. A mature table grape produces 25–40 large bunches of grapes depending on how much space the vine has. A couple of vines can produce surplus to freeze, dry or make into juice.

Pests: Birds, raccoons and other animals do the most damage. Powdery mildew infects European varieties, but American and American hybrid varieties are resistant. Blister mites can cause puckered spots on grape leaves, but even large numbers do not affect the harvest; if necessary, spraying sulfur when vines are dormant will control them.

Varieties: Seedless American/American hybrid grapes: Himrod (very early white); Interlaken (very early green); Price (very early blue); Canadice (early red); Sovereign Coronation (early blue-purple); and Vanessa (early red). There are other early and midseason varieties for warmer areas of the coast; late varieties won't have enough heat to ripen.

Kiwi

The fuzzy (grocery store) kiwi fruit is hard to manage in a small yard: you need both a female and a male plant, and they are large and extremely vigorous. The hardy kiwis (see "Varieties," below) are less rambunctious and easier to manage, but also produce smaller fruit and less weight of fruit.

Culture: Grow vines in moderately fertile soil and avoid overfertilizing with nitrogen. Vines do best in full sun, in the warmest part of the garden (as for grapes). It can take 5–7 years for female fuzzy-skinned kiwi plants to flower, but once vines begin fruiting, they come into heavy production rapidly.

Harvest and Storage: A mature fuzzy kiwi vine can produce hundreds of pounds of fruit. Pick them before they ripen, in late September to early October. The skin of the fuzzy kiwi will be brown, without a green tinge; the smooth skin of hardy kiwi remains green. Store for 3–4 months or even longer in ideal conditions (35–41°F/2–5°C). As needed, remove fruit from cold storage and hold at room temperature to ripen. As the storage period lengthens, the time it takes to ripen when at room temperature decreases.

FIGURE 11.4. Fuzzy-skinned kiwi is an amazingly productive vine!

Pruning: Fuzzy kiwi vines grow 10–20 feet (3–6 meters) in a season, but can be kept much smaller with regular pruning. Prune vines in both winter and summer; the vines produce many strong shoots, which need to be kept pruned back.

Pests: None. Animal are not usually a problem, because the fruit is picked while still green.

Varieties: The fuzzy-skinned kiwi (*Actinidia deliciosa* or *A. chinensis*) have egg-sized fruit with rough skin. Females: Saanichton, Hayward; Male: Chico Male.

Hardy kiwi (*A. arguta*) have small fruit (up to ¾ inch long/1–2 cm) with a smooth skin that doesn't have to be removed before eating. Varieties: Issai (self-fertile) and Ananasnaja (needs a male pollinator). Other kiwis, some with variegated leaves, also produce small, tasty fruit (e.g., *A. kolomikta*).

Peaches, Nectarines

Peaches on the coast are a hit-or-miss crop because they flower early, when cold rainy weather may keep bees away. Fruit quality often doesn't approach that of fruit grown in hotter climates, but fresh peaches and nectarines are a treat nonetheless.

Culture: Grow peaches and nectarines in the warmest part of the garden. If you can, plant the tree against a south- or southwest-facing wall of a building that has enough of a roof overhang to keep winter rain off of the tree and prevent peach leaf curl. Most varieties are self-fertile, but not all, so check whether your tree needs a pollinator.

Pruning: Trees can be trained into an open center structure or trained against a wall or trellis. Fruit is produced on 1-year-old branches (the previous season's growth); therefore, trees should be pruned heavily each year. As a general rule, remove about two thirds of the branches during the winter or head back the shoots by a third to avoid having fruit develop at the ends of long branches. To control excessively vigorous growth, continue pruning in summer, removing watersprouts and heading back long branches.

FIGURE 11.5. Early Redhaven peach ripens well in my garden most years—but not always.

Harvest and Storage: Fruit is ready to harvest when they part from the branch with a gentle tug. Where raccoons and other animals make it difficult to achieve tree-ripened fruit, pick fruit slightly green and ripen indoors.

Pests: Brown rot; peach leaf curl: there is no point in growing peaches susceptible to this disease unless you are prepared to spray trees, or you can grow them under a structure to keep off rain during the infection period in February and March.

Varieties: Early varieties (e.g., Early Redhaven) have the best chance of ripening in coastal gardens. There are several varieties with some level of resistance to peach leaf curl: Frost (good degree of resistance, widely available); Q-1-8; Avalon Pride; Oregon Curl Free. Genetic dwarf peaches and nectarines (e.g., Golden Prolific) can be grown in large tubs and moved under a roof overhang during the leaf curl infection period.

Pears

There are both European pears (the well-known, pear-shaped fruit) and Asian pears (rounder, with a crisper texture; also called "apple pears").

Culture: Pears enjoy good, well-drained soil, but tolerate less-well drained and heavy soils better than other fruit trees. Grow two varieties of pears to ensure pollination or grow multi-graft trees. Asian and European pears are not good pollen trees for each other because they don't bloom at the same time (Asian pears bloom later).

Pruning: Even dwarf pears tend to become rather large trees, but can be kept to 12–15 feet (3.5–4.5 meters) in height with pruning. They can also be espaliered. Left to their own devices, pears tend to grow tall, with upright branches. Prune to keep trees shorter and train the branches to spread at wider angles (use spreaders if necessary to hold branches in place while they are young). Once early pruning establishes the basic shape of the tree, they don't need much pruning.

FIGURE 11.6. The arrow shows where the stem of this Red Bartlett pear will snap from the branch when ready to pick.

Harvest and Storage: Although pears can ripen on the tree, don't let them. They are much better picked slightly green and ripened off the tree. Pears are ready to pick when the stem on the fruit snaps cleanly from the branch when you lift up the fruit. Hold the pears in a cool, dark place to finish ripening. Winter pears are ready to pick in late September to late October. Sort the fruit and put it in cold storage. After a month in cold storage, winter pears ripen when they are brought to room temperature. They keep for about 3–4 months — longer if held in ideal cold storage at 35–41°F (2–5°C). Fruit will begin to ripen in cold storage by late December.

Pests: Pear trellis rust; pear sawfly is occasionally a problem: the larvae look like tiny black slugs on the leaves and chew holes between the leaf veins. Wash them off of leaves with a stiff stream of water; they don't show much inclination to climb back up the tree.

Varieties: Summer European varieties: Bartlett (early); Clapps Favorite (early); Flemish Beauty (mid-season). Winter European varieties: Bosc (harvest in late September); Seckel; Anjou; Doyenne du Comice (harvest in October). Many varieties of Asian pears are available.

Plums

With sweet, juicy and colorful fruit, plum trees are productive and easy to care for. Two main groups are commonly grown: European plums, which are oval shaped with very sweet flesh and skins; and Japanese plums, which are larger and rounder, with tart skins. European plums generally bloom later, so have a better chance of being pollinated than Japanese plums in coastal spring weather, which is typically cool and rainy.

Culture: Many, but not all, plum varieties are self-fertile, so you can harvest a good crop from a single tree; multi-graft trees are also available. Fruit of European plums usually doesn't need much thinning, but Japanese plums bear heavily in some years and should be thinned to 6 inches (5 cm) apart.

Pruning: Only semi-dwarf rootstock is available for plums; however, trees can be kept pruned to 10–15 feet (3–4.5 meters) high. Once tree shape is established, European plums don't need much pruning beyond removing crowded branches. Japanese plums put on a lot of shoot growth each season, so keep the vertical shoots pruned out in the summer, and prune dormant trees as well.

Harvest and Storage: Enjoy tree-ripened fruit immediately; plums picked before they are completely ripe keep in the refrigerator for over a month. For longer storage, they can be frozen, canned or dried.

Pests: Aphids; brown rot.

Varieties: European plums (all self-fertile): Opal, Victoria, Stanley, Italian prune, Damson. Japanese plums (all self-fertile): Santa Rosa, Golden Nectar, Shiro. Plum hybrids: Crosses between plums and apricots or peaches (plumcots, pluots) are becoming more widely available. Check your local nurseries for availability, and ask how well these have been growing for gardeners in your area.

Raspberries

Once raspberries become established, you may wonder why you planted such an invasive plant that sends up shoots everywhere — until you taste that first handful of ripe raspberries, of course.

Culture: Set plants 2–3 feet (60–90 cm) apart in rows. They do best in cool, moist soil, so keep plants deeply mulched. They should have some kind of support to hold the canes upright because they get quite tall. They can be tied to two or three parallel wires a foot or two apart running along a fence or between posts.

Pruning: Simple method for pruning raspberries: When plants are dormant, cut down all canes that bore fruit last year. The bark on these will be darker gray and rougher compared to the smooth bark on canes that grew in the last growing season. You can prune all varieties this way, but everbearing varieties can also be pruned in two stages. These raspberries produce a fall crop on the top third of new canes and a crop the following summer on the lower part of those same canes. When plants are dormant, prune off just the top part that has fruited and allow the bottom of the canes to produce fruit next year. Then prune out that entire spent cane the following winter. Try to keep only five to ten new canes per plant. Pull, cut or dig out weaker shoots and those that come up away from the main plant. Raspberries tend to spread widely, so keep on top of this tendency by pulling wandering shoots.

Harvest and Storage: Enjoy raspberries immediately or freeze or preserve them.

Note: When picking, hold the bucket away from the branch to avoid the risk of a stinkbug falling into the bucket. They are common in bramble fruit and drop when disturbed. If they drop in the bucket, they will fire off a stink that taints all the berries.

Pests: Raspberry crown borer is sometimes a problem in older plantings. The larvae overwinter in cocoons at the base of canes. In March, they start feeding on the buds of new shoots, then burrow into the lower part of canes, which die back. In early spring, pull back the soil and look for larvae to destroy before they move into the canes; prune out attacked canes at the base.

Varieties: Summer bearing: Tulameen ripens late June to early August; Malahat ripens mid-June. Everbearing (fall-bearing): Autumn Bliss ripens August to September; Heritage ripens August to November. By planting a couple of plants of several different varieties, you can extend fresh harvest from June to early November.

Rhubarb

I know rhubarb isn't really a fruit, but everyone thinks of it as one, so here it is. Tuck a plant into the back of a flower bed or in a corner where it won't be disturbed and enjoy this earliest fresh "fruit" of the year.

Culture: It would be the rare household that needs more than one of these large, productive hardy perennials. Plant offsets or crown divisions in late fall or early spring, and keep plants well-watered and mulched. Every spring, apply a thick layer of compost.

Pruning: Snap off flower stalks when they form later in the summer.

Harvest and Storage: Start harvesting for a week or two when plants are 2–3 years old; by the time plants are 5 years old or more, you can harvest up to 8 weeks. Remove stalks by pulling them, instead of cutting them, which leaves a stub that can rot back into the crown. Holding the base of the stalk, tug it sideways or twist it slightly, and the stalk will pop off at the crown.

Pests: None. Well, almost none: Deer are not supposed to eat it, but they do.

Varieties: Most gardeners get a plant from another gardener and don't know the variety. Some people prize plants with the reddest stalks: Crimson Cherry, MacDonald, Strawberry. Others like Victoria, a vigorous, old variety with greenish stalks.

Strawberries

Strawberries thrive in coastal gardens. There are two main types: June-bearing varieties and everbearing (day-neutral) varieties that fruit from late June to October. Although not exactly the same thing, everbearing and day-neutral strawberries act the same way in coastal gardens to produce berries all season, so they are treated the same.

Culture: Start a new bed with certified vi-rus-free plants. For everbearing varieties, space plants 1 foot (30 cm) apart; space June bearers 18 inches (45 cm) apart. The wider spacing accommodates the greater number of runners that develop on June-bearing va-rieties. Set plants with the crowns slightly above the soil line. Well-spaced plants in fertile soil produce well for 3 years or more. However, beds usually become crowded and overgrown after several years in one place, which reduces pollination and increases Bot-rytis infections on the fruit. I plant half of my total area of strawberries new each year, so that I have one new bed and one older bed. Top dress beds with compost in the spring. Mulch plants with leaves in the fall to protect the crowns from frost heave.

FIGURE 11.7. Tristar is a winner — as this September harvest shows.

Pruning: Remove excess runners (these are shoots that will eventually pro-duce new plants on the end). Everbearing varieties generally produce fewer runners, so require less pruning than June bearers. You can leave a couple of runners from each plant to develop new plants to fill in the bed or peg down the developing plantlets in pots of soil set among the plants (still attached to the runner). In early fall, when the new plants are well rooted, cut the runners and plant them out.

Harvest and Storage: Strawberries have a short shelf life, but freeze well and make classic jam.

Pests: Birds; slugs; Botrytis.

Varieties: June-bearing: Sequoia, Rainier, Hood, Puget Reliance, Tillam-ook. Everbearing/day-neutral: Tristar (large berries, excellent flavor, resists red stele root rot and powdery mildew); Hecker (smaller berries, resistant to viruses and verticillium wilt); Quinault (soft berries, good flavor, susceptible to Botrytis); Seascape (large, showy berries).

Glossary

Annuals: Plants that normally produce flowers and seeds in their first year of growth (they complete their life cycle in a single growing season). Annual vegetables include beans, peas, squash, lettuce, radishes, mustard greens and Chinese cabbage.

Biennials: Plants that normally produce flowers and seeds in their second year of growth, after they experience the period of winter. They complete their life cycle in the second growing season. Common biennials include carrots, cabbage, kale, leeks, beets and parsley.

Biennial bearing: Some fruit trees, particularly apples, tend to produce a big crop one year and hardly any crop the next year. By stringently thinning the apples in the heavy crop year, the tree can be kept from exhausting its energy reserves so that it can continue producing a moderate crop every year.

Bolting: Sending up a flower stalk and going to seed. Plants may bolt in response to unusually warm weather, cold weather, long day lengths or poor growing conditions that stress the plants.

Cloche: Low plastic or glass covers used to cover seedlings or tender plants to keep them warm in cool weather.

Coldframe: Any structure smaller than a greenhouse, designed to let in sunlight and trap heat through clear panels (glazing) on the roof.

Damping off: A disease of seeds and seedlings caused by soil fungi. Infected seedlings rapidly fall over as the stems collapse at the soil line. Infected seeds fail to send up shoots.

Day-neutral: Day-neutral strawberries flower and develop fruit regardless of day length, in contrast to spring or June-bearing strawberries that flower and fruit for three weeks during the longest days of the summer.

Determinate (tomato): Also called "bush" tomatoes. Plants put out flowers at the tips of shoots, so they stop producing new shoots and flowers after reaching full size. Plants are small and ripen fruit early over a short period; therefore, they are a good choice for Pacific Northwest gardens.

Espaliering: A system of training plants, usually fruit trees, to grow along a wire trellis, flat against a supporting wall or fence. Although shoot growth must be rigidly controlled to keep the trees two dimensional, trees can be very productive in small spaces.

Everbearing: Fruit varieties that yield a harvest over a long period. Everbearing raspberries produce both a summer and a fall crop of berries. Everbearing strawberries produce fruit from spring to fall. In the short summer of the coastal climate, the cropping period for "everbearing" strawberries is about the same as that of "day-neutral" strawberries (June to early October).

Floating row covers: Feather light, spun-bonded polyester or polypropylene fabrics used to cover plants to keep in heat. They allow in sunlight and rain and are light enough to rest on the leaves of plants, without supporting frames or hoops. Also used to prevent pest insects from laying eggs on plants.

Glazing: A transparent material used to cover greenhouses, tunnels or coldframes, usually glass, flexible or rigid plastic, or fiberglass.

Humus: The dark brown residue of decomposed organic matter in the soil. It is a major source of nutrients for plants. It also coats soil particles and helps stick them together, which improves soil structure.

Indeterminate (tomato): Also called "vine" tomatoes. Plants continue to grow new shoots and flowers until the weather is too cold for tomatoes. If not pruned, vines become quite large. They need a long growing season to mature a full crop. To encourage ripening of fruit already on the plant, prune off new flowers and cut tips of new shoots starting in mid-August.

Larva (plural, *larvae*): Immature stage of insects. Caterpillars, grubs and maggots are all larvae.

Manure tea (compost tea): A brew made by soaking a shovelful of composted manure or garden compost in a bucket of water. After soaking 2–5 days, the dark brown liquid can be strained off, diluted to a pale brown tea color, and used as a liquid fertilizer.

Mesclun: A blend of lettuce and other salad greens sown together as a mixture. Mesclun is usually harvested by cutting all of the young leaves from one section of a bed at once and leaving the plants to grow another crop of leaves.

Pathogens: Living organisms that cause diseases, including viruses, fungi, bacteria and other microorganisms.

Perennials: Plants that live year after year and continue to grow after they flower and fruit. Common perennials include fruit trees, strawberries, artichokes and asparagus. Tomatoes, peppers and eggplants are actually perennials, but they are not hardy enough to survive winter unless they are kept in a heated greenhouse.

Pupa (plural, *pupae*): Immobile stage of many insects between the larval stage and the adult stage.

Rocambole: A type of garlic that has a woody central flower stalk. Usually strong flavored and easy to peel.

Savoy or savoyed: Leaves that are naturally crinkly, crumpled or puckered. Some varieties of cabbage, Swiss chard and spinach have heavily savoyed leaves.

Scape: A kind of central flower stalk, such as found in Rocambole garlic.

Stucco wire: Heavy galvanized, welded wire with a 2-inch square mesh, usually 4 feet or 1 meter wide; it is sold by the running foot or roll at lumber and builders' supply yards.

Transpire/transpiration: The movement of water from the roots up through the stem and to leaves. When the water reaches the leaves, it evaporates into the air and cools the plant.

Vermiculite: A natural mineral called mica that expands when it is heated. The resulting particles are fluffy and lightweight.

Vernalization: A plant's response to winter cold or a short period of cool spring weather that results in flowering some months later. Usually occurs after full-grown biennial plants overwinter in the garden; however, if spring seedlings are large enough, a late cool period in April or May can cause them to flower prematurely — usually in July or August. Plants that most readily switch to "flowering mode" after a spring cold chill include onions, leeks, Swiss chard, beets, celery, celeriac and some cabbage family plants.

Resources

Soil Testing Laboratories
British Columbia
Agrichem Analytical, 409 Stewart Rd., Salt Spring Is., BC, V8K 1Y6
Tel: 250-538-1712 Web: agrichem.ca

MB Labs, 10115 McDonald Park Road, Sidney, BC
Tel: 250-656-1334 Web: mblabs.com

Pacific Soil Analysis, #5–11720 Voyageur Way, Richmond, BC, V6X 3G9
Tel: 604-273-8226

Norwest Labs, #104, 19575-56A Ave. Surrey, BC, V3S 8P8
Tel: 1-800-889-1433 Web: contractlaboratory.com

Washington and Oregon
A & L Western Agricultural Laboratories, Portland Office,
10220 SW Nimbus Ave., Bldg. K-9, Portland, OR 97223
Tel: 503-968-9225 E-mail: rbutterf@al-labs-west.com Web: al-labs-west.com

Soil & Plant Laboratory, Inc.
13547 SE 27th Place, Suite 3B, Bellvue, WA 98005
Tel: 425-746-6665 Fax: 425-562-9531 E-mail: splabnw@flash.net
Web: soilandplantlaboratory.com

Utah State University Analytical Lab (serves PNW gardeners)
4830 Old Main Hill, 166 Ag Science Bldg., Logan, UT 84322-4830
Tel: 435-797-2217 E-mail: usual@usu.edu Web: usual.usu.edu

An OSU Extension Services publication lists all testing labs,
Laboratories Serving Oregon: Soil, Water, Plant Tissue, and Feed Analysis. 2008.
Web: extension.oregonstate.edu/catalog/html/em/em8677/

Soil sampling instructions: *Soil Sampling for Home Gardens and Small Acreages*
Web: extension.oregonstate.edu/catalog/pdf/ec/ec628.pdf

Compost Information and Products

Compost Fundamentals. A thorough, scientific and practical review of everything there is to know about composting from Washington State University Whatcom County Extension. Web: whatcom.wsu.edu/ag/compost/fundamentals/index.htm

Fish and Wood Waste Compost Products

Check websites for store locators.

Sea Soil™ by Foenix Forest Technology Inc., seasoil.com. Widely available in British Columbia. Web: seasoil.com

Earthbank™ Fish Compost, fishcompost.com. Available at garden suppliers on Vancouver Island. Web: fishcompost.com

Oly Mountain Fish Compost® from North Mason Fiber Company, northmasonfiber.com. Available in Washington state.

Tools and Equipment

Lee Valley Tools is a US and Canadian mail-order supplier of tools, with an extensive line of garden tools. Ten-year garden journals, min-max thermometers, rain gauges, dehumidifier packs useful for seed storage. Local retail stores in British Columbia: Victoria, Vancouver, Coquitlam. Online catalog and ordering: leevalley.com.

Scarecrow® motion-activated animal deterrent is a sprinkler with a motion detector that automatically detects animals moving in the area. As they approach, it repels them with a short but startling burst of water. Sold widely in garden centers. For more information: contech-inc.com/products/scarecrow

Garden Advice and Pest Identification

Master Gardener Association of British Columbia
Web: bcmastergardeners.org
Includes list of local chapters and a Plant Information Line (year round):
Tel: 604-257-8662, or e-mail: plantinfo@bcmastergardeners.org

University of British Columbia Botanical Garden
Web: ubcbotanicalgarden.org
Hortline: Call 604-822-5858 on Tuesdays and Wednesdays from 12:00 pm to 3:00 pm.
Online forums: ubcbotanicalgarden.org/forums

Western Washington State Master Gardeners, Washington State University
Web: gardening.wsu.edu. Includes "Ask an Expert" forum and many online factsheets.

Oregon State University Master Gardener Program
Web: extension.oregonstate.edu/mg
Provides a list of all local Master Gardeners contacts by county as well as links to
online factsheets.

Pest Management

West Coast Gardening: Natural Insect, Weed & Disease Control. Linda Gilkeson. 2006.
Trafford Publishing. 154 pp. Detailed entries for common pests of vegetables and
fruit, lawns and ornamentals in south coastal BC and Pacific Northwest gardens.
How to identify insects and diseases, prevent pest problems and use safe, effective
controls, including beneficial insects. Canadian orders web: lindagilkeson.ca;
U.S. orders web: trafford.com/Bookstore

Garden Insects of North America: The Ultimate Guide to Backyard Bugs. Whitney
Cranshaw. 2004. Princeton University Press, Princeton, N.J. 656 pp. THE definitive,
up-to-date photographic reference for identifying insects and looking up life cycles
(does not provide control information).

Tree Fruit

Organic Tree Fruit Management. Linda Edwards. 1998. Certified Organic Associations
of British Columbia. 240 pp. Covers organic pest and disease management, information on soil fertility and nutrition in tree fruit, management tools available to the
organic grower. $40 plus shipping. Available from: COABC, Box 577, Keremeos, BC
V0H 1T0. Web: certifiedorganic.bc.ca

Seed Saving Books and Organizations
Books

How to Save Your Own Vegetable Seeds. 5th edition. Seeds of Diversity, Canada.
Excellent, how-to manual on home vegetable seed production from Seeds of Diversity: Canada's Heritage Seed Program. Gives detailed instructions for saving seeds
from common vegetables. 48 pages, well illustrated with photos. $12.00 (includes
postage) from: Seeds of Diversity Canada, P.O. Box 36 Stn Q, Toronto ON M4T 2L7.
Web: seeds.ca Toll-free phone: 1-866-509-7333.

Saving Seeds as If Our Lives Depended on It. Dan Jason. 2006.
Both a personal overview of how seed affairs have gotten to be what they are today
and a practical beginner's guide to saving seeds and the joys thereof. Published by
Salt Spring Seeds. 54 pp. $12. Available by mail order from web: saltspringseeds.com.

Organizations
Organic Seed Alliance
P.O. Box 772, Port Townsend, WA 98368
Non-profit supporting the ethical development and stewardship of seeds; carries a complete listing of organic seed suppliers in the region. Tel: 360-385-7192
E-mail: info@seedalliance.org Web: seedalliance.org

Salt Spring Seed Sanctuary
Box 444, Ganges PO, Salt Spring Island, BC V8K 2W1.
A charitable organization dedicated to preservation and promotion of heritage seeds and networking to encourage local food and seed production; carries a listing of seed and gene bank resources. Become a member: Tel: 250-537-5269
Web: seedsanctuary.com

Seeds of Diversity Canada
P.O. Box 36 Stn Q, Toronto ON M4T 2L7
If you are interested in heritage seeds, you may want to become a member.
Toll-free phone: 1-866-509-7333 Web: seeds.ca

Seed Companies (All Have Online Catalogs)
Canada
West Coast Seeds
3925-64th Street, RR#1, Delta, BC V4K 3N2
Phone: 604-952-8820 Toll-free fax: 877-482-8822 Web: westcoastseeds.com
A full range of good summer garden varieties, with an especially large selection of winter hardy vegetables. The only Canadian supplier I know of for winter varieties of cauliflower and broccoli. Widely available in seed racks at nurseries. Will ship some items to USA.

Salt Spring Seeds
Box 444, Ganges PO, Salt Spring Island, BC V8K 2W1
Tel: 250-537.5269 E-mail: dan@saltspringseeds.com Web: saltspringseeds.com
Locally grown seed and many unique vegetables and herbs, with tomatoes a specialty and an outstanding selection of garlic and dry bean varieties.

Seeds of Victoria
395 Conway Road, Victoria, BC V9E 2B9
Tel: 250-881-1555 Web: earthfuture.com/gardenpath/Seeds_Catalogue.htm
Limited selection, but all locally grown and certified organic seed.

Full Circle Seeds
P.O. Box 807, Sooke, BC, V0S 1N0
Tel: 250-642-3671 Web: fullcircleseeds.com
Organic OP heritage seeds with a speciality in tomatoes and lettuce, some hardy
greens. Only source for "Unique" leeks.

William Dam Seeds Ltd
Box 8400, Dundas, Ontario L9H 6M1
Tel: 1-905-628-6641 Web: damseeds.ca
Supplier of only untreated seed, with many European varieties, including red torpedo
onions, Namenia and a selection of corn salad varieties. Includes a large selection
of winter greens, especially chicory, endive and kale, and many root vegetables not
found elsewhere.

USA

Territorial Seed Company
P.O. Box 158, Cottage Grove, OR 97424-0061
Tel: 800-626-0866 Fax: 888-657-3131 Web: territorialseed.com
In addition to an extensive spring catalog with a large selection of summer crops,
TSC has a special summer catalog with many varieties of winter greens, lettuces,
winter broccoli and cauliflower for the Pacific Northwest; rare source for Roodnerf
Brussels sprouts. Widely available in seed racks at nurseries. Will ship seeds to Canada.

Victory Seed Company
P.O. Box 192, Molalla, Oregon 97038
Tel: 503-829-3126 E-mail: info@victoryseeds.com Web: victoryseeds.com
Pretty good selection of heirloom varieties adapted to local climate; a few winter
broccoli and cauliflower, winter hardy lettuce cultivars.

Abundant Life Seeds
P.O Box 279, Cottage Grove, OR 97424-0010
Tel: 541-767-9606 Fax: 866-514-7333 E-mail: info@abundantlifeseeds.com
Web: abundantlifeseeds.com
Certified organic seeds: lots of tomatoes, some interesting greens, very few cabbage
family varieties.

Seeds of Change
Tel: 1-888-762-7333 Web: seedsofchange.com
Orders accepted for both US and Canadian addresses. Very large selection of certified organic OP and hybrid seeds for commercial growers and home gardens, including selections for container growing. Widely available in seed racks at nurseries.

International

Thompson & Morgan, Seedsmen
Canada: 47-220 Wyecroft Road, P.O. Box 306, Oakville, ON L6J5A2
Toll free: 1-877-545-4386 Web: thompsonmorgan.ca
USA: P.O. Box 4086, Lawrenceburg, IN 47025 Web: tmseeds.com
A British seedhouse with distributors in Canada and the US. Not as many winter varieties as they used to carry, but worth checking out the Royal Horticultural Society merit winners and other UK varieties. Their online catalog will drive you nuts with random search results.

Chiltern Seeds
Bortree Stile, Ulverston, Cumbria, LA12 7PB, England
Web: chilternseeds.co.uk
One of the only European seed houses that still sells retail internationally. Source of many excellent winter vegetables suited to the Pacific Northwest, including celtuce, many varieties of purple sprouting broccoli, winter cauliflower, broad beans, parsnips and other winter vegetables beloved of British gardeners.

Index

Bold page numbers indicate main discussion of topic, *italic* page numbers indicate figures and tables.

root bound plants, 109
root crops, 9, 36, 93, 145
root flies, 185–186
rototilling, 47–48, 68–69
rutabagas, 22, *31*, *115*, **255**

S
sage, 23
salad greens. see leafy
    greens; lettuce; *specific
    leafy green*
Salmonella, 49
salsify, *31*, *115*
sand, 47
sandy soil, 45, 47
San Juan Islands, 85
scab. *see* apple scab; potato
    scab
scales, *181*
scallions, 29
Scarecrows, 136, 218
scare tapes, 218–219
SeaSoil, *60*, 105
season adaptation, 25
seaweed fertilizer, liquid,
    60, 65
seaweed meal, 59, *60*
seed banks (in soil), 88–90
seed banks (repositories),
    24
seedbeds, 71–72
seed catalogs, 25–28
seedlings
    mulches and, 87
    plastic sheets for, 95
    starting indoors, 99–109
    thinning, 78–79
seeds
    germination test, 117
    preparing seedbed,
        71–72
    sowing, 72–73, 74–78,
        105–106
    storage, 114–116
    treated, 76

watering, 73–74
    see also seedlings
seed saving, 26, 109–114
self-fertile flowers, 11–12
self-watering contain-
    ers, 151
semi-dwarf fruit trees, 120
shade, 16, 17, 142
shallots, *31*
sheep manure, 49
sheet composting, 51–52
silt, 45
Sitona lineata, *31*, **195–196**
slugs, 87, *181*, 191, **197–198**
snails, *181*, **197–198**
snap beans, **223–224**
soaker hoses, 83–84, 86
sod, in pathways, 21
sodium bicarbonate, *181*
soft brown scale, *180*
soil
    acidity, 61–62
    cultivation, 65–69
    depth, 43–44
    fertility, 44–45
    for fruit trees and
        bushes, 122–123
    organisms in, 6–7
    potting mixes, 104–105
    seasonal drainage pat-
        terns, 17
    structure, 47–48
    temperature, 74–76
    tests, 61, 62, 63
soil-borne diseases, 30
Solanaceae (nightshade
    family), 29
sowbugs (*Porcellio spp.*),
    198–199
sowing, 72–78, 87
space limitations, 30, 32–37
Spanish onions, 99
Sphaerotheca spp., 27, 121,
    180, *181*, **210–211**
spider mites, *180*

spinach, **248**
    crop rotation, *31*, 36
    cross-pollination risk, *111*
    disease resistance, 27
    ease of growth, 24
    flowering, 10
    germination tempera-
        ture, 75, 77
    seeds, 113, *115*
    spacing, 29
    sunlight requirements,
        16
    winter protection, 93, 97
spinach leafminer (*Pego-
    mya spp.*), **196–197**
spinosad, *180*, 187
sprinklers, 83
squash, **249–252**
    crop rotation, *31*
    germination tempera-
        ture, 75
    growth cycle, 7
    hardening off, 107
    planting transplants, 80
    pollination, 12, *12*, 13, 214
    pumpkins, *31*, 75, *115*
    seed storage, *115*
    sowing, 73
    spacing, 32
    summer
        disease resistance,
            26–27
        ease of growth, 22
        quantity to plant, 29
    sunburn, *107*, 213
    using non-garden space,
        33
    vegetative growth, 9, *9*
    winter
        crop rotation, 37
        ease of growth, 23, 24
        quantity to plant, 29
        starting indoors, 99
        trellising, 90
squirrels, 220

staking, 90–93, 124, 149
steer manure compost, 48
stomata, 9
straw, 88
strawberries, **272–273**
    in containers, 152–153
    diseases, *203*
    ease of growth, 23
    harvest dates, 122
    interplanting, 36
    irrigation, 125
    stress, effects of, 10, 82, 176
    structure of soil, 47–48
stucco wire, 92
subsoil, 44
succession planting, 33–34,
    33
sulfur, 7, 45, 59, *61*, *181*
summer crops, space re-
    quirements, 28–29
summer oils, *180*
summer squash. *see* squash
sunburn, *107*, 213
sunflower family, 29
sunlight
    effect on dormancy, 8
    garden microclimates, 17
    for garden site, 15–17
    for greenhouses, 142
    for plant growth, 5–6
    seedling requirements,
        102–103, *103*
Sunshine Organic Planting
    Mix, 105
Swedes. *see* rutabagas
sweet basil, 8, 145
sweet marjoram, 8
Swiss chard, **252–253**
    crop rotation, *31*
    cross-pollination risk, *111*
    ease of growth, 22
    effect of temperature, 10
    germination tempera-
        ture, 75
    growth cycle, 7–8

About the Author

LINDA GILKESON is a keen organic gardener with a passion for insects and 25 years of gardening experience on the west coast. After earning a Ph.D. in entomology, she worked as the research director of a biological control company and then for the British Columbia government coordinating programs to reduce pesticide use. She is the author of *Year Around Harvest: Winter Gardening on the Coast* and *West Coast Gardening: Natural Insect, Weed and Disease Control*. Linda is also a regular instructor in Master Gardener programs and is kept busy giving talks and workshops on organic gardening and pest management for community education programs, garden clubs and other groups. She currently lives on Salt Spring Island where she enjoys harvesting food from her garden all year round.

Visit her web site at www.lindagilkeson.ca

If you have enjoyed *Backyard Bounty*, you might also enjoy other

BOOKS TO BUILD A NEW SOCIETY

Our books provide positive solutions for people who want to
make a difference. We specialize in:

Sustainable Living • Green Building • Peak Oil
Renewable Energy • Environment & Economy
Natural Building & Appropriate Technology
Progressive Leadership • Resistance and Community
Educational & Parenting Resources

For a full list of NSP's titles, please call 1-800-567-6772 *or check out our website at:*

www.newsociety.com

NEW SOCIETY PUBLISHERS